INDUSTRIAL MOVEMENT

Industrial Movement

Experience in the US and the UK

P.M. TOWNROE
University of East Anglia

SAXON HOUSE

© P.M. Townroe 1979

Published by
Saxon House,
Teakfield Limited,
Westmead, Farnborough, Hants., England

British Library Cataloguing in Publication Data

Townroe, Peter Michael
   Industrial Movement.

   1. Business relocation — Great Britain
   2. Business relocation — United States
   I. Title
   338.6'042'0941   HC260.D5
ISBN 0 566 00279 5

Printed in Great Britain by
David Green (Printers) Ltd, Kettering, Northamptonshire

Contents

Preface

This review of the major sources in the literature on industrial movement in the United States and the United Kingdom was undertaken under contract for the Economic Development Administration of the US Department of Commerce. Both countries, at various levels of government, have operated policies which seek to influence the volume and spatial distribution of the flows of industrial moves. In both countries a body of literature has grown up seeking to analyse these flows of movement, to study the influence of the various policy measures upon the flows, and to analyse the impact the flows have upon the areas of origin and destination. The emphasis and focus of the two literatures has been rather different, in part due to the different statistical bases available and in part due to the different focus and emphasis given to spatial economic policy. Therefore, although there are similarities in the concerns and approaches revealed in the literature relating to each country, there are also contrasts. These contrasts include differences in coverage of sub-topics within the general subject area, differences in the intensity of study, and differences in the methodologies used. Both the similarities and the contrasts suggest significant utility is to be gained by bringing together the two bodies of literature into a common review.

One problem in bringing together the writings on a particular subject area is to know when to draw limits to bibliographic search. The literature on the general topic of the location of industry is much larger than that on the subject area of industrial movement. The term 'industrial movement' has been used throughout this review to refer to the process of opening new industrial plants. This is the common British usage. In some American material, the same term has been widened to include the process of expansion and contraction of employment within existing plants as well as openings and closures, the idea of 'movement' coming from relative rates of growth and decline between areas. This review is limited however to the process of opening new plants, this being the prime (but not the only) concern of most area development policies. The wider literature on patterns of industrial location and of locational change in the two countries is not systematically reviewed, and has been used only to set the context for the consideration of industrial movement.

The literature examined has been limited in another way as well. In both countries a huge reservoir of potentially relevant research results exists in the theses of university research students and in the unpublished or limited circulation papers of the professional staffs of government departments and agencies. Although reference to this kind of material is sometimes made in the sources which have been examined for this review, these research results have not been sought or referred to here for three reasons. Firstly, a direct time constraint on the preparation of this review in the face of a large literature of books and academic journal articles. Secondly, the view that for a review such as this to be useful to policy makers and administrators as well as to research workers, a limit must be placed on coverage of those references which subsequent work fails to suggest are of more than narrow or local interest and of limited enhancement to general knowledge in the field. Thirdly, the belief that significant results from this sort of material tend, in the end, to pass the relevant screening processes to emerge in journal paper or book form. On similar grounds very little use has been made of professional or industrial magazines or journals. This book tries to be more of a 'where-are-we-now?' study of the knowledge of the industrial movement process in the United States and the United Kingdom, than an exhaustive bibliographic listing and commentary.

Separate bibliographies of the American and British literature are provided at the end of the book, with a third (shorter) bibliography of general references or references to a limited number of industrial movement studies in non-US or UK countries. An outline of the chapter-by-chapter contents of the review is in the following introduction.

I am indebted to David Keeble, Gunter Krumme and Graham Gudgin for comments on a first draft. I would also like to thank Gerlad L. Duskin of the Office of Research in the Economic Development Administration for a sympathetic introduction in to the ways of the US Federal Government and to many useful references in the American literature on industrial mobility.

Finally may I apologise to all of those British and American social scientists to whose published research work in this field I have done less than full justice. I can only hope that this review will encourage newcomers to the field to seek out the cited books and papers.

Peter M. Townroe
University of East Anglia,
Norwich.

October 1978

Acknowledgements

The research for this volume was undertaken while the author was an academic visitor to the University of Washington, Seattle and the University of California, Berkeley under grant number PF-551 99-7-13358 for the Office of Economic Research of the Economic Development Administration of the US Department of Commerce. The views expressed are those of the author and must not be taken to represent the views of the sponsoring agency.

Figures 2.1, 4.1, 4.2 and 4.3 are reproduced from M.E.C. Sant, *Industrial Movement and Regional Development,* 1975, pages 65, 116, 117 and 72 by permission of Pergamon Press Ltd. Figure 5.1 is reproduced from chapter ten of R.J. Chorley and P. Haggett (eds), *Socio-Economic Models in Geography,* 1967, page 365 by permission of Metheun and Co. Ltd. Figure 6.1 is reproduced from P.M. Townroe, *Industrial Location Decisions,* 1971, page 13 by permission of the Director of the Centre for Urban and Regional Studies, University of Birmingham. Figure 9.1 is reproduced from D.E. Keeble, 'Industrial Geography', *Progress in Human Geography,* 1 (2), 1977, page 308 by permission of Edward Arnold (Publishers) Ltd.

Introduction

This review brings together the available British and American literature on industrial movement in order to meet three objectives. Firstly, to describe what is known about the patterns and characteristics of industrial movement at three different spatial levels: i.e. the city, the region and between regions. Secondly, to present the understanding that has been built up in both countries by both theoretical and empirical studies of the process of industrial movement at the micro-level, that is, at a level of the individual firm seeking a new location for a plant. And thirdly, to discuss the link between industrial movement and urban and regional social and economic policy in both countries, suggesting both the limitations and the potential for those policy instruments which seek to influence industrial movement. These three objectives are met in the successive chapters of the review.

This introduction is in two parts. The first part sets out the definition of the principal terms associated with industrial mobility as used in this review, and then discusses the principal sources of information on industrial mobility available in the two countries. The second part outlines the contents of the nine chapters following.

Definitions and sources

As indicated in the preface, the term 'industrial movement' in this study follows the British usage and refers to the process of opening new industrial establishments, both factories and offices. Thus, industrial 'moves' may consist of 'transfer moves' and 'branch plant moves'. A transfer, as the word implies, is a relocation involving the closure of an existing unit of a company accompanied by the opening of a new establishment in a new location. Branch plant moves are openings of new plants and new sites, without the closure of existing units of the company. Overall, 'movement' means the process of locating in new or vacated premises away from the previous premises owned by the company, whether or not those previous premises are closed down or sold as a result of the move. It is clear that some moves may take place over a period of time, the establishment of an initial branch leading subsequently to a complete transfer of operations out of an existing plant.

The use of this restricted definition of industrial movement means that this study and review is very much focussed on the process of choosing new industrial plant locations and the geographical patterns resulting therefrom. Many American studies have followed this same usage of the term industrial movement; but others have widened it to include the growth and decline of activity within existing industrial establishments; the gross total of 'movement' therefore including both the opening and closing of plants and changing distributions at existing sites. These studies analyse patterns of geographic change in industrial activity by small areas. The activity is recorded in statistics of output or employment or floorspace, statistics which say nothing about the opening and closure or change of ownership of sites or buildings. While changes in the levels of activity at a given site or location may be linked to a wide range of economic forces having an influence over space on the given industry, the process of locational decision making within the company for these changes in level is rarely explicit. The choice of a new site, on the other hand, necessarily involves explicit locational choice. And, although those many public policy agencies in both countries concerned with the local economic prosperity of an area now realise that a policy interest should perhaps be taken in the fortunes of existing companies, the prime thrust of area development efforts in both the United States and the United Kingdom has been towards the attraction and guidance of companies investing in new plant and equipment in new locations.

Chapters 2, 3 and 4 of this study will not be able to keep to the narrow confines of the usage of industrial movement outlined above; and these chapters in particular will outline some of the major changes in the distribution of industrial activity at the three separate spatial levels of the city, the region, and the nation to include both the influence of new plant openings and the changing intensity of use of older establishments. Similarly, subsequent chapters will not always confine themselves to the discussion of the movement of manufacturing industry, which is the prime focus of this study. The majority of industrial policy all over the world has focussed upon manufacturing as the most spatially footloose sector of industry and as the sector most susceptible to the influence of public policy. In both the US and the UK, however, as in all other advanced industrial countries, the proportion of total employment accounted for by manufacturing is continuing to decline. In 1975 the proportions in the two countries were 23 per cent and 33 per cent. Employment growth is now strongly centred in the service sector, and increasingly policy makers have been turning to these sectors as sources of potentially mobile jobs. The movement of offices is discussed in particular in chapter 2.

Information on industrial movement in the two countries comes essentially from three sources: from the analysis of small area based statistics on changes in employment and output by industrial sectors; from the study of statistics relating to 'flows' of industrial moves, as previously defined; and from interview and postal questionnaire surveys of companies recently involved in choosing new plant locations. Further, but less important, sources of understanding include case studies of movers, surveys of locational attitudes of non-movers, statistics on the industrial response to distribution of industry policies and anecdotal accounts of responses and opinions in the press and in trade and professional journals.

Analysts of industrial movement in the United Kingdom have been especially fortunate in that in 1968 the central government department then responsible for the national distribution of industry policy, the Board of Trade (now the Department of Industry), published a set of summary statistics on the national pattern of industrial movement between fifty sub-regions of the United Kingdom for the period 1945 to 1965 (Howard, 1968). This initial publication contained a preliminary analysis of the characteristics of the inter-sub-regional moves, and further work followed from a number of research studies (e.g. Keeble, 1971; Lever, 1972; Townroe, 1973; Rhodes and Moore, 1976; Sant, 1975; Taylor, 1977). These studies and others included analysis based on additional but unpublished government statistics which increased the detail by area and sector, and extended the coverage to 1971. [1] Any movement across a sub-regional boundary was recorded in most areas for cases in which at least ten people were employed by the establishment involved, whether the move was to new or to secondhand premises. Both transfers and branch moves were distinguished and allocated an origin as well as a destination, the origin of a branch plant being taken as that area in which the recognised headquarters plant of the company was located, except after 1965 from when it was 'the location of the unit (manufacturing or non-manufacturing) which gave rise to the new development'. The sub-regional boundaries were such that all significant city-to-hinterland, city-to-city, and region-to-region moves could be recorded. Moves within a city, being always within a sub-region, were therefore not recorded (except in aggregate for 1966–71). These statistics now form the cornerstone of any overview of industrial movement or distribution of industry policy in the United Kingdom. [2]

Research workers in the United States have not been so fortunate in having an easily accessible data base to work from. They have therefore, like other British colleagues, turned to survey techniques or to analyses of employment and output data from small areas over a period of time.[3] Recently however, direct data on industrial movement in the sense used here has been generated, using the Duns Market Identifiers file of manufacturing establishment data collected by the Dun and Bradstreet corporation. Struyk and James (1975), for example, used this data in their analysis of changes in the location of industry within four major metropolitan areas, as did Jusenius and Ledebur (1977) for their work in Ohio. Schmenner (1978) also used this source for his work on industrial change in Cincinnati. Each manufacturing establishment is recorded by a geographical code and a unique identification number, together with four digit SIC (Standard Industrial Classification) product codes and employment in the plant with additional information on the parent firm. This file was first compiled in 1965, and comparison over time allows the identification of establishments which have moved out of, or migrated into the areas and those which have commenced or ceased operating.[4]

A number of large American real estate and commercial brokerage firms, such as Coldwell Banker of Los Angeles, have assembled files similar to those of Dun and Bradstreet, and these files have sometimes been sold to individual city authorities for planning and economic development policy purposes as well as used for commercial analyses. These files have not, however, been available for published research studies.

The detail of the Dun and Bradstreet data has been matched in the UK by the Glasgow University Register of Industrial Establishments (GURIE), relating solely to Glasgow (Firn, 1973; Cameron, 1973); and in data banks for the North West of England prepared by Dicken and Lloyd (1978) and for the East Midlands region by Gudgin (1978). Individual local urban planning authorities have undertaken special exercises to evaluate patterns of movement, but these have usually been one-off exercises rather than the maintenance of updated records. Establishment data has also been provided by the records of the United Kingdom Factory Inspectorate, the body responsible for the health and safety at work legislation, but these records have severe weaknesses as a data source.[5]

In both countries access to relevant data sets, either for direct statistical analysis, or as a basis for the sample design of a survey, has been a problem for research workers interested in industrial movement. Commercial sensitivity and the disclosure limitations placed upon the government departments and the statistics they collect from industry will continue to place barriers across sets of relevant information which already exist in both the public and the private sectors.[6] The ad hoc and indirect approaches used in the past in this field to generate information about industrial movement will therefore continue.

A chapter-by-chapter outline

Chapter 1 briefly examines the broad patterns of population and employment change in the United States and the United Kingdom over the past twenty years or so to provide a background and context for the examination of industrial mobility in the two countries. It provides a preliminary indication of the importance of industrial mobility for the changes outlined and links this to the basic interests of public policy in industrial movement and to industrial mobility as seen from the perspective of an individual company.

Chapter 2 examines industrial movement within the city or metropolitan area, linking the processes of suburbanisation and decentralisation away from the urban core areas to the changing locational requirements of industry. This chapter builds particularly on studies of Boston and Glasgow. It also introduces the phenomenon of office mobility, and considers the role of the older urban areas as an incubator for new industrial activity and as a seed bed for mobile plants. Moves within the city-region are examined in chapter 3; in particular the moves into the non-metropolitan areas of the United States contiguous with the metropolitan areas which have recently shown fast population and employment growth, and the moves to those new towns and expanding towns in the United Kingdom designed to receive population dispersed from the largest cities. Chapter 4 considers the longer distance industrial movement between the major regions of each country, focussing in particular on the moves influenced by regional development programmes.

Thereafter, the perspective shifts to the individual firms and to the plant in a new location. Chapter 5 reviews some of the strengths and weaknesses of alternative theories of industrial location for the study and analysis of industrial movement. Chapter 6 brings together those studies which have sought to describe and analyse locational decision making procedures within companies; while chapter 7 highlights the experience of the transition into the new plant; and chapter 8 discusses some of the major problems companies have discovered in both countries in settling into their new factory and adjusting to a new environment.

A further chapter on the impacts of mobile industry on the local community was considered for this point. However, the literature on this subject is very extensive and a review of American experience has recently appeared (Summers et al., 1976).

The final chapter provides a summary of the principal themes in the industrial movement literature of the two countries. These themes are related to the wider considerations of patterns of urban growth, of policies for regional development, and of the problems facing industrial managers in new industrial plants. The chapter concludes with a number of suggestions for future research activity.

Notes

[1] The exact definitions and areas used for the collection of these statistics are given in Howard (1968, p.36)and Sant (1975, Appendix A and B.)
[2] Recent reviews of the UK distribution of industry policy include Cameron (1974)and Sundquist (1975).This policy will be outlined and discussed further in chapter 4.
[3] Leone (1972) has reviewed alternative American data sources.
[4] A very detailed monitoring of industrial change in Texas is undertaken by the Bureau of Business Research at the University of Texas at Austin, published in the annual *Directory of Texas Manufacturers*. This source allowed Rees (1978a) to build up a picture of nearly four thousand location decisions between 1960 and 1975 in the Dallas-Fort Worth and Houston areas.
[5] See Lloyd (1973). This data has been used by Dicken and Lloyd (1978) in their studies of Manchester and Merseyside.
[6] Hansen (1973, p.33), for example, discusses this problem in using the *County Business Patterns* statistics published annually by the US Department of Commerce. Difficulties with British data are discussed by Firn (1973, p.708) in evidence to a parliamentary committee on regional economic development.

1 Changing patterns of population and employment in the United States and the United Kingdom

Over the past twenty years or so, very significant spatial shifts have occurred in the directions of population and employment change both in the United States and the United Kingdom. These shifts have been partly influenced by the results of public policy decisions, while they also reflect underlying changes in social and economic forces in each country. The influence of public policy has been both explicit, in terms of area development programmes and land use planning policies, as well as being implicit in the pressures coming from the secondary effects of those public sector policies with principal objectives which are essentially non-spatial, such as in defence, housing or industry. The underlying social and economic changes of greatest relevance to the shifts in the directions of change of population and employment are probably those most closely associated with a rising real standard of living in both countries: increased consumer incomes leading to increased ability to choose where to live and to work, linked to a shift in the pattern of employment away from agriculture and manufacturing industry and toward service sector occupations.

The broad patterns of these shifts in the directions of change in the distribution of both population and employment will be outlined in this chapter. These changes serve as a necessary context for the discussion of the phenomenon of industrial movement in the United States and the United Kingdom and for the comparison of the literature available in the two countries. Then the section headed 'Industrial change and industrial movement' offers an initial response to the question: 'How important is the role played by industrial movement in the changing pattern of population and employment in the two countries?' The chapter concludes with an introduction to industrial movement from the perspective of the individual plant or company.

Recent patterns of population and employment change in the United States

Throughout the present century the growing population of the United

1

States has increasingly found its home in the city, while the population in rural areas has declined both relatively and absolutely. By 1970 three out of four people lived in an urban area, with the majority of the urban population concentrated particularly in the larger cities. Migration away from the farms of America in excess of the natural increase meant that by 1971 the farm population had been reduced to less than 10 million or under 5 per cent of the population. Throughout the 1940s, 1950s and 1960s, one half of all the counties in the US had lost population.

In the 1960s, although the metropolitan areas continued to grow faster than the total population, their percentage rates of growth slowed compared with the 1950s, as shown in Table 1.1. In particular, the growth rates of the largest metropolitan areas slowed compared with the relatively smaller cities. By the end of the 1960s the process of increasing the concentration of the national population in the seventy-odd major metropolitan centres seemed to be coming to an end; but deconcentration at the local or metropolitan scale, so strong in the previous twenty years, showed no sign of slowing. The strong inter-regional migration flows to the West, Southwest and the Southeast continued, with rapid industrial growth and extensive retirement migration to all of the Sunbelt South. The other major migration flow of the post-World War II period, that of rural blacks to the Northeastern cities, was beginning to dry up. These changes allowed Berry to summarise in 1973:

> Growth in the United States is now largely metropolitan growth in all the larger urban regions; the concentrative migration process resulting from industrial urbanization has ended. Migration takes place between metropolitan areas on an interregional scale and intraregionally through an accelerating dispersion of people and jobs outward into the expanding metropolitan periphery. Nearly 40 million Americans change their homes each year. Roughly one in fifteen Americans — a total of 13 million people — migrate across a county line. And the outward urge dominates, into zones of superior residential amenity. In the two decades 1950—1970 the average population density of all urbanized areas in the United States dropped from 5,408 persons per square mile to 3,376; for central cities the decline was from 7,786 to 4,463. Many of the central cities that grew in the wave of industrial urbanism are now experiencing declining populations. Declining central cities lost more people in the decade than were lost due to migration by declining rural counties. The list includes Baltimore, Boston, Philadelphia,

2

Table 1.1
Population of the United States by place of residence, 1950 to 1970

Area	Population 1950	1960	1970	Percentage change 1950–60	1960–70	Average annual change 1950–60	1960–70
Standard metropolitan statistical areas [1]	94,579	119,595	139,419	26·4	16·6	2·3	1·5
Central cities	53,696	59,947	63,797	11·6	6·4	1·1	0·6
Outside central cities	40,883	59,648	75,622	45·9	26·8	3·8	2·4
Non-metropolitan areas	56,747	59,728	63,793	5·3	6·8	0·5	0·7
Total	151,326	179,323	203,212	18·5	13·3	1·7	1·3

[1] The 243 SMSA's defined in 1970.

Source: US Bureau of the Census. *Statistical Abstract of the United States.*

3

Pittsburgh, Chicago, Detroit and St. Louis; fifteen of the twenty-one central cities with a population exceeding one-half million in 1960 lost population in the decade. Almost all metropolitan growth was, as a result, concentrated in the decade in rapidly-dispersing suburban territory.

In short, there has been a shift in the locus of new growth — residential industrial, commercial — to the expanding suburban and exurban segments of the daily urban systems on an intra-regional scale, as well as to the nation's 'rimland' on the inter-regional scale. Many suburban areas now provide all the essential services formerly concentrated in the city core; new outlying locations provide for shopping needs, jobs, entertainment, medical care and the like. And along with suburbanization has come an extensive sorting-out process. Suburban communities are internally homogeneous, while highly differentiated from each other along class, age and ethnic lines, just as the white suburbs are differentiated in their turn from the central cities in which the nation's blacks and other racial minorities are increasingly concentrated.

The essential driving force resides in *social* rather than economic dynamics (Berry, 1973, p.36).

The growth of the suburbs between 1950 and 1970 was much faster than the overall increases in the populations of the Standard Metropolitan Statistical Areas (SMSA) central cities. This gain is understated by Table 1.1 because of annexation of some suburban areas by central cities. Allowing for this annexation, 22·9 million people were added to metropolitan suburbs between 1960 and 1970 (Zimmer, 1975, p.26). Within metropolitan areas, many central cities lost population, so that 2·3 million people were lost to 130 central cities between 1960 and 1970. The patterns and the forces in this suburbanisation of the American urban populations are well documented and reasonably well understood (e.g. Clawson, 1971; Zimmer, 1974; Hansen, 1975).

The 'problem' regions of the United States in the 1950s and 1960s were those parts of the country which Friedman and Miller (1965) and others have termed the 'intermetropolitan periphery'. Except for the thinly populated areas of the interior of the country (most of the plains and mountain states), the intermetropolitan periphery includes those areas which intervene among metropolitan regions, such as Appalachia, Northern New England, or the Ozarks. These areas had low growth and declining industries, poor social and economic infrastructure, low incomes, and all the problems associated with a declining population, selective outward migration, and poor standards

of health and education.[1] These areas nevertheless contained
approximately one-fifth of the American population.

Since 1970 a further shift in the pattern of urban population growth
seems to have occurred. Growth of the metropolitan areas has
continued, but at a lower percentage rate (0·9 per cent from 1970 to
1974). The central cities of metropolitan areas having a population in
excess of one million in 1970 lost population at about 1 per cent per
year from 1970—74, while the central cities in the remaining smaller
SMSA's grew at nearly twice the rate of the suburban rings in these
larger cities, showing an absolute increase of 3·3 million from 1970—
74 compared with 219 million previously.

The more significant change in the early 1970s, however, is the
increase in the rate of growth of the non-metropolitan counties of the
country. This growth is a sharp break with earlier trends. Between
1970 and 1974 the population living in these counties increased at
more than twice the annual rate of the 1950s and 1960s, the growth
being felt particularly strongly in counties designated metropolitan
since 1970 (Barabba, 1975, pp.41—6). Non-metropolitan areas and
metropolitan areas overall now seem to be growing at approximately
the same rate; 4 per cent 1970—74, taking into account territory
designated metropolitan since 1970. A major factor for this change in
trend appears to be that since 1970 there has been a net outward
migration from those metropolitan areas with populations in excess of
three million; and the group of SMSAs with populations of between
one and three million in 1970 also would have suffered a net
migration loss had it not been for heavy inward migration into the
retirement and recreational cities: Miami and Tampa-St. Petersburg in
Florida, and Phoenix, Arizona. Of the fifty largest cities in 1970,
thirty-eight had lost some of their population by 1975. Of the large
metropolitan areas only Pittsburgh had lost population overall in the
1960s.

Barabba (1975, p.47) has calculated that between 1970 and 1974
the proportion of metropolitan residents living in the suburbs rose
from 54 to 57 per cent, the suburbs gaining 6·5 million people or 8·4
per cent of the 1970 total. The central cities lost about 2 per cent of
their population in this period; the growth which was taking place
occurred only within the suburbs. In the largest cities, for example in
New York and Philadelphia, central city losses have not been made up
by suburban gains.

The revival of population growth in the non-metropolitan areas has
been primarily the result of a reversal of the long standing pattern of
outward migration. The reasons for this reversal are not fully understood, although a number of possible factors have been suggested

5

(Beale, 1976; McCarthy and Morrison, 1978). These include improved accessibility, allowing longer commuting distance and shorter journey times for recreational visits; a strengthening desire for a rural or small town residential environment, perhaps for retirement in an improved climate with an opportunity to experiment with new life-styles; employment growth in manufacturing concerns shifting further from the large cities; employment growth in energy extraction industries; and the growth of areas containing a state capital, a senior state college, a prison, or a large military installation.

The role of manufacturing jobs in this revival of the non-metropolitan areas, although not dominant, is important. Between 1970 and 1974, the non-metropolitan areas gained 643,000 manufacturing employees, 65 per cent of the national increase. Most of the remaining increase was concentrated within the suburban rings of the smaller metropolitan areas.

Among the economic factors operating on employers to encourage these shifts in manufacturing are the higher, relative costs of operations within metropolitan areas due to higher land costs, labour costs, utility costs, taxes and congestion. Problems of security add to these costs. The outward migration of white collar and skilled blue collar workers from the central cities to the suburbs and beyond for social reasons deprives inner city employers of their previous pool of labour. They therefore move, following the labour, perhaps attracted further to untapped pools of labour in small towns for labour intensive activities.[2] The Interstate highway system has improved access for all transport, while new systems of corporate organisation and control have allowed large multiplant companies to operate units performing relatively routine functions, to be decentralised far away from a controlling head office. Difficulties with environmental and land use planning controls have discouraged industrial investment in some areas;[3] while many federal state and local government financial and infrastructure incentives have sought to promote lagging areas.

One of the most important results of the shifts in population and job patterns since 1970 has been the relative economic decline of the states of the Northern Industrial Tier as a group and of their major industrial cities in particular. This 'decline' has been primarily a problem of population outward migration and of relatively high rates of unemployment. Rates of new job creation have dropped dramatically compared to the 1960s. One reaction of popular opinion to this new situation has been to blame the complementary rise of the Sunbelt states and to call for a redirection of federal spending back towards the Northeast. However, analysis has shown that the relative levels of economic development between the two regions are more

6

balanced than this reaction suggests. The South still has a relative poverty problem to counter the unemployment problems of the Northeast, and Jusenius and Ledebur (1976; 1977) have suggested that a simple reswitching of federal expenditure is no substitute for the rather different sorts of economic development policy best suited to each region.

> At best, the evidence is mixed and fails to support the unequivocal claim that the Northern Industrialised States should benefit from a reallocation of Federal program benefits which diminishes the flow of benefits to States in the South. (Jusenius and Ledebur, 1976. p.34)

This brief summary of recent changing trends in the distribution of population and employment in the United States has focussed on the national aggregate picture.[4] A fuller geographic picture will emerge in the next three chapters. At the national level however certain of these trends have had consequences which have encouraged a public policy response to promote area development, principally by the federal government.

The United States has no policy comparable to the regional economic development policies of most countries in Western Europe. For reasons which are both constitutional and ideological there is no strong central policy to direct and induce a spatial redistribution of economic growth so as to alleviate areas of economic distress and to promote regional development. What policy responses there are in the United States are diffused both within the federal government between programmes which have only partly area based objectives and also between the federal government and the state and local governments. The resulting low profile of area based economic policy sometimes leads Europeans to an inadequate appreciation of those policies which do exist.[5]

There are approximately 1,030 programmes of domestic assistance by the US federal government. Of these forty-two concern themselves with area based economic development. The Economic Development Administration (the EDA) of the Department of Commerce is the principal federal agency. But the programmes of other federal departments and agencies also concern themselves with aspects of population and employment distribution; in analysis, in funding and in regulation.[6] A well known example is the mortgage insurance programme of the Federal Housing Authority. Often these programmes have implicit or unintended effects on the spatial pattern of development. Another example is the interstate highway programme. The activities of the plethora of state and local governments and local public agencies likewise have a cumulative impact. The continental scale of the country and the federal constitution perhaps do not permit the sort of coherent population distribution and regional economic development policy strived for in many European countries, West and East. These barriers exist independently of the stronger (but weakening) cultural and philosophical restraints on government interventions in the United States.

In fact involvement by the federal government in the geographical pattern of economic growth in the country has a very long history.[8] Interest in the colonisation of the West and in developing transportation infrastructures goes back to the Land Act of 1785. Experience with programmes to foster regional economic growth (largely through public works) was gained in the New Deal, and in the sixteen years after the end of the Second World War there were a succession of congressional attempts to involve the federal government further in the economic development of the more underdeveloped areas of the country. This congressional pressure eventually resulted in the 1961 Area Redevelopment Act. This Act was revised and extended in the 1965 Public Works and Economic Development Act (PWEDA), which is the current (but amended) ruling legislation.

In the PWEDA Congress gave a mandate to the newly formed Economic Development Administration (EDA) to encourage self-sustained economic growth in depressed areas. This was to be achieved primarily by financial assistance for programmes of public works but also by guiding, encouraging and funding the planning capacity of local governments and development agencies. Areas requesting aid must submit an 'Overall Economic Development Plan'. Business loans, a major instrument in the 1961 Act, were continued but given a lower priority in the 1965 Act. The EDA was also given limited authority to conduct worker training programmes.

At the same time, early experiments with regional planning in the 1930s, leading to over forty state planning commissions by 1935, were revived in the Appalachian Regional Development Act of 1965 establishing a commission covering parts or all of thirteen states with programmes in health, housing, vocational education, soil conservation, and timber development, as well as in public works.[9] Title V of the 1965 Act led to further commissions being established for eight other regions. These commissions were however without project funds or any administrative jurisdiction. The commissions now cover all or part of forty-six states and still have only limited assistance funds in spite of the revisions of the 1975 Regional Development Act (RDA).

8

Regional planning was also encouraged under Title IV of the Act by which the Secretary of Commerce could designate multicounty development districts, each of which would contain two or more redevelopment areas plus at least one centre which showed promise of economic growth.[10]

Since 1965 the EDA has had a fairly turbulent legislative history. Important qualitative changes have been introduced which have widened the responsibilities of the Agency. The EDA programme has moved from an essentially rural and remedial focus to include urban problem areas and the prevention of distress. As Martin and Leone (1977) in their history of the EDA have pointed out, equity and welfare objectives have been recognised and encouraged. The EDA has also been given, since 1971, a counter-cyclical role in the management of the national economy, lessening the distinction between chronic and temporary distress; and a role in disaster relief expenditures. The EDA is now much larger than was ever anticipated in the mid-1960s, with a budget planned for the fiscal year of 1979 in excess of $620 million (although this includes expenditure on administration and services). Further growth may come from proposals made early in 1978 by the Carter Administration to extend federal economic development activity in urban areas. The EDA has also had to coordinate its activities with other important recent federal legislation, in particular the 1973 Comprehensive Employment and Training Act, 1972 Rural Development Act and the 1974 Community Development Block Grant programme.

Expectations of the EDA have not really been matched by its funds or its powers. Relative to the expenditures on area development by the governments of most European countries (as a percentage of GNP), the budget of the EDA is small and is vastly overshadowed by the expenditures of other federal programmes. And the American political process ' . . . encourages diffusion and discourages focus' (Martin and Leone, 1977, p.109), so that the effectiveness of the EDA programmes has been weakened by an inability to use strong tools selectively. This has led to calls for a strengthening of the powers and the resources of the agency (e.g. Jusenius and Ledebur, 1977).

Compared with the United Kingdom therefore, explicit central government policies directed towards regional economic development have had a very limited influence on industrial mobility in the United States. The choice of new industrial locations has been much more strongly but indirectly influenced by the totality of other federal expenditures; although the pattern of this overall influence is very difficult to assess. However, in contrast with the United Kingdom, the influx of industrial investment into particular individual communities

9

in the United States has been very strongly influenced by *local* programmes to promote industrial growth, depending largely on local initiative and funding. These programmes have included the use of industrial development bonds, loans and loan guarantees and local tax concessions (Hellman et al., 1976). The role of these incentives in influencing industrial mobility will be considered in later chapters.

The changing pattern of population and employment distribution in the United Kingdom

Many of the forces which encouraged migration to the larger metropolitan areas and suburbanisation of both homes and jobs in the United States in the 1950s and 1960s were also present in the United Kingdom; although with less strength and with stronger constraints imposed by elements of public policy. Overall comparison might, at first sight, seem to be difficult or inappropriate. After all, the UK has one-quarter the total population of the US living on 2·7 per cent of the land area. The principal industrial areas of the country are no more than 400 miles apart, and there are few truly rural areas, well outside the urban field of large metropolitan areas. When, in subsequent chapters, we examine inter-regional industrial mobility, the meaning of 'region' will clearly mean something rather different in scale between the two countries. However, strong similarities in the processes of industrial mobility in the two countries do exist, and one starting point for seeing these common forces is in the pattern of suburbanisation.

Hall and Clawson (1973) have compared in some detail the pattern of land conversion in the Boston-Washington megalopolis and the London to Lancashire metropolitan axis or 'coffin'. Both countries experienced significant increases in population in the 1950s and 1960s, the peak increase in net population in the UK coming in 1962 with a rise of 500,000 assisted by immigration from the Commonwealth. Both have experienced a marked deceleration in this increase in the early 1970s as birth rates fell; the UK population stabilising by 1975. In spite of overall rising population, in some areas within both countries the population has declined in the last thirty years. In 39 per cent of all administrative areas in the UK the population declined between 1951—61. These areas included agricultural parts of the country and also the inner cities. The growth was concentrated in the suburban rings around the metropolitan areas and in the smaller free standing cities. The total demand for new homes in the UK was also encouraged by a high rate of household formation, which between

1951 and 1961 was running at 2·2 times the increase in population.

In examining megalopolis England (which contained 33·8 million people in 1971), Hall and his team of research workers (Hall, 1974) showed how the 34·7 per cent of that population which could be classified as suburban in 1951 had increased to 41·7 per cent in 1971. This suburban shift accounted for the total increase in population of 3·5 million in the 'coffin' area. The suburban shift in employment was slower to come. In the 1950s, parts of the area were still experiencing a centralising of employment, but through the 1960s the decentralisation of employment accelerated, and by 1966 the 25·5 per cent of employment classified as suburban in 1951 had grown to 28·3 per cent. Thus, over the two decades, initially radial commuter journeys into the urban cores increased, but this was then followed by rising ring-to-ring journeys to new suburban jobs, following the US pattern.

The suburban spreading within the metropolitan areas of the UK has not progressed as far or as fast as in the US. Higher real incomes, lower petrol prices, higher car ownership, and heavy investment in the road system have all encouraged and permitted greater suburbanisation in the US. Also, the spread has not been significantly resisted by land use planning policy as in the UK. Less stringent zoning and density requirements as well as easier permissions for shopping developments and employment centres, have all allowed lower overall densities in American urban areas. Conversely, the loss of population in the inner cities and the problem of deprivation and social malaise have been relatively greater in the American experience than in the British. Both land use planning controls on the private sector and the very important role of public housing (in both inner city slum clearance areas and in peripheral housing estates) in the UK have modified the extent to which the American experience has been followed; but the underlying pressures have pointed in the same direction. And as we shall see in the next chapter, mobile jobs have led and (more usually) followed this outward movement of population to the edges of the built-up areas.

One further influence on the growth of population and of jobs around the larger conurbations in the United Kingdom has been the programme of planned community developments. These public sector initiatives include the large suburban public housing estates, with limited accompanying local employment opportunities, and the new towns and the expanded towns, in which housing has been planned to be phased in with the expansion of the employment base. The self-standing new and expanded towns, all separated from their metropolitan 'parent' by at least the width of a 'greenbelt', a zone or collar of extremely restricted development, have been responsible for only a small portion of total new house construction in their regions. The new and expanded towns, for example, only accommodated some 18 per cent of the total 1951–66 increase in population outside London in the South East region. But the influence of these planned communities on the pattern of industrial mobility in the UK is far more significant, especially in the Southeast and East Anglia regions. For example (Keeble, 1976, p.85), the eight new towns and two expanded towns in the outer metropolitan area received mobile industry from London which resulted in a net increase of 51,000 manufacturing jobs between 1959 and 1966, or 27 per cent of the total net manufacturing employment growth in the OMA (Outer Metropolitan Area), in this period. And in East Anglia, the seven main expanded towns accommodated 11,000 jobs or 29 per cent of the total net manufacturing growth of the East Anglia region. Industrial immigration into these towns will be examined further in chapter 3.

The new towns have also played a role in British regional economic development policy, the public policy influence which has restrained the growth of population and of employment in the more prosperous and fast growing areas of the United Kingdom while at the same time actively promoting economic growth in those areas with slow growth, persistently high unemployment, and relative social and economic deprivation. The dimensions of the British regional problem and the evolving policy responses over the past forty-five years are well known and have been extensively analysed and discussed. (Recent overviews include Cameron, 1974; Sundquist, 1965, chapter 2; Keeble, 1976, chapter 8.) The policy of controls, incentives and leading infrastructure has been a fundamental influence on industrial mobility in the UK, far more so than any federal or state policy in the US. This review will return to some of the specific ways in which British regional policy has influenced industrial mobility in later chapters. But in making comparisons with the United States it needs to be remembered that over the past thirty years all new industrial factory floor space over 5,000 square feet (with some variation) has required a special permit, an Industrial Development Certificate, from the central government before the investment can be sanctioned by a local land-use planning authority.[11] And that by the mid-1960s, financial incentives to mobile industry were being offered over 40 per cent of the land area of the country, an area containing 20 per cent of the total population.[12]

To conclude this introduction to the context for industrial mobility in the United Kingdom, we may briefly outline the spatial distribution of population and employment change nationally. In 1971, the South East region (with London as its centre), contained 7·4 million people or 13 per cent of the total UK population. In the period between the two world wars the region had grown at two and one-half times the rate of population growth of the country as a whole. This faster rate of growth continued after the Second World War, so that between 1951 and 1961 London and the Southeast region received 530,000 in migrants from Scotland, Northern Ireland, Wales and Northern England from Yorkshire and Lancashire to the Scottish border, or two-thirds of the total net outward migration from the regions. (Sundquist, 1975, p.53.) Half of the new jobs in the country in this period were being created in the Southeast. The pattern has changed since the 1950s, modified by government policy, and perhaps also by improved inter-regional communications. By the late 1960s, 40 per cent of investment in new manufacturing jobs was occurring in those same regions suffering from outward migration. By the early 1970s outward migration had slowed for Scotland (which lost 95 per cent of its natural increase between 1961 and 1971) and had ceased for Wales. Net migration into the London region was brought to a halt. But the 'drift to the South', a focal point for regional policy, had not completely stopped. Rather, it had been dispersed. For London continued to receive the largest stream of inward migrants of any region in the country. But these migrants were more than offset by the outward migration of Londoners, retiring to coastal towns in the Southwest and East Anglia regions, or moving to long distance commuting centres in adjacent regions. Across the whole country the dominant North—South migration streams of the 1950s and 1960s were replaced by more complex interactions, with greater emphasis on local and intra-regional migration flows than on inter-regional flows.

The 'regional problem' has not ceased in the United Kingdom, in the sense that the assisted areas — Scotland, Northern Ireland, Wales, Northern and Northwestern England and parts of the Southwest and the Yorkshire and Humberside regions — continue to exhibit above average unemployment rates, lower incomes, and high relative scores on indices of economic and social deprivation; but disparities have been reduced. The 220,000 or so jobs, according to an estimate by Rhodes and Moore (1973, p.99), which had been created in the assisted areas as a result of regional policy between 1963 and 1971, reflect a degree of success for the policy, and disparities that would have been wider without the policy. Indeed, compared with the United States and many European nations with active regional policies, welfare differences between the regions of the UK are small; as Cameron suggests in his summary of the dimensions of the British

13

regional problem:

> In sum, the differences in welfare across the British regions are small; rural depopulation has already occurred to a very great extent; the domination of the primate city has declined at least if measured in terms of population and despite inter-regional migration processes which constantly shape the balance of population in favor of the South East, East Anglia and the West and East Midlands; and the overall regional changes in population distribution, both historically and forecast, are on a modest scale. However, a high level of unemployment in some regions, low activity rates, and generally apalling environmental conditions create a continuing need for active measures to improve regional economic performance and the regional physical environment. (Cameron, 1974, p.77)

Beneath the policy influences, four underlying factors have shaped the changing regional balance of employment and population in the United Kingdom over the past thirty years. The first is the suburbanisation which has already been referred to. The second is the continuing importance of the London metropolitan area: as a location for economic activity, as a magnet for migrants, as the centre of cultural, political and economic power of the nation; and up to the late 1960s, with the West Midlands Conurbation, as a continuing reservoir of new and potentially mobile job opportunities.

The third factor, by way of contrast, has been the depth and the extent of the industrial structural change that has been required in the depressed regions. The run down of employment in the basic industries of all or major parts of those regions, industries such as coal mining, shipbuilding, textiles, iron and steel manufacture, and heavy engineering, went further and took longer than was envisaged at the end of the 1940s. [13] This process was largely completed, however, by the mid-1970s, and the unwelcome pressures of necessary industrial structural change are now being felt across many industries and more uniformly across the regions of the country.

The fourth factor, following the experience of the US, is the reducing role of manufacturing employment in the total economy, and the shrinking contribution manufacturing makes to the creation of new job opportunities. The potential flow of mobile manufacturing jobs, traditionally the base for regional development policy, can only be maintained by ever tighter controls over new manufacturing jobs. If this is felt to be undesirable, regional policy has to look to the expansion of companies indigenous to the assisted areas, or to the

14

service sectors of industry as a source of job mobility.

Further influences on population and employment distribution are present (the exploitation of North Sea oil, the motorway system, changing local and regional government structures and powers, increasing state intervention in industrial investment planning, etc.). However, since 1971, the slow growth rate of the UK economy, with a sluggishness in industrial investment accompanying the slow down in population growth, has led to a certain stability in the patterns outlined. [12]

Industrial change and industrial movement

How important is industrial movement, as defined for this review, for the changing patterns of employment and population distribution in the two countries as just outlined? This is an extremely difficult question to answer, quantitatively and with confidence. Because of the inadequate recording of investments in new branch plants and in complete relocations ('transfers') in both countries, a full picture of movement is not possible. Even where details are available (as in the case of the UK for the inter-subregional moves between 1945 and 1971), there is still a problem in deciding a cut-off date in relating the number of moves to the employment generated by those moves; for it is the employment totals which are usually the prime focus of policy and which are the usual indicators to relate to general sectoral and spatial changes in industry.

There are three possible ways to attribute an employment total in an establishment to movement. The first is to use the estimate of employment to be generated by the investment put forward by the company concerned before the move. Companies are often required to do this in seeking financial incentives or locational licences and permissions. Alternatively, the employment total may be taken after the initial build-up to full production in the establishment, but before supplementary investment takes place. The relevant time lag is difficult to identify, but in the majority of mobile plants it is in the order of two to five years. The third way, and the one the UK government was forced to follow in the collection of its 1945–65 movement statistics (Howard, 1968), is to total the employment in each mobile plant at the end of the period of study (in the UK case end-1966) no matter when during the study period the move-in took place. Thus, some plants will have had much longer to build up employment, and to subsequently expand, than others.

In addition to these statistical difficulties, it is obvious but

15

important to remember that the major part of employment change in a given area will be due to the expansion and contraction of existing industrial establishments, without industrial movement (as suggested by Figure 1.1). For example, Stanback and Knight (1970, p.222) quote the example of Manchester, New Hampshire in the 1950s. Manchester gained 8,071 jobs between 1950 and 1960: by a rise of 14,548 jobs in expanding industries (electrical and other machinery, printing, food plants, and most significantly, 6,459 jobs in services), and a fall of 6,477 jobs in declining sectors (textiles, agriculture). Some sectors experienced both expansions and decline at different establishments within the sector. Stanback and Knight took account of these gross changes in their general analysis of employment change from 1950 to 1960 across 368 metropolitan labour markets of the US. They show, for example:

> Intra-regional relocation of employment in individual industries played a relatively minor role in regions whose transition was most important. For the Southeast region, only 380,000 job changes were attributable to intra-regional relocation of employment within individual industries, whereas total regional transition . . . accounted for nearly 2 million jobs. Approximately four-fifths of the total transition in the Southeast occurred as a result of employment gains in one industry being offset by employment losses in other industries. (Stanback and Knight, 1970, p.220)

More recent aggregate evidence for the United States for the period 1970 to 1972 is summarised in Table 1.2. This table clearly shows the dominance of plant deaths and expansions and contractions in overall employment change and the relatively minor importance of plant movement; although this is at a very coarse regional scale, intra-regional movement being incorporated as transfers and branch plants in the deaths and births columns. Acquisitions will also be an important influence on these changes. Rees (1978) for example, in his study of the Dallas-Fort Worth area found that an acquisition decision was more common than a branch plant decision, especially for locally based companies. And Hamilton (1978) in his UK study found that 43 per cent of his 1,486 firms in manufacturing had been involved in acquisition or merger activity between 1960 and 1972. Only 14 per cent of his firms did not make explicit locational changes in production or office jobs through closures, relocations or new facilities. Nearly all of the firms (95 per cent) claimed that they had altered the relative importance or functions of their existing units,

16

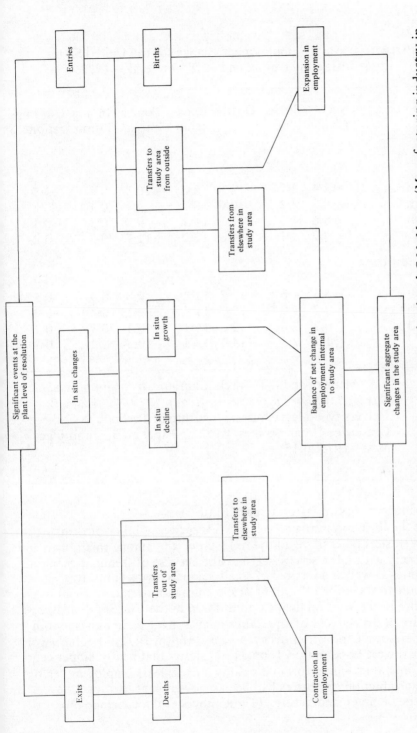

Figure 1.1 Components of industrial change. Source: P.E. Lloyd and C.M. Mason, 'Manufacturing industry in the inner city: a case study of Greater Manchester', *Transactions of the Institute of British Geographers*, New Series 3 (1), 1978, p.79.

17

Table 1.2
Percentage average employment change for the United States
by industry and region, end − 1969 to end − 1972.

Area	Net Change	Births	Deaths	Expansion	Contractions	In-migration	Out-migration
Manufacturing							
Northeast	−12·4	2·7	−12·8	8·0	−10·3	0·4	−0·5
North Central	− 8·2	2·2	−10·0	8·7	− 9·1	0·1	−0·2
South	− 5·6	4·2	−12·2	11·3	− 9·0	0·3	−0·1
West	− 9·7	4·3	−14·3	12·0	−11·7	0·2	−0·2
All Industries							
Northeast	− 6·3	4·6	−12·2	11·2	− 9·8	0·4	−0·5
North Central	− 3·2	4·9	−10·7	11·7	− 9·1	0·2	−0·2
South	0·2	7·6	−12·3	14·1	− 9·3	0·3	−0·2
West	− 1·9	7·3	−14·1	15·3	−10·5	0·2	−0·1

Source: P.A. Allaman and D.L. Birch, *Components of Employment Change for States by Industry Group 1970−72*, Harvard University − Massachusetts Institute of Technology Joint Center for Urban Studies, Working Paper no.5, Cambridge, Mass., 1975, p.15.

contributions to the aggregate pattern of change.

At the local intra-urban level, very extensive mobility of firms between sites takes place all the time, especially among small firms and especially within the service sector. But because of frequent changes of names as well as addresses of small manufacturing firms, it is difficult to trace the full extent of intra-urban movement. In an exercise in the West Midlands Conurbation in the UK, Smith arrives at a figure of 30 per cent of all establishments involved in movement in the metal trade industries over ten years (Smith, 1972). Keeble's work in Northwest London (1971, pp.31−2) shows that nearly 80 per cent of all manufacturing firms in his study area in 1963 employing ten or more production operatives had been involved in at least one move since beginning manufacture. (These moves did not include those to

contiguous sites, and 61 per cent were of less than ten kilometres).
Movement between sites by smaller manufacturing firms within urban
areas is probably greater than has generally been appreciated in the
literature, even though overall mobility accounts for only a small
proportion of aggregate changes as shown in Tables 2.3 and 2.4.

British government statistics for the movement of manufacturing
branches and transfers between and within fifty sub-regions of the UK
from 1966 to 1971 are shown in Table 1.3, compiled by Sant (1975,
p.38).

Table 1.3
Generalised distribution of origins and destinations of
industrial establishments in Great Britain, 1966—71

	Origin and Destination			
	Within same subdivision	Within same region excl- uding (1)	Within GB excluding (1) & (2)	Total
By destination				
Assisted area destinations	939 (52%)	205 (11%)	660 (37%)	1,804 (100%)
Other destinations	926	408	254	1,588
By origin				
Assisted area origins	939 (71%)	205 (15%)	183 (14%)	1,327 (100%)
Other origins	926 (45%)	408 (20%)	731 (35%)	2,065 (100%)
Total moves	1,865	613	914	3,392

Source: M.E.C. Sant, *Industrial Movement and Regional Development*,
Pergamon, 1975, p.38.

All of these moves are for plants employing ten or more people. They
do not include moves in from overseas nor entirely new firms, or
acquisitions of an establishment by another firm. Employment in
these 3,392 moves in the six year period involved 1·5 per cent of the
total employment in manufacturing. Sant further shows the significance of manufacturing movement between sub-regions 1945—65 for

19

the total change in employment in each sub-region in Great Britain from 1951 to 1966 (Figure 1.2). This map shows how, in some sub-regions, industrial movement has been an extremely important contributor to employment change, either complementing the growth of the service sector in the face of declining agriculture or of slowly growing indigenous manufacturing, countering a net decline in indigenous manufacturing. Some of these patterns of movement will be returned to in later chapters, but the overall significance of movement for individual regions may be gained by the following statistics.

The 2,756 moves recorded between sub-regions between 1945 and 1965 created 762,000 jobs by the end of 1966, or about 8·5 per cent of the total UK manufacturing workforce. The 921 moves to the peripheral areas (the principal policy assisted areas of the UK) created 345,000 jobs. By the end of 1966, 26 per cent of all manufacturing jobs in Wales, and in Devon and Cornwall were attributable to moves over the previous twenty years. Rhodes and Moore (1976, p.27) suggest that about 165,000 jobs in mobile manufacturing plants in 1971 had been induced by the operation of regional policy over the period 1960 to 1971. The annual movement rates per 1,000 UK plants in manufacturing between the eleven regions of the UK were 1·44 from 1946–51, 0·74 from 1952–59, 1·56 from 1960–65 and 2·08 from 1966–71 (Keeble, 1976, p.133). One result of this movement has been to increase the number of multiplant companies which are now multi-regional as well. For example the proportion of Hamilton's (1978) 1,486 firms which were multi-regional in 1972 was 64 per cent compared with 41 per cent in 1960.

Two further aspects of industrial movement are of importance for changing patterns of employment distribution. The first is of limited but increasing significance to the United States, but has been of considerable importance to the United Kingdom; industrial inward migration by foreign owned companies. Foreign investment is normally analysed in aggregate or by sector but the internal spatial distribution is also important not only for individual recipient regions but also because foreign investors have a wide choice when considering alternative locations in a county. They are therefore more likely to make that choice on the basis of a detailed economic calculus than domestic migrant firms (Townroe, 1972), and they are perhaps more susceptible to the influences of area development policies. In the UK from 1945 to 1965 258 foreign owned manufacturing concerns were established. By the end of 1966 these plants employed 108,500 people. This flow of movement was especially significant to Scotland, the destination of one-third. (The impact of US investment in the UK has been studied by Dicken and Lloyd (1976), and in particular in

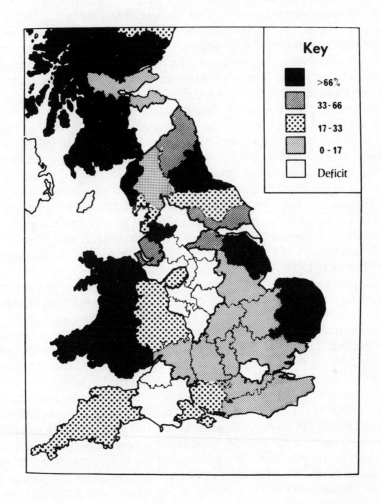

Figure 1.2: The contribution of industrial movement to employment
change.

(Key: $\dfrac{\text{Net employment in moves (1945–65)}}{\text{Change in employment (1951–66)}}$ x 100)

Source: M.E.C. Sant, *Industrial Movement and Regional Development*,
Pergamon, 1975, p.65.

Scotland, by D.J.C. Forsyth (1971). Similarly, in the US, foreign investment, particularly West German, has been especially important in the Carolinas. Japanese investment has also been building up in the West Coast states.

The second aspect of industrial movement of importance for employment distribution is plant closure as shown in Tables 1.2 and 2.3. Transfer moves (one-third of the 1945—65 UK total inter-subdivisional moves) imply shutdown of a plant by the firm concerned. Normally, however, the premises will be re-occupied by another company. The number abandoned or transferred to new uses is not known. More is known about closures by inward migrant companies. Approximately one-quarter of the inter-regional moves between 1945 and 1965 in the UK had closed by the end of 1965 (as had 7·9 per cent of the 1966—71 moves by the end of 1971). This might be regarded as a failing of policy or management, or as part of a natural economic adjustment process (especially where firms have moved again to get larger premises); but it is a phenomenon of obvious concern when the firms closing down have been in receipt of public area development funds and are important employers in a given locality. Closure of plants has been analysed, both in aggregate (Sant, 1976; Atkins, 1973; Hamilton, 1978), and at a more local level (R.W. Schmenner, 1978; P. Dicken and P.E. Lloyd, 1978).

In particular, concern at the falling levels of employment in the manufacturing sector within Greater London has led to recent studies which show that plant closures have been a far more important contributor to the fall than outward migration of plants, as previously suspected. Dennis (1978), for example, shows that between 1966—74 among plants employing twenty or more people in manufacturing 44 per cent of the decline of 390,000 jobs in Greater London was attributable to factory closure unconnected with industrial movement. Movement from London accounted for 27 per cent of the fall, while shrinkage in plants remaining in the capital comprised 23 per cent of the fall (the remaining 6 per cent being a decline in firms employing under twenty people). The loss arising from movement was due more from unplanned moves (11 per cent) than from moves to the assisted areas (9 per cent) or from moves to the new and expanding overspill towns (7 per cent). The transfer of production out of London by large multiplant companies accounted for a large part (41 per cent) of the decline. This picture has been reinforced by the detailed study of Gripaios of 359 firm closures in the South East part of Inner London between 1970 and 1975. Seventy-four per cent of the closures resulted from firm closures, and over half of the ninety-two plants relocating did so within Greater London. Gripaios (1977) concludes

22

that locational factors were primarily responsible for the factory closures, and that neither industrial structure nor decentralisation policy had much direct influence.

Industrial movement and locational efficiency

The relationship between industrial movement and the changing pattern of employment distributions may also be viewed from another perspective entirely. Because, as we shall see, companies involved in transferring industrial plants and in establishing new branch plants are, by and large, the fastest growing and most successful companies in the economy, the pattern of their choice of location will be important for two reasons. Firstly if, for whatever reason, the location chosen does not optimise the potential efficiency of the firm, then there is an opportunity cost attached to the chosen site for the firm, and a cost to society as a whole for the resources used by the firm. There may also of course be a direct cost or an opportunity cost to society attached to an optimal choice of location by the firm because of negative externalities. An underlying rationale of restrictions and permissions and of incentives and inducements for new industrial investments is to bring private and social costs into some sort of rough balance. Therefore, the managerial efficiency with which the task of choosing a new location is undertaken is of interest and importance for the improvement of the productivity of industrial investments, and for the design and the effectiveness of area development policy. There are indications that the process of locational choice in many industrial concerns is executed in a manner unlike many other choices facing the managements of companies. Uncertainty as to both procedure and to the extent of the decision environment is high, the lessons of precedent usually absent, and the relevance of criteria for choice ambiguous. Therefore studies of industrial movement which have concerned themselves with the procedures of decision making may contribute at both the corporate level (by improving the quality of decisions), and at the public policy design level (making instruments more effective).

The second reason that the study of locational decision making in industrial moves is important is that the choices by the faster growing and more successful companies in the economy will reflect both the changing locational needs of industry and the changing relative advantages of different areas of the country. The significance of certain locational factors, such as transportation costs, may be diminishing while the importance of others, such as access by employees to high amenity environments, may be increasing. These

23

changes in turn mean that regions or parts of regions previously attractive to industrial investment may lose favour, while other areas become viable and profitable as potential locations. Not only are these changes important for any long term distribution of population policy and the planning of long term public investments, but they are also important in predicting areas of growth and decline in indigenous non-mobile industry, and in the planning of area development policy responses.

The literature in the two countries which has concerned itself with locational decision making and the issues a company has to face in moving to a new location and in running in a new plant is examined in chapters 6, 7 and 8.

Notes

[1] Hansen (1973, p.84) quotes a table of seventeen such indicators of economic and social distress for the Ozarks Region. See also Ledebur (1977).

[2] The size of these pools is often increased by return-home migration when a new employer is announced (Thompson, 1975, p. 190).

[3] A large petro-chemical investment by the Dow Chemical Company in California, for example, was withdrawn early in 1977 in the face of environment objections and the requirement of over fifty permits to be obtained. The investment is now planned for Yugoslavia.

[4] Extensive analyses of regional and industrial growth in earlier periods in the United States are to be found in Pred (1966) for the period between 1800 and 1914; in Perloff et al. (1960) for the period 1870—1954; in Creamer (1963) for 1947—61; in Fuchs (1962) for 1929—54; and in Stanback and Knight (1970) for 1940—60.

[5] See recent reviews by Hansen (1974) and Sundquist (1975). Also the US : UK comparison by Choguill (1977).

[6] These include the Departments of Housing and Urban Development of Labor, of Agriculture, of the Interior, of Transportation, and of Health, Education and Welfare, and such agencies as the Army Corps of Engineers, the Forestry Service, the National Environmental Protection Agency, the Inland Waterways Commission.

[7] Under the fifty-one states, which themselves have almost total power to initiate land use planning and economic development policies, there are some 3,000 counties of varying size and power, within which are 5,000 legally incorporated cities of less than 50,000

population, as well as the larger cities, each with local planning powers. The country is also covered by nearly 90,000 special districts responsible for such matters as schools, sewerage, drainage, parks, water supply, air pollution, transportation planning and regulation, and area-wide planning. Many localities have special agencies for the promotion of economic development. One author suggested 14,000 in 1966 (C.L. Hamman, p.11).

[8] See Martin and Leone (1977, chapter 1).

[9] Although in fact S470 million of a total appropriation of $769 million was spent on highways. The Appalachian programme has been evaluated in different respects by Rothblatt, 1971; Hansen, 1973; Newman, 1972 and Rondinelli, 1975.

[10] Section 302 of the 1974 Extension Act has extended this aid to city and state planning agencies. This form of assistance is reviewed by Gillette (1976).

[11] The IDC control and its service sector counterpart, the Office Development Permit system, operated since 1965, are discussed in chapter 3. IDC's are not required in the development areas.

[12] The available 1976 package of incentives in the different categories of area is outlined in Townroe (1976, pp.56—7 and pp.183—8). The important labour subsidy, the Regional Employment Premium, was withdrawn at the end of 1976.

[13] See Brown (1972), especially chapter 6.

[14] Except in the East Anglia and Southwestern Regions, the fastest growing regions 1971—76 in terms of population. Retirement migration has been one influence on that growth, but has been exceeded by immigration of people of working age.

2 Intra-urban industrial movement

Because of the relatively limited research investments into the study of the location and movement of industry within cities in both the United States and the United Kingdom, the core of this chapter relies on research results from a restricted number of cities: Glasgow and London in the United Kingdom; Chicago, New York, Cincinnati, and the four Struyk and James (1975) cities — Boston, Cleveland, Minneapolis-St. Paul, and Phoenix — in the United States. Analysts have considered the changing patterns of employment in many other cities, and there are a number of partial reviews of industrial movement; but patterns of industrial movement have received the most complete attention in these nine cities.

This chapter begins by extending the review of intra-urban workplace locations briefly considered in the last chapter, and by considering some of the changing forces on industrial locations in cities. It will then be possible to see how these forces are reflected in the patterns of industrial movement in the cities listed above with particular attention to the discussions in the literature on the suburbanisation of manufacturing. Office moves within cities are influenced by rather different sets of forces to manufacturing plants and so are treated separately here. Elements of the discussion of the city as an incubator of ideas, innovations, new jobs and industrial moves are then examined in the final section.

The pattern of workplace locations in a city may change as a result of six processes as shown in Figure 1.1:

1. The expansion and contraction of employment in existing plants
2. The birth of entirely new plants
3. The death or disappearance of an existing plant
4. Relocations (or transfers) within the city
5. Establishment of a new branch plant by an existing city company
6. In-migration of branches or transfers from firms previously or presently based outside the city

Statistics of employment change by area will reflect the net impact of all of these processes. This chapter will be particularly interested in 4. and 5. but, as we shall see, the impact of 1. dominates all else.

Changing intra-city workplace locations

The interpretation of the available statistics on workplace trends within American and British cities has resulted in some ambiguity and conflict for essentially three reasons. Firstly, the quality and coverage of the principal statistical sources used has been uneven. Secondly, strong underlying changes have been taking place in population patterns and migration flows and it is not clear whether these changes lead or are led by changes in job location. And thirdly, employment totals, especially in manufacturing and for small areas, tend to be very sensitive to cyclical swings in the fortunes of the national economy. These three factors qualify the essentially simple picture of a progressive suburbanisation of employment in the larger cities, and of manufacturing as being the sector to disperse most quickly.

However, in spite of these qualifications, there is no doubt that the long run trend in workplace location in both American and British cities has been towards a lowering of densities and a lowering of the density gradient city centre to periphery. The only exception to this trend has been the concentration of certain office occupations in the urban core, but this concentration has also been facing strong pressures for dispersal.

The trend towards dispersal in American cities is very deep seated. Creamer (1935) for example, traced patterns of deconcentration of both jobs and population in 200 industrialised counties back to 1899, and Mills (1972) has shown falling density gradients in manufacturing employment back to 1920. The trend was reversed during World War II but continued thereafter, associated with falling population densities and rapid expansions of residential suburbs. Kitagawa and Bogue (1955) showed this reversal in World War II in their study of manufacturing suburbanisation 1929 to 1947, in 162 standard metropolitan areas. This study demonstrated great variation between cities in the degree of suburbanisation, but overall found that manufacturing employment in the period was more centralised than population, and that rapid population growth was a prerequisite for any extensive change in the degree of suburbanisation. The post World War II expansion of the residential suburbs of cities in the United States has been reviewed by Zimmer (1975, pp.28–40). Using 1965 city boundaries, a study quoted by Harrison (1974, p.8) showed that the percentage of metropolitan manufacturing jobs in eight large SMSAs located within the central city fell from 88·6 per cent in the 1900–18 period to 60·8 per cent in 1967. Kain's study (1975, pp.86–94) using 1950 central city boundaries, shows how the suburban share of manufacturing employment in forty SMSAs rose between 1948 and

27

1963 from 33·1 per cent to 51·8 per cent; in wholesaling from 8·2 per cent to 28·6 per cent; in retailing from 24·7 per cent to 45·4 per cent; and in services from 15·2 per cent to 31·3 per cent. The suburban share of the population rose from 36·0 per cent to 54·3 per cent in the same period.

This changing suburban—central city balance has also been reflected in falling average density gradients over time, with an acceleration of the flattening post World War II. Between 1940 and 1963, according to Mills (1972, p.46), in six SMSAs the average density gradient of population fell from 0·67 to 0·36; while the gradients in manufacturing 1939 to 1963 fell from 0·77 to 0·68; in retailing from 0·90 to 0·41; in services from 1·12 to 0·5; and in wholesaling from 1·24 to 0·59. Proportionately, decentralisation has occurred most rapidly in wholesaling. More recently, Kemper and Schmenner (1974) have considered the density gradients for manufacturing in five SMSAs, using a better data base than Mills,[1] for the period 1967 to 1971. They find continuing decentralisation falling central densities and flattening density gradients. Overall, employment is less centralised than the manufacturing firms themselves, indicating that larger firms, on average, locate at greater distances from the city centre. Sectorally, little consistency in the pattern of centralisation could be found in the five cities, except that in all cases the apparel industry and printing and publishing were heavily centralised.

Similar, although not so extensive, patterns of decentralisation are also found in the United Kingdom (Hall, et al., 1972); although planning controls with a strong bias to the conservation of agricultural land, and the philosophy of 'green belts' around the major cities, have kept decentralisation lower and densities higher than they probably would have been in the absence of the controls. Decentralisation of manufacturing employment has been examined in detail by Keeble (1968) in London and by Henderson (1974) and Bull (1978) in Glasgow. Bull finds, like Gripaios (1977) in South East London and Schmenner (1978) in Cincinnati, that suburbanisation is much more the result of the pattern of plant closures and plant births and of relative rates of expansion than of intra-urban industrial movement.

Using a sample of over 3,000 building permits, Newman (1967) found that from 1954 to 1965, 49 per cent of all new private non-residential building in US, SMSAs was outside the central cities. By type of building industrial construction (63 per cent) was the highest, and office building (27 per cent) was the lowest.[2] In Boston, Detroit, Los Angeles, New York, Philadelphia, San Francisco and Washington DC, the proportion of industrial building outside the central city was in excess of 75 per cent; but, with the exception of

28

New York, office building in these same cities outside the central city was also well above the national average. Although sectors of employment such as public utilities, local government and finance, insurance and real estate have been increasing in the central cities, they have been increasing elsewhere in the metropolitan areas also. Business, professional and technical services occupations have been growing especially rapidly in the suburbs.

In the late 1960s and early 1970s there have been some indications that the trend towards suburbanisation has changed. The absolute decline in central city employment, including manufacturing, has been reversed, as shown in Table 2.1, and in some SMSAs the suburban share of jobs has stabilised. Cohen (1972) examined the thirty SMSAs studied earlier by Kain and found that for the 1963 to 1967 period, compared with 1958 to 1963, twenty-five of the thirty cities had increasing central city employment compared with fifteen in the earlier period; while only eleven increased in manufacturing employ-ment in the first period, twenty-one did so in the second. Other studies support this picture of a steadying of suburbanisation, although with many qualifications about data and the impact of cyclical swings in the economy (Harrison, 1974, pp.14—26). Public sector jobs (federal, state and local) have been an especially important contributor to the maintenance of central city employment. In 1966, 68 per cent of all public sector jobs in fourteen SMSAs were in the central city rather than the suburbs (Harrison, 1976, p.28). The government sector accounts for approximately one-fifth of all jobs in metropolitan areas and has grown nearly twice as fast as private sector employment since World War II.

Ganz and O'Brien (1973) have interpreted these recent changes more strongly, arguing a significant revival of the economies of the central cities at the end of the 1960s. They show that thirty large central cities gained 1·5 million jobs between 1960 and 1968, or one-quarter of the total job gains in their metropolitan areas. This gain was concentrated in finance, insurance, communications, business services, recreation and tourism, personal services and government services. The claim of central city revival has been critically examined by James (1974). James argues that the apparent reversal in the fortunes of the central cities documented by Ganz and O'Brien is transitory and reflects cyclical forces, in particular the strong national growth of employment 1958 to 1967. James is thus closer to the pessimistic views of the employment fortunes of the inner city of Long (1971), who focussed on St. Louis, and of Sternlieb (1971) who focussed on the older North Eastern cities. James argues, with Kain, that economic, transportation, technological, and social pressures will

29

Table 2.1
Thirty large metropolitan areas: change in employment

	Central city (1)	'Suburbs' (2)	Total metro-politan (3)	Central city (4)	'Suburbs' (5)	Total metro-politan (6)
	Thousands			Annual Percentage		
1958—63						
Manufacturing	−264	393	129	−1·3	6·0	0·3
Retail	108	546	654	1·0	7·7	3·6
Wholesale	− 48	145	97	−0·7	8·2	1·2
Selected services	173	205	378	2·6	7·9	4·1
Total above	− 31	1,289	1,289	−0·1	4·8	1·8
Local government[a]	52	n.a.	n.a.	1·6	—	—
Total	21	n.a.	n.a.	0	—	—
1963—67						
Manufacturing	139	679	818	0·9	4·8	2·7
Retail	59	350	409	0·6	4·6	2·5
Wholesale	57	171	228	1·1	8·4	3·2
Selected services	141	165	306	2·4	5·9	3·5
Total above	396	1,365	1,761	1·1	5·1	2·8
Local government[b]	110	n.a.	n.a.	3·1	—	—
Total	506	n.a.	n.a.	1·3	—	—

[a]1957—62   [b]1962—67

Source: Benjamin I. Cohen, Trends in negro employment within large metropolitan areas, *Public Policy*, 19 (4), 1971, p.614.

continue to encourage decentralisation of job locations.

What have been the attractions of suburban sites to industry? In general terms, factors which have been suggested include: [3]

Space Suburban locations have provided sites for single storey factories, warehouse and retail establishments, at a relatively low land cost and with room for subsequent expansion. Suburban growth has been most rapid in the most strongly growing industrial sectors, but also in those companies undergoing modernisation in all sectors. The space requirements of many sectors of manufacturing have been changing. Flow-line integrated production processes require single storey buildings, and it is extremely difficult and costly to assemble large tracts of land close to city centres (W.F. Lever, 1975b). Workers' car parking requirements add to the pressure for more land.

Labour supply Population growth and employment growth have fed one another. Companies have moved to suburban sites to pick up pools of labour, only in turn to generate yet more residential growth. The flight to the suburbs has been stimulated by Federal Housing Authority standards and loan facilities as well as tax reliefs on mortgage payments (M. Clawson, 1971, pp. 41—4). But overall there is a close interdependence between jobs and housing choices, as studies of workplace and residential populations in the suburbs suggest (A.M. Guest, 1976a and 1976b). Unfortunately this resulted in a mismatch of employment and residence for low paid and minority workers, unable to afford the housing or the transportation to gain access to suburban jobs. [4] Available female labour in particular has been found to be important in British studies (Henderson, 1974). Lower labour costs and better skills may be obtained by moving a plant or opening a branch.

Transportation Throughout the 1950s and 1960s, the network of limited access highways has been extended, both between cities and around and within cities. With falling costs of truck transportation relative to railroads, suburban sites with access to the freeway system have been popular for industrial expansion for industry selling away from the city. And even for local wholesalers and manufacturers serving local markets, Evans (1975, pp.268—74) has demonstrated theoretically how a change from a radically focussed transport system to a complete cross urban transport system will encourage movement to sites away from the central city.

Communication technology Improvements in telecommunications equipment and in data processing have reduced the need for relatively routine production operations in a company to be close to managerial decision making centres or to city centre agglomeration economies.

31

This permits locations of activity in the suburbs and beyond, while control and strategic functions can rest in an office still located in the city centre.

Urban services Related to the above, urban services, including business services and public services and utilities, have been diffused throughout metropolitan areas, or are priced without regard to location. Agglomeration economies within urban areas have reduced in significance for most sectors of industry.[5]

Taxation Differential rates of property and business taxation central city to suburbs, have been a further encouragement to decentralisation. The effects tend to be cumulative. As firms begin to move out, the tax base falls. But expenditures do not fall but rise frequently. So tax rates in the central city are forced up, and more economic activity moves out.

Social factors Rising crime and congestion and the 'flight of the middle classes' may lead business owners or senior managers to search for suburban locations to meet their own convenience and place preference.

Pollution and land use planning controls Zoning, planning restrictions on mixed land uses in residential areas, and noise, smell, and emission regulations may all discourage a company from trying to expand or even to retain an existing unit in a central city area.

Markets In the larger cities, many smaller suburban firms will be selling to larger suburban firms. Larger firms will lead smaller firms to decentralise, or will encourage their creation in the city outskirts.

In both the United States and the United Kingdom the force of decentralisation of manufacturing jobs dropped with the fall in manufacturing jobs in the 1973—74—75 recession. But overall there is little evidence of a reversal of the suburbanisation trend, the trend resulting from both growth and then movement of central city companies and from indigenous and new firm growth in the suburbs. The relative rates of expansion and contraction within plants rest on earlier decisions as to the location of new plants, branch units or relocations (Wood, 1974).

Intra urban patterns of movement in manufacturing industry

A Pressures to move

In considering the destination choice by manufacturing firms within

32

cities, we may envisage these firms facing a rent gradient with a peak close to the historic core of the city, or the central business district, and flattening slopes as distance from the core increases. There are some minor peaks in non-core sub-centres of the city. And for some smaller firms rentals may rise in suburban locations where only recently constructed property is available. An individual firm will seek a satisfactory location, balancing off the land costs or rental prices against the other spatially variable costs across the land area of the city.[6] Some firms will seek a central location. These tend to be firms locating operations with low land to output requirements, but which would benefit from the external facilities most readily and cheaply available near the urban core. Other firms seek more peripheral locations: those needing more land relative to output or reacting to the various pressures outlined in the previous sections.

Some firms will be pushed into making this destination choice by external forces. These forces may be the direct result of the decisions of public policy. Urban renewal and slum clearance are the most obvious; but higher taxation, or new land use or pollution control restrictions, may result indirectly from the decisions of public policy. A slum clearance programme of housing for example may deprive a core plant of its labour force, now rehoused in the suburbs.[7] (This is perhaps more common in the United Kingdom with its larger proportion of public sector housing than in the United States.)

It will be more common, however, for firms to undertake a choice of destination as a result of internally generated forces, even if in many cases there is considerable inertia and delay (D. Stone, 1974, p. 65). Table 2.2 is not untypical of a number of industrial surveys which have asked the question: 'Why did you move?' This table is taken from a British government survey of 500 plants, which moved between 1964 and 1967, and although it includes long distance mobility as well as intra-urban movement, the pressures to choose a new location at all are not dissimilar for the different lengths of move eventually undertaken. As the table shows, growth and the need for more space are the prime pressures on movement. Locating a new plant to meet the demand from a new market will be more common among longer distance moves, but will be a factor for some intra-urban moves. Similarly for moves in response to problems of labour recruitment, either of numbers or of changing quality. But the expansion of production is the major force behind both relocations and the establishment of branch units. This expansion may be associated with changes in technology or with new products involving new processes requiring single storey factory buildings. The price of land then becomes an increasingly important element in the

Table 2.2
'What caused you to consider opening a new plant in a new location?'

		Percentage of all respondent firms		
		Major reason	Minor reason	Outstanding single reason
1	To permit an expansion of output	83	8	20
2	Inadequate existing premises or site	50	11	8
3	Unsatisfactory labour supply at existing location	40	11	15
4	Inducements and facilities made available by official bodies	27	14	2
5	Opportunity to purchase or rent premises or site at new location	20	8	3
6	Too far from established or potential markets	19	1	9
7	Refusal or expected refusal of IDC	12	4	5
8	Town Planning difficulties	11	3	4
9	Lease or former premises fell in, or good offer received	5	2	3
10	Desire to be in more attractive surroundings	4	8	1
11	Too far from supplies, actual or prospective, of materials or services	3	2	1
12	More profitable to operate elsewhere, no other postulated reason being major	1	–	1
13	No one outstanding reason	–	–	28

Questions 1–12 were asked of 531 firms.

Question 13 was asked of 492 firms, having been added after some interviews had taken place.

Source: Department of Trade and Industry, Inquiry into Location Attitudes and Experience, *Memorandum submitted to the Expenditure Committee (Trade and Industry Subcommittee) on Regional Development Incentives,* (Session 1973–4) p.532, HC 85 - 1, HMSO, London.

investment calculus of the expansion.

Supplementary questions asked in the same British government survey expanded the answers listed in the table:

1 *Expansion of output* The desire to expand the output of existing products was important for more than three times as many firms as the need to provide for a new line of products. This expansion factor was more important for branch plant moves than for transfers and its dominance in this survey is supported by the results from many other locational surveys.[8]

2 *Inadequate premises* This factor is closely associated with the previous factor: the reason that the existing site was fully occupied being more important than a desire for reorganisation. One firm in eight was influenced in some (often minor) degree by traffic congestion. Security has been suggested as an additional factor in some American studies.[9] All of these reasons, as expected *a priori*, are more important for transfer moves than for branch plant locations. Both of these first two factors were also found to be particularly important (for 76 per cent and 87 per cent of relocating firms) for fifty-three movers from London to the new and expanded towns between 1970 and 1975 (Dennis, 1978, p.71). Also for the 1971–75 transfer moves in Cincinnati (Schmenner, 1978, pp.4–71).

3 *Unsatisfactory labour supply* A shortage of female labour was the outstanding single reason for movement for one firm in nine. In contrast a shortage of male labour was the dominant factor for only 3 per cent of respondents. Shortage of skilled labour and difficult labour practices were important for only a small minority of firms. Overall, this group of reasons was relatively more important (as expected) to labour intensive industry, to moves originating within Greater London, and to those moves also motivated by an expansion of output.

4 *Inducements* Two-fifths of all respondents were influenced in some degree by inducement and facilities, the influence being strongest (understandably) for moves to assisted areas and new and expanded towns, and for moves originating overseas. It was a major reason for only 15 per cent of moves among the largest 500 British companies, and for only 11 per cent of transfer moves.

5 *Opportunity to purchase or rent premises or site* Smaller firms, those in labour intensive industries, and transfer moves, were all more likely to react to the stimulus of a new plant solution to existing difficulties. They were attracted to the immediacy of the solution. But this was a supplementary factor, being the outstanding single reason for only 3 per cent of respondents.

6 *Markets* Distance from existing and potential markets was the

outstanding factor for only 5 and 3 per cent of respondents. One per cent moved because the market location had changed. This factor is much more important among American companies operating at a state or continental scale. The McMillan survey, for example, of 500 new plants lists markets as the major factor for the choices of new location (T.E. McMillan, 1965). There is little evidence of companies moving out to suburban locations for predominantly market reasons.

7 *Industrial Development Certificates* This peculiarly British factor was the outstanding factor for only 3 per cent of respondents because they had actually been refused permission to extend an existing site or to build on another site within the local area; and for another 2 per cent of respondents because they expected such a refusal. This factor was particularly important for the subgroup of engineering companies moving from within the West Midlands conurbation.

8–12 The remaining factors were of minor importance, both to respondents overall and to most separately identified subgroups. Town planning difficulties were relatively more important for transfer moves, for whom expansion was not a major motive, and for single plant firms based in the largest cities. The falling-in of a lease was one of the most important motives for movement among the non-expanders and for single plant transfer move firms. Fifteen per cent of moves in the paper, printing, and publishing section listed this as a major reason, the highest percentage of any sector. Amenity seems to be less of a reason for moving than a reason for choosing one location rather than another once the decision to move has been taken. The motive of moving to be closer to a supply of components was unimportant in all subgroups considered. The desire to be closer to a supply of raw materials was a major factor for firms in the food, drink and tobacco industry (17 per cent), in chemicals (12 per cent), and in the brick, pottery, glass and cement industries (13 per cent).

13 *No outstanding reason* The fact that over one-quarter of firms involved in movement could not list a single outstanding factor stresses the multi-dimensional aspect of a decision to move in many companies.

Among all of these factors listed in this British survey it is noteworthy that labour costs are nowhere cited as a reason for movement (although labour costs are possibly included in the third factor). This is in contrast to American evidence. Mueller and Morgan, for example, list labour costs, together with unionism, as a reason for relocation by 32 per cent of employment in their 239 firms in Michigan (1962, p. 212).

Unfortunately, there is no large scale survey which has distinguished the pressures for movement among short distance intra-urban movers from those influencing the longer distance moves. It would seem that the pressures to move on any subgroup of firms moving both locally and further afield are broadly similar, the main differences arising in the reasons for choosing one new location rather than another: but the intra-urban moves are more commonly transfers by smaller firms, suggesting that the external push factors (lease, town planning, labour supply) are relatively more important than the internal push factors of growth and expansion and the attraction of inducements for these movers, compared with moves away from the urban area of origin.

B Dispersal patterns

How far can we enlarge upon the general characterisation, outlined in the first part of this chapter, of a progressive suburbanisation of manufacturing industry in British and American cities, in which industrial mobility plays a significant role? Two studies in particular help us: the work of Struyk and James (1975) on four American cities and the analysis of industrial movement within the Clydeside conurbation by Cameron and his co-workers (G.C. Cameron, 1973).

It might be thought that the development of modern urban road systems reduces the significance of distance within the city for the location of manufacturing industry, and that the location of new plants will not need to relate to the city centre in the way it has done so in the past (and as implied by rent gradient theory). Perhaps urban land is becoming increasingly homogeneous in its locational attributes for manufacturing industry. This thesis of locational randomness of new manufacturing development was examined by Cameron in his study of plant migration, births and deaths, in separate areas within the Clydeside conurbation.

At the beginning of the period (1958), three out of four manufacturing plants in Clydeside were located within eight kilometres of the centre of the city; one in four was within one kilometre. (Table 2.3) By 1968 the number of plants within a two kilometre radius of the city centre had fallen by one-quarter, much faster than the 8 per cent fall for the whole metropolitan area. This 'loss' was due to both a low birth rate and to a heavy loss of transferred plants. Elsewhere, nearly every other area gained plants absolutely and relatively. In the outer part of the central city (2 to 8 kilometres from the city centre) these gains tended to be the result of a new immigration of plants, but further out a high birth rate also contributed to the increase. The birth rate tended to increase with distance from the city centre, while the death rate showed little spatial variation. New plants tended to

Table 2.3
Changes in industrial plants, Clydeside conurbation, 1958 to 1968

	Average number of establish.	Birth rate[ii]	Death rate	Immigrtn. rate	Out-migrtn. rate
Central city[iii]					
Ring 1	501·5	16·3	27·1	5·6	24·5
Ring 2	371·5	16·0	32·3	17·5	30·1
Ring 3	242·5	16·5	25·6	28·5	16·5
Rings 4—8	603·0	19·1	27·7	20·9	14·6
Sub total	1,718·5	16·8	28·2	16·8	21·1
Sub-centres[iv]	403·0	30·3	34·5	18·1	5·5
Non-urban quadrants[v]					
South East	157·5	41·3	30·5	13·3	3·2
Other	122·5	40·8	28·6	16·3	9·8
Sub total	280·0	41·1	29·6	14·6	6·1
Total	2,401·5	21·9	29·4	16·7	16·7

[i](Stock 1958 + Stock 1968) - 2

[ii]All rates of change are in numbers of plants per zonal average total, per cent.

[iii]In kilometre rings from conurbation centre.

[iv]Ten sub-centres within the conurbation but outside the central city, including East Kilbride and Cumbernauld New Towns.

[v]The remaining conurbation areas outside ii and iii.

Source: G.C. Cameron, 'Intra-urban location and the new plant', *Papers and Proceedings of the Regional Science Association,* 29, 1973, pp.1—16.

locate further from the city centre than was average for the total stock of establishments, confirming the general suburbanisation thesis; although the evidence is not available for whether this effect is the result of progressive leap-frogging of plants away from the city centre, or whether the result comes from both inner city centre to periphery moves as well as outer city centre moves, and from moves within the inner periphery to locations further out. An industry-by-industry analysis indicated that new plants tended to replicate the locational pattern of the parent industry, again arguing against the randomness thesis.

When establishment size is brought into the analysis, Cameron finds, like Moses and Williamson in Chicago (1967, p.27) that smaller firms move shorter distances than larger ones and that smaller new plants tend to locate closer to the city centre. In Glasgow 54·9 per cent of the new plants 1958 to 1968 were located within the central city but they only accounted for 24·6 per cent of the 1968 employment in all the new plants.

Struyk and James' study of intra-metropolitan industrial location in Cleveland, Minneapolis-St. Paul, Boston and Phoenix unfortunately only present spatial shifts in terms of number of employees rather than number of plants involved as well. As Table 2.4 shows, the net natural increase that they found (births minus deaths) considerably outweighed the influence of net migration, but the contrasting influences of migration on the central city and on the rest of the metropolitan area stands out. In all four cities mobile establishments contributed to an outward shift of employment. This contribution was especially strong in Cleveland and Minneapolis-St. Paul. In Boston there was more cross migration: and in Phoenix what little movement there was occurred mainly within the central city boundaries. The pattern of births and the destinations of mobile plants in the four cities tended to be reinforcing.

Struyk and James (1975, chapter 10) also suggest a dichotomous pattern of intra-urban locations, which contributes to industrial mobility. They examine the hypothesis that locational activity within urban areas is influenced by the clustering of industry at specific locations and by the externalities that are associated with such concentrations. Using a definition of 'concentration' under which an industry is classified as concentrated in a zone if the employment in that zone in that industry is more than twice that which would have been present in that zone if the total SMSA employment was evenly distributed across the metropolitan area, the net changes of employment by zone in each city are linked to the presence and absence of concentrated industries. Using a regression procedure, the authors

Table 2.4
Components of net employment change in central cities and rest of
the metropolitan area, 1968 relative to 1965 (number of employees)

	Total net change	Net immi-gration[a]	Net natural increase	Net change in stationary establishments
Boston				
Central City	− 2,965	−2,362	−10,735	10,132
Rest of SMSA	14,182	664	− 8,870	22,748
Cleveland				
Central City	−18,646	−4,441	−11,144	− 3,061
Rest of SMSA	4,636	4,606	− 4,240	4,383
Minneapolis-St. Paul				
Central City	−14,599	−2,764	− 6,200	− 5,635
Rest of SMSA	6,007	2,869	− 1,446	4,422
Phoenix				
Central City	9,495	− 86	374	9,216
Rest of SMSA	4,813	36	3,205	1,573

[a]The net number of jobs moving from central city zones may not
equal the number moving into SMSA-ring zones, because the employment count for 'origin' firms is for 1965 while that for 'destination'
firms is for 1968.

Source: R.J. Struyk and F.R. James, *Intra Metropolitan Industrial
Location*, Lexington Books, Lexington, Mass., 1975, p.96.

demonstrate that concentrated industry responds differently to a set
of locational influences (which includes variables for externalities,
scale effects and specific industry linkages) than non-concentrated
industry. The concentrations are relatively more important in more
centralised locations, suggesting that general external economies are

the most important influences on the locational behaviour of concentrated industries. When this effect is analysed for migrant firms only, the analysis shows, for example, that external economies are important in the apparel and printing and publishing sectors, are unimportant in food processing and are of declining importance in the machinery industry. An important policy conclusion is that the locations of non-concentrated industries are more likely to be influenced by non-externality factors (which might include transportation facilities, local markets and inducements) and so be able to be more strongly influenced by the instruments of public policy; but that there will continue to be considerable demands for space, especially among smaller firms, within these industrial concentrations, and in areas accessible to the urban core. [10]

The overall pattern of industrial migration out from the city centre, qualified by cross-movement to retain or enhance advantage of external economies by certain sectors of industry, is reinforced by other studies. Stone (1974) for example in his study of 309 outward migrants over a nine year period in Boston, lays particular stress on the pool of high level labour skills for particular industries in the core areas of the city. Steed (1976) shows how these external economies, however, may be changing in nature and are becoming less important than they used to be and less associated with the central core of the city. In Montreal and Toronto the downtown areas in the 1960s attracted a much smaller proportion of new plants than in the 1950s in two industries, clothing and printing and publishing, normally associated with high externality requirements. Schmenner (1978, pp.4—27 — 4—44) in his detailed work on Cincinnati again shows net decentralisation and the short distance moved by many plants. Only 24 per cent of his sample of 219 plant moves between 1971 and 1975 moved more than six miles, 31 per cent moved within the same zip code and another 21 per cent moved to an adjacent zip code. Although 39 per cent of the moves were decentralising, 16 per cent were in the reverse direction; the remaining 45 per cent remaining approximately the same distance from the CBD (Central Business District). Longer distance moves were less likely to be 'across town' moves, being more likely to be larger, faster growing and decentralising.

C Intra-urban zonal attraction

Industry moving within the city will react to the general pattern of spatially based economic forces operating upon the location of

41

economic activity. The extent to which movers react to identifiable forces was tested by Moses and Williamson (1967, pp.211—22) in their analysis of 2,000 Chicago firms moving between 1950 and 1964 to 582 zones within the city. Using regression modes in which the number of destinations per unit area were the dependent variables, rather indifferent results were obtained using the following independent variables: the distance of the zone from the core as a proxy for the rent gradient; the population density in the zone as a proxy for the wage gradient; the percentage of transportation land in a zone minus highway land as a reflection of access to non-highway transport; access to freeways by a dummy variable if a freeway was in or adjacent to the zone; the percentage of vacant industrial and commercially zoned land; a dummy for land within the City of Chicago; and the percentage of land in a zone in manufacturing use. The statistical quality of the results was improved by grouping the zones into three areas, and splitting the moves into branch plants and transfers. The strongest equation was for branch plants locating in the north of Chicago, 66 per cent of the variance being explained. The only consistently significant variable (in 6 out of 8 equations) was the percentage of manufacturing land, positive in all but one of the equations, although the sector with the highest percentage of such land had the lowest density of destinations.[11]

A similar regression analysis has been applied by Cameron and his co-workers to 1,133 movers in Glasgow for the period 1958 to 1968, using 742 zones, aggregated into 60 basic zones (G.C. Cameron et al., 1975). This study used three forms of dependent variable: numbers of in-migrant plants to a zone, the employment in those plants; and, for comparison, the 'in-situ' employment expansion. Closures of new plants by the end of the period were ignored; and the 'in-situ' expansion figures included net growth in new plants and interzonal relocations as well as net growth in plants remaining in the zone throughout the period. Over half the moves (607) were within or between zone transfers (56 moving more than once), the remainder being new single plant companies (351) branch plants originating outside the Clydeside conurbation (118) and local branch plants (57).

The independent variables in this study were: zone to city core distance as a measure of access to the external economies of the core; zonal employment densities, as a proxy for the rent gradient; a measure of vacant land and property in each zone;[12] the proportion of land not in manufacturing, as an indicator of possible town planning restrictions and of the lack of local linkages; the proportion of land in transportation uses; potential zonal access to labour using private transport, derived from a local transportation study and an indicator of the local labour markets; a similar variable of access by public transport; and an index of zonal access to freight flows within the total urban area.

The results show an improvement over the Chicago model, 75 per cent of the variance of total plant destinations being explained by the model, and 50 per cent of the variance of total employment destinations. The most satisfactory variables are: access to the core, vacant land and building space, the proportion of land use in manufacturing and accessibility by public transport for labour. The model works much more satisfactorily for those zones within the City of Glasgow than for those in the periphery of the conurbation. This suggests that the influences of accessibility and the rent gradient on movement destinations are more important for central city mobility than for moves to or within the periphery; or that this model has not included variables which are especially important for the peripheral destinations. The missing variables may include the rezoning of land to industrial use, accessibility to the inter-city transport networks, the search for particular categories of labour, the desire of owners and managers for high amenity or low home-to-factory travel time, or the attraction of lower taxes outside the central city.

Intra-urban movement of offices

All the discussion in the previous section has been in terms of the intra-urban mobility of manufacturing industry. And yet, as noted earlier, manufacturing is a declining sector in terms of employment in both the US and the UK, and the full tertiary sector accounts for the majority of jobs involved in the processes of industrial mobility within the city. Much of the service sector mobility is, however, associated with small offices or retail outlets, in moves over very short distances which do not fundamentally influence the spatial structure of employment in the city. The offices of large organisations on the other hand are more analagous to the factories of manufacturing industry, being influenced by a city wide pattern of economic locational forces. These forces, plus public policy interventions, give rise to an intra-urban pattern of office mobility, not dissimilar to that found in the manufacturing sector. (P.W. Daniels, 1975, chapters 7 and 9)

There are, however one or two very important differences which influence the locational patterns of office development. The first is essentially institutional. In both the US and the UK the majority of office floorspace is leased rather than owned by the user. This even applies to many office based organisations and administrations in public sector industry and in local, state, and national governments. Often the leases are fairly short term with frequent rent reviews. This means that office based firms face a more frequent stimulus to move than is the case with manufacturing firms. And because the requirements of most office firms in terms of fixtures and fittings in their buildings are not so very different from all other firms, there are fewer constraints on moving than is the case with manufacturing.

This renting characteristic of offices means that it is more difficult for government to influence either the volume or the direction of flow of office movement.[13] The renting characteristic also means that the location of new construction is planned by property companies and financial institutions to maximise the market opportunity for rental: usually the centre of the city. Construction costs vary little between city centre and suburb. Office firms looking for rental floorspace are often therefore forced to go to central locations, even though the most efficient locations for them individually, availability of floor space aside, are outside the highly priced central area.

However, the second important difference of very many office firms from the average manufacturing concern is that locations within or close to the CBD are felt to be both efficient and necessary, even at high rental rates. This is because of the particular pattern of external economies resulting from agglomeration for many office firms. Local linkages in the form of easy, quick, and cheap contact between individuals both within the office organisation and with other office organisations are (or are thought to be) a prime requirement for efficient and profitable operation. Face to face meetings are preferred to contacts in the form of a letter, memo, telex message, or telephone conversation. This desire for face-to-face contact encourages office firms to cluster together and to gain mutual benefit from the presence of each other. Thus, agglomerations to offices grow up, as in the City of London or on the Island of Manhattan. And even within these agglomerations specialisms occur, as for example with the grouping of banks and stock-brokers around Wall Street; the past concentration of consulting engineers in the Victoria and Westminster areas of London; the advertising and media companies in mid-town Manhattan; or the focus of printing and publishing in the Fleet Street and Covent Garden areas. Specialised services then grow up around the larger firms.

The pattern of spatial specialisation of office activities in central London has been linked to an analysis of the forms and patterns of communications used by firms, sector by sector (J.B. Goddard, 1973), based upon information gathered in a communications audit. Full details of the internal and external communications of a sample of individuals within the office firms are collected from a 'contact diary' filled in over a period of days by each respondent. The pattern established in the analysis of those diaries allows a single office organisation to assess the dependence upon face-to-face communication, and whether there are 'blocks' or sub-units of the organisation which may be dispersed to lower cost non-central city locations. Key negotiating and decision making functions, and functions with a high level of external communication may need to be retained in the central city. This approach to office location was pioneered in Sweden where communication audits have also been undertaken in manufacturing concerns (G. Tornquist, 1970 and 1973). The technique has been used to assist in the planning of the dispersal of government offices from Central London (Hardman, 1973).

One result of these studies in London has been to demonstrate that a high proportion (over 80 per cent) of the communications which take place between office organisations in Central London could in fact readily be undertaken outside the centre. So many office functions could in fact decentralise. And in the case of London, with some of the highest rentals for office floorspace in the world, office decentralisation has been occurring. Between 1963 and 1975, 1,761 office firms known to the Location of Offices Bureau[14] had moved or were in the process of moving within or out of Greater London. Seven hundred and five of these moves were within the Greater London area (in a radius 8 to 10 miles from the centre), and over half of all the moves were within the direct hinterland of the city, as shown in Table 2.5, two-thirds being within forty miles. Many of these moves were undertaken by small firms, as shown in Table 2.6, half of the total employing less than 25 people, and only 181 employing over 200 people (although the largest 10 per cent of moves accounted for 59 per cent of the total jobs involved). The smaller firms tend to move over smaller distances, so that the 73 per cent of moves which are under forty miles account for only 61 per cent of the total jobs moved.[15]

Much of the London movement out of the centre has been to a limited number of suburban office complexes, usually based upon a railway interchange. Croydon is the largest, but others include Watford, Slough, Kingston-upon-Thames, Potters Bar, Hounslow and Romford. Rents can drop by 50 per cent and more between city centre and suburb, and an office firm can achieve considerable financial savings by moving to a suburban location without damaging necessary ease of contact with the city centre or forcing all the staff to move house. (P.W. Daniels, 1977, p.267) This suburbanisation has not been typical of other large British cities however. In Leeds, for

45

Table 2.5
LOB clients moved and moving 1963—75 by distance

Distance from Central London	No. of moves	Percent. of moves	No. of jobs	Percent. of jobs
Inside GLC area	705	40	46,410	35
Beyond GLC area — 19 miles	147	9	7,702	5
20—39 miles	426	24	29,067	21
40—59 miles	120	7	11,051	8
60—79 miles	129	7	17,339	12
80 miles and over	234	13	26,036	19
Total	1,761	100	140,605	100

Source: LOB Annual Report 1974—75, p.37.

Table 2.6
LOB clients moved and moving 1963—75 by size

Size of move in jobs	No. of moves	Percent. of moves	No. of jobs	Percent. of jobs
Under 25	872	50	8,943	6
25—49	293	17	9,925	7
50—99	235	13	15,330	11
100—199	180	10	23,806	17
200—499	128	7	36,829	26
500 and over	53	3	45,772	33
Total	1,761	100	140,605	100

Source: LOB Annual Report 1974—75, p.35.

example, 45 per cent of 830 office firms surveyed had moved in the previous twenty years, some moving two or three times; but nearly all this movement was in the city centre (M.V. Facey and G.B. Smith, 1968). Individual firms have established themselves in spacious suburban surroundings in provincial towns, and in some of the new towns, but outside London office complexes of a large number of firms and buildings are still focussed on the centre of cities.[16]

In the United States also, the central city has held its attraction for many office firms and this is reflected in the central city office construction boom of the past fifteen years or so. Between 1960 and 1972 gross office floorspace in Manhattan increased by 104 million square feet to a total of 244 million square feet, a 74 per cent rise. In central Chicago over the same period the increase was over 50 per cent. Gains of 60 to 90 per cent were found in Atlanta, Boston, Cleveland and Dallas, while Houston, Minneapolis-St. Paul and San Francisco increased by over 100 per cent. But as Table 2.7 shows although the non-CBD totals were small in these cities, the growth rates of office floorspace away from the city centres were very high indeed.

Unfortunately, there has been no research into how far the suburban growth of office employment is associated with a decentralising movement, or with inward migration from outside the metropolitan area, or with the growth of existing firms.

Table 2.7
Growth of office space in nine SMSAs (in million gross feet)

City	Central City CBD		Rest of SMSA	
	1960	1972	1960	1972
New York	140	244	135	239
Chicago	48	73	1	15
San Francisco	19	34	3	18
Atlanta	11	20	12	29
Minneapolis-St.Paul	10	20	1	25
Houston	11	22	4	20
Boston	18	29	1	10
Dallas	10	16	3	13
Cleveland	8	15	—	4

Source: Adapted from G. Manners, The office in metropolis: an opportunity for shaping metropolitan America, *Economic Geography*, 50, 1974, Table One.

The degree of intra-urban mobility

Reference was made in the last chapter to the difficulty of establishing the full extent of industrial mobility in an area (because of lack of plant based records and statistics, details of closures, changes of name, etc.); but such estimates as have been published suggest that considerably more movement takes place than is commonly supposed. The degree of mobility will be especially high within urban areas, particularly among small single plant firms. Schmenner (1978, pp.5–34) for example estimates that between 80 and 90 per cent of all moves are local moves, finding that between 1971 and 1975 in Cincinnati 11 per cent of all of the area's manufacturing plants moved, and 17 per cent were newly established. The new firm of the typical entrepreneur in the manufacturing industry will commence operations in a nursery unit. This may be the basement or the garage of a house, a 'lock-up' garage, a small workshop in older buildings, a corner rented in a larger factory or warehouse, a 'flatted' factory in a multi-storey building, or under the arches of a railway viaduct or freeway bridge. More common now is the nursery unit (of perhaps 1,500 square feet or less) offered on a public or private sector industrial estate. It may be hypothesised that because of the dependence of this new operation on urbanisation economies, the first location is likely to be towards the centre of the city. As, and if, the firm is successful, the need for more space increases while the dependence upon urbanisation economies decreases, and a sequence of moves takes place, typically moving away from the urban core.

Movement will also take place among small but growing firms in the suburban areas. New companies, linked to previously decentralised operations as customers or suppliers, go through a similar sequence of moves to find more space; although the sequence may involve fewer moves as the space to expand at any one given site is more likely to be available in suburban locations. As we have seen in the section headed 'Pressures to move', these sequences of movement associated with growth will only be part of the full pattern of industrial mobility in the city. Movement also takes place because of labour supply problems, a lease falling in, town planning problems, changing markets etc. The total scale or degree of mobility from and within the city has received considerable attention as evidence of the city as an incubator of economic activity. If the economic environment of the city is necessary to allow new ideas, new products, new processes and new organisations to grow, then any policy which detracts from that environment will have a harmful effect on the long term prospects for economic growth of the city and the nation. Once again, we are facing the question of the importance of local external economies for manufacturing industry in highly developed economies like the United Kingdom and the United States. Should these externalities of the city for industry be fostered? Should any policy, such as town planning regulations, which detracts from the positive influence of externalities, be resisted?

The scale of industrial movement within and from the city, without allowing for the impact of policy on whether movement takes place, is also important for policies of intra-regional and inter-regional development dependent upon a flow of mobile industry from the city which may be 'steered' or induced to desired destinations. A city acts as a 'seed bed' of industrial moves for both transfers and branch plants. How much movement is there? Can policy 'generate' movement?

Tables 2.3 and 2.4 have already shown the scale of industrial migration in one British and four American cities. Further evidence for Merseyside and Manchester in the UK comes from Dicken and Lloyd (1978). They find that the fall in manual employment in manufacturing in inner Merseyside between 1966 and 1975 (a fall of nearly 20,000 jobs) came about primarily from closures (complete and relocations): 22·5 per cent of the 1966 base employment. There was also a 12 per cent fall due to net contraction, countered in part by openings accounting for 10·5 per cent of the initial labour force. In Manchester a loss of 40,000 jobs was due more to closures, 50·3 per cent of the base, than to an in-situ contraction of 6·1 per cent. Entries to the area gave new jobs to 12·9 per cent of the base. Somewhat in contrast, births and inward migrants gave 40 per cent of the gross job creation on Clydeside between 1958 and 1968 (J. Firn and K. Swales, 1978).

Struyk and James (1975) discovered that between 1965 and 1968 in their four study areas — Boston, Cleveland, Minneapolis-St. Paul, and Phoenix — the total employment associated with moving, new and closing establishments represented 17 per cent of the 1965 base employment; and 37 per cent of the establishments listed in 1965 had been involved in relocations or new plants and closures by the end of the period. The study revealed a larger contribution of industrial mobility to changes in geographic distribution than the authors anticipated. Table 2.8 brings together their results for the four cities.

The original 'incubator' hypotheses, taken from Hoover and Vernon, was that ' . . . small manufacturing establishments will find it advantageous to locate initially at high density, central locations within the metropolis. This advantage is due to any number of factors including ready access to rentable production space, raw materials, labour, and other services.' [17] The work of Struyk and James and of Cameron, already referred to, does not give strong support to what Leone and Struyk have called the 'simple' incubator hypothesis. Births of new manufacturing enterprise were not disproportionately concentrated in either the core of the metropolis, or the central

49

Table 2.8

Numbers of relocating, new and closing establishments and employment in Cleveland, Boston, Minneapolis-St. Paul, and Phoenix 1965–68

Establishments	Relocations	New	Closures
Cleveland	664 (13·8)[1]	464 (10·0)	655 (14·1)
Boston	567 (9·8)	354 (6·1)	779 (13·4)
Minneapolis-St. Paul	485 (15·9)	374 (12·3)	548 (18·0)
Phoenix	106 (4·7)	290 (24·4)	240 (20·2)
Employment			
Cleveland	17,199[2](5·8)	7,708 (2·5)	23,092 (7·8)
Boston	13,998 (4·7)	3,884 (1·3)	23,849 (8·0)
Minneapolis-St. Paul	12,462 (8·3)	9,297 (6·2)	16,943 (11·3)
Phoenix	2,465 (4·7)	6,380 (12·1)	2,821 (5·3)

[1]Numbers in brackets are percentages of the 1965 base.

[2]The employment of relocating establishments at their original location.

Source: R.J. Struyk and F.R. James, *Intra Metropolitan Industrial Location,*Lexington Books, Lexington, Mass., 1975, Tables 2.6, 3.5, 4.5 and 5.4.

industrial district, or the traditional manufacturing locations in Boston, Cleveland, Minneapolis-St. Paul and Phoenix, even when the rates were adjusted for an industry mix. Table 2.3 shows strong birth rates in areas outside the central city in the Clydeside conurbation.

These results led Struyk, James and Leone to what they have termed the 'complex' incubator hypothesis, which incorporates the growth and relocation of new manufacturing establishments.[18] The study of the four American cities showed that employment in new establishments is generated in zones in the city, which already have a large number of manufacturing employees in plants of below average size, but which are not the traditional manufacturing centres dominated by larger plants, often branches or subsidiaries of large corporations. The complex incubator hypothesis suggests that new plants will grow faster and be more likely to relocate than older plants, and that the relocation will involve decentralisation out to lower density areas and lower rents, as suggested in the opening paragraph of this section.

This hypothesis was examined with data for New York for the period 1967 to 1969.[19] It was found that young plants did have both higher growth rates and higher probabilities of relocation; but that, within the first three or four years of the life of the new plant, relocations were over very short distances and normally within the general core area of the city. (Unfortunately there was no testing of the relocation of new plants in sub-centres in the outer areas of the city, where the Cameron study found high birth rates but low outward migration rates as shown in Table 2.3). After this early period, the New York study did find decentralising relocations but this appeared to be much more a function of their rate of growth than of age. The patterns of movement of these new plants are complex including some centralisation, but the study found that plants relocating outside the zone of origin generally grow more than those relocating within the zone of origin; and that this holds good for plants originating in the CBD as well as others. However, the younger plants which relocate outside the zone of origin grow more slowly than their older relocating counterparts. This may be because the period after the first long (zone to zone) relocation of a new plant is a time for consolidation before further growth is attempted. Unfortunately there is insufficient research on intra-urban manufacturing mobility to be able to assess whether the pattern of this suburban incubation serves the same function and is as productive overall for new plants as incubation in the inner urban areas.

Notes

[1] Establishment data by zip codes rather than using just the central city and metropolitan area totals. The Mills technique yields estimates which are very dependent upon the assumption that a negative exponential function correctly describes the distribution of employment.

[2] Other types were: business, stores, community, educational, hospital, and institutional, and amusement.

[3] In addition to the factors listed here, Kitagawa and Bogue (1955, pp.121–2) also attributed high degrees of suburbanisation in particular cities to: topography, late industrialisation, the type of manufacturing, the inability of the city to annex suburban areas, a failure of older central area industries, a failure to zone sufficient industrial land, the

presence of a large satellite industrial city, and the promotion of industrial sites by the rail-roads. They suggest that industry has been more influenced by *site* factors than *location* factors within metropolitan areas, and that suburbanisation has been led by the large multiple stage semi-independent plant.

[4] Although Mooney's study (1969) of the employment conditions of negroes in ghettoes in the twenty-five largest SMSAs between 1948 and 1963 suggests that their geographic separation is of less significance than aggregate demand conditions and the changing structures of employment in the central cities, the expanding employment opportunities being largely for female workers. For a contrary view, see D.K. Newman (1967, pp.7—13). Newman demonstrates how getting to a suburban job imposes a greater burden on central city residents than is experienced by suburban commuters into the central city, particularly given the greater dependence of poorer central city dwellers on public transit.

[5] Agglomeration economies in urban areas are still significant for a limited number of industrial sectors and categories of company and industrial process although no longer tied to the urban core. In other sectors and categories, Stanback and Knight (1970, p.263) have suggested that services in manufacturing industry have been increasingly internalised within the total structure of large firms. So that a new plant relies on the firm's headquarters or other specialised units, which may well be in another city. See also Pred (1976) for a discussion of this effect.

[6] The extent to which companies seek satisfactory rather than 'optimum' locations and the extent to which they undertake a full calculus of locational costs is discussed in chapter 6.

[7] See P.M. Townroe (1971, p.39) and M. Mann (1973) for British examples of this. Although Henderson (1976, p.65) shows that firms in Glasgow between 1958 and 1968 were not more likely to relocate if initially located in a slum clearance area.

[8] D.E. Keeble (1972) brings together the British evidence. See also W.T.M. Molle (1977) for evidence from the Netherlands.

[9] This reinforces Cameron's conclusion (G.C. Cameron, 1970, p. 163).

[10] Op.cit.p.221. Destinations per square mile in the north, west, and south sectors were 1·21, 1·00 and 0·43, while the percentage of land in manufacturing was 1·9, 3·1 and 4·4. The authors suggest that this result may be due to the influence of a high proportion of non-white population in the southern sector.

[11] Total industrial acreage in each zone in 1964 divided by the average stock of plants and multiplied by the number of plants which

left the zone or died within the zone, 1958—68.

[12] The UK government has operated an Office Development Permit control in London and the South East region since 1965, and has offered limited inducements to office firms in the assisted areas, but without the strong influence on the location of new investment that has resulted from the controls and incentives for manufacturing. The ODP limit was raised to 30,000 square feet in June 1977.

[13]The Location of Offices Bureau is a government sponsored agency promoting office decentralisation from London, and office moves to the assisted areas, as well as office development in inner urban areas throughout England and Wales.

[14] These figures capture perhaps only half of the total number of jobs involved in office movement in and from London: many firms will not approach the Location of Offices Bureau for help and advice (J. Rhodes and A. Kan, 1971, p.15).

[15] Gosforth, in the suburbs of Newcastle-upon-Tyne is one exception to this. In Greater Manchester inward migrant office firms have been attracted to suburban centres such as Altrincham, Stockport, Horwich and Wilmslow.

[16] R.A. Leone and R. Struyk, 1976, p.325. The Hoover and Vernon study of the New York region showed that over 60 per cent of firms with sixty employees or less was concentrated in the core area (1962, p.46). The recent work of Rees (1978b) supports the 'simple' incubator hypothesis in the case of Dallas - Fort Worth. And Schmenner's Cincinnati study (1978, pp.4—121) also supports only the 'simple' hypothesis although the incidence of births in the control areas was less than in most suburbs and fringe areas.

[17] Op.cit., p.327.

[18] Op.cit., pp.327—30.

3 Intra-regional industrial movement

The fastest percentage growth rates of manufacturing employment in the United States since 1970 have been in those non-metropolitan areas of the country within the sphere of influence of the metropolitan areas. Many industrial companies which in the 1950s or 1960s would have decentralised to metropolitan suburbs in order to expand and to find cheap sites and an adequate labour force now appear to be moving further out. In the United Kingdom, many companies were encouraged to decentralise further than the suburbs throughout the 1950s and 1960s by public policy; by land use planning restraints on metropolitan expansion using 'green belts', and by the programme of new and expanding towns. Some companies in both countries were encouraged to move even further, to new regions away from the home base. These further moves will be considered in chapter 4. The focus of concern of this chapter is the industrial movement within a region, using the notion of the city region. The moves discussed here are those decentralising from a principal metropolis to smaller towns and cities within the city region, or the moves between the smaller centres. Therefore the discussion of this rather ill defined group (and more on definitions below) concentrates on transfers and branch plant moves over distances of perhaps 20 to 100 miles.[1]

The first section of this chapter will establish the importance of industrial movement to what has been termed the 'inter-metropolitan periphery', after spending a few paragraphs on the definitional problem. The evidence on both the patterns and the casual factors in this sort of movement is very limited in both countries. This section will try, however, to identify the key locational variables, discussing in particular the importance of links past and present with the dominant metropolis. The encouragement given to this movement by urban development restrictions and by taxation in the central city is considered in the next section. This is followed by a brief section on office moves and research and development unit locations outside the main metropolitan area. Section five is more or less exclusively British in content, describing industrial movement to the new and expanding towns, the planned satellite dispersal centres. A minority of these urban development schemes have been designed as part of programmes of development for lagging regions. The focus here, however, is on those schemes, surrounding the major urban centres, which were designed primarily for purposes of limiting urban expansion and as contributions to urban public housing and slum clearance. Evidence will be drawn principally from the schemes around London in the South East and East Anglia regions and around Birmingham in the West Midlands. The chapter concludes with a brief discussion of the impact of incoming mobile industry on smaller communities.

An outreach of suburbia?

With some prescience in an article published in 1965, Friedmann and Miller (J. Friedmann and J. Miller, 1965) looked forward to a blurring of the economic and sociological distinctions between metropolitan areas in the United States and the areas constituting the inter-metropolitan periphery. This periphery is made up of those parts of the country which lie between the main metropolitan areas, but which are influenced by the life and vitality of the city. Using core areas of at least 300,000 people and a radius of two hours driving time (or approximately 100 miles) as their 'urban fields', Friedmann and Miller (p.324) derived a system which covered 35 per cent of the land area of the country (the remainder being mainly the thinly populated Great Plains and Rocky Mountain States) and included between 85 and 90 per cent of the population. Within each 'urban field' there is an inter-dependency between the metropolitan core and the non-metropolitan periphery.

In the past, growth has been centred on the cities. Much of the inter-metropolitan periphery suffered both demographic and relative economic decline.[2] Outward migration of population was selective and debilitating and the structure of industry was outmoded, with high shares of declining or low growth sectors. But Friedmann and Miller foresaw a reversal of these trends:

> Looking ahead to the next generation, we foresee a new scale of urban living that will extend far beyond existing metropolitan cores and penetrate deeply into the periphery. Relations of dominance and dependency will be transcended. (p.313)

And this reversal implies a changing spatial pattern of economic activity:

> The urban field of the future . . . will be a far less focussed region than today's metropolitan area. The present dominance of the

metropolitan core will become attenuated as economic activities are decentralized to smaller cities within the field or into the open country, but because proximity will continue to account for a good deal of local interaction, the urban field will be a coherent region. (p.315)

Development in the inter-metropolitan periphery would result from four uses of the land: *recreation,* to include camps, parks, resorts, etc., *institutions,* including education, research, health and administration; *community construction,* for holidays, retirement, art colonies, etc., and *economic activities,* which might include agri-business, warehouses, insurance companies, and research and space intensive manufacturing. [3] And the location of the economic activities would be increasingly determined by the location of the labour force, a labour force which evidence has since shown has a marked preference for rural or small town residential environments.[4]

The concept of the urban field is really the older geographical idea of the city region, given economic and sociological characterisation relevant to the circumstances of the late twentieth century in a very prosperous nation. And the inter-metropolitan periphery bears similarities to the ideas of 'exurbia' or the 'urban penumbra', or to the outer metropolitan area concept used in the definition of metropolitan economic labour areas in the United Kingdom.[5] Empirically, the Friedmann-Miller urban field is probably closest to Berry's identification of 173 regions, based on commuting patterns in 1960 in the US. These regions, known as Bureau of Economic Analysis (BEA) regions, were based on the Doxiadis definition of daily urban systems, with an average radius of ninety miles (B.J.C. Berry, 1973). Conceptually however, the idea of the urban field is probably closer to the 77 first order urban spheres of influence and the 292 first and second order urban spheres of influence identified by Huff, using a simple gravity model to allocate counties to urban centres (D.L. Huff, 1973).[6]

Berry, like Friedmann and Miller, but writing in 1970, also foresaw a changing relationship between 'the nation's seventy odd truly metropolitan centers' and corresponding areas of urban influence (B. J.C. Berry, 1970, p.341 and pp.347—51). Berry saw the Friedmann-Miller forecasts as conservative, and, as we saw in chapter 1 looked to 'the emergence of entirely new societal frameworks' (p.348) in which '. . . gradients of distance-accretion will replace those of distance-decay (from central cities). Persons of greater wealth and leisure will find homes and work among the more remote environments of hills, water and forest, while most will aspire to this as an ideal.' The basis of this will be the diffusion of electronic technology, reducing the frictions of moving goods and people. The metropolitan centres will no longer be dominant centres of innovation, and the focal points of transportation and communication networks. Economies of localisation and urbanisation will cease to be important in many sectors of economic activity. Labour markets will be able to be less specialised and less concentrated.

The reversal in the relative growth experience of the central cities plus suburban rings versus the non-metropolitan areas, foreseen by both Friedmann and Miller and by Berry, now seems to have occurred. 'A turning point has been reached in the American urban experience. Counter-urbanisation has replaced urbanisation as the dominant force shaping the nation's settlement patterns. A similar tendency has been noticed in other western nations.' (B.J.C. Berry and Q. Gillard, 1977, p.1) The evidence suggests that this reversal was job-led, i.e. the employment expansion, particularly in basic or exporting sectors, preceeded the population expansion in the non-metropolitan areas. In 1970 Haren used unpublished data to show that manufacturing employment in the United States between 1962 and 1969 grew at 2·4 per cent per annum in the 193 largest labour market areas, but at 3·7 per cent per annum elsewhere. The large labour markets accounted for 71 per cent of total national manufacturing employment in 1969, but only 63 per cent of new manufacturing jobs. The non-metropolitan areas gained 167,000 jobs per year over the period, 99,000 of these being in the smaller labour markets of the South. About half of the gains in the smaller labour markets nationally, or 20 per cent of the overall total, were the result of new or mobile plant additions and expansions in rural and semi-rural communities. These moves were over a very diversified range of industry.

This growth of manufacturing jobs in the non-metropolitan areas has continued into the 1970s. Between 1970 and 1974 manufacturing employment (although by type of residence) in these non-metropolitan counties which have *not* been designated metropolitan since 1970, grew by 683,000 or 13·9 per cent. Manufacturing employment in metropolitan areas grew by 407,000 or 3·0 per cent. (The national growth in manufacturing was 5·3 per cent.) The suburban rings of the smaller metropolitan areas also rapidly expanded manufacturing employment, at 12·7 per cent, but this was only somewhat faster than their population growth of 11·5 per cent. The growth of population in the non-metropolitan counties defined above was only 4·2 per cent. These changes are shown in Table 3.1. These changes and their broad implications have been discussed by many, including Beale (1976), Tucker (1976), Vining and Strauss (1977),

Table 3.1
Population and manufacturing employment by type of residence in
the United States: 1970 and 1974

(Numbers in thousands. 1970 metropolitan area definition)

Type of residence	Numerical change 1970—74	Percentage change 1970—74	Numerical change 1970—74	Percentage change 1970—74
United States, total	8,130	4·1	1,050	5·3
Metropolitan areas, total	4,985	3·6	407	3·0
Central cities	−1,226	− 1·9	− 66	− 1·1
Suburban rings	6,212	8·4	473	6·0
Metropolitan areas, 1,000,000+	1,570	2·0	− 66	− 0·8
Central cities	−1,310	− 3·8	− 139	14·3
Suburban rings	2,881	6·4	73	1·5
Metropolitan areas 1,000,000	3,415	5·9	474	8·2
Central cities	84	0·3	73	2·8
Suburban rings	3,331	11.5	401	12·7
Non-metropolitan areas, total	3,144	5·0	643	11·0
In counties designated metropolitan since 1970	870	10·4	− 40	− 4·2
Outside counties designated metropolitan since 1970	2,274	4·2	683	13·9

Source: US Bureau of the Census, Statistical Abstract of the United
States.

Ledebur (1977), and Weinstein and Firestine (1978).

McCarthy and Morrison (1978) conclude from their detailed analysis at a county level that this non-metropolitan growth is fundamentally due to three factors. The first   the increasing accessibility of these areas, permitting both longer distance commuting, more intensive recreational use (promoting service jobs) and the decentralisation of manufacturing. The second is that previous advantages of proximity for both manufacturing and government related activities have lessened, this industrial trend being complemented by increase in the revival and growth of employment in energy extraction. And the third factor is made up of less definable changes in the American life style. These changes include earlier retirement and more leisure; and a desire for a rural or small town living environment, even at the expense of higher salaries. The problems posed by these changes for the older metropolitan industrial centres are severe and far reaching. They have been surveyed for both the Great Lakes Region and the Northeastern Region by the Academy for Contemporary Problems and a number of public policy responses have been discussed (R.R. Widner, 1977a and 1977b).

Patterns of population and manufacturing employment and manufacturing employment growth in the United Kingdom over the past twenty-five years do not show such a clear cut reversal in the fortunes of the non-metropolitan areas. This may be partly because the relevant analysis has not been undertaken, but it is also because the influence of planning and urban development policies confuses the available evidence. It is also more difficult to see a 'turn-around' in non-metropolitan areas due to changing economic and social forces similar to these operating in the United States, when the metropolitan areas (or Standard Metropolitan Labour Areas — SMLAs)[7] contain 79·3 per cent of the population (in 1971) and the 126 metropolitan areas are in so many cases so close together.[8] The principal changes between 1951 and 1971 in population and total employment are shown in Table 3.2.

Table 3.2 shows that although the strongest growth in both population and employment in both decades was in the metropolitan rings, the outer metropolitan rings accelerated in population growth markedly in the second decade, while employment started to expand again after previous decline. These changes may be interpreted as a widening of the urban fields of the main metropolitan centres. This widening has extended commuter hinterlands. They may also be interpreted as a change in the relative attractiveness of small urban centres. These patterns, however, were over-shadowed by the influence of a (relatively) small number of new towns and town

Table 3.2

Population and employment change by urban zone, 1951 to 1971, in Great Britain

	Population change %		Employment change %	
	1951—61	1961—71	1951—61	1961—71
Urban cores	1·9	− 2·8	6.7	− 3·1
Metropolitan rings	13·3	17·2	6·6	15·0
SMLAs	5·7	4·4	6·7	1·4
Outer metropolitan rings	3·1	9·8	−0·4	3·9
MELAs	5·3	5·2	5·6	1·8
Unclassified areas	− 0·9	− 1·4	−5·5	− 0·7
Great Britain	5·0	5·0	5·1	1·7

Source: R. Drewett, J. Goddard and J. Spence, *British Cities: Urban Population and Employment Trends 1951—71,* Research Report 10, Department of the Environment, London, 1976, p.10.

expansion schemes. Six of the top ten fastest growing SMLAs in population terms 1951—61 and 1961—71 contained towns of this sort. Similarly, six of the top ten fastest growing SMLAs in employment terms 1951—61; and nine of the top ten 1961—71.

Another analysis of the growth and decline in manufacturing employment within the South East region between 1966 and 1971 highlights this general picture of dispersion. Keeble (1976, p.269) shows how in this period London and the ring of industrial satellites surrounding the metropolitan area lost manufacturing jobs; and in contrast growth occurred in areas on the periphery of the region, in South Hampshire and West Sussex, on the Kent/Sussex border, and in ten local areas in the north of the region. Much of this growth was focussed in small towns and rural areas; growth occurring in 39 of the 44 local areas which employed less than 5,000 manufacturing workers in 1966. Only seven of the twenty centres employing over 20,000 in manufacturing recorded a net expansion of employment. Much of this dispersion was due to intra-regional industrial mobility. Keeble (1976, pp.271—2) shows how between 1966 and 1974, 96 per cent of the 42,000 manufacturing jobs recorded as crossing sub-regional boundaries in the South East resulted from outward flows, away from

Greater London, as opposed to either inward or orbital flows. This movement was over larger distances to the south of London than to the north, coastal locations proving especially attractive. This flow to the periphery contrasts with the 1945–65 period when 60 per cent of the employment in all moves between sub-regions within the South East moved to destinations within thirty miles or so of central London. Keeble (1976, p.273) concludes that this longer distance movement within the South East resulted from improved radial communications, planning constraints and external diseconomies in larger centres, and from a search for available labour; but especially from a rising valuation in residential space preferences for attractive environments. This matches American conclusions (e.g. Ledebur, 1977).

An analysis of patterns of dispersion since 1971 has not been undertaken for Great Britain as a whole, but it might be expected that both the absolute and relative changes have slowed down. Inward migration from overseas has slowed, the birth rate has dropped and the economy has been growing only sluggishly. Therefore it would be surprising to find the continuing and growing buoyancy of the non-metropolitan areas, experienced recently in the United States; except that growth held up by on-going investments in those new and expanding towns still too small to be classified with their immediate commuting hinterland as metropolitan.

It is clear in both countries that the relative growth rates of non-metropolitan areas, or the inter-metropolitan periphery, has a lot to do with changing pressures on the location of manufacturing industry. These pressures are expressed in patterns of industrial movement.

Industrial moves into non-metropolitan areas

The evidence on the characteristics of intra-regional industrial mobility is very limited in both countries. The previous section has suggested that considerable decentralisation beyond the suburbs, but within the region, has taken place in all of the regions of both countries. Three individual examples will highlight this.

Employment in the motor vehicle industry in the United States grew in the 1940s by 294,000 and fell in the 1950s by 28,000. Fifty-eight per cent of the increases and 86 per cent of the decreases to give these net figures occurred in the Great Lakes region (T. Stanback and R.V. Knight, 1970, p.213). The regions' share of national employment in the motor industry fell from 81 per cent in 1940 to 74 per cent in

1960; but Detroit's share fell from 47 per cent to 29 per cent. Eight thousand job losses in Detroit were offset by 71,000 job increases in the smaller metropolitan areas and the non-metropolitan areas in the surrounding region.

Much of the change in the balance between Detroit and the surrounding region in this one industry will, however, have been the result of the expansion and contraction of employment at existing sites. This process is seen again in a recent study of New Jersey[9] (F. J. James and J.W. Hughes, 1973). During 1967 and 1968, 283 manufacturing establishments employing twenty or more relocated within the state; 57 moved into New Jersey from other states; 262 new manufacturing establishments were formed; and 189 establishments were closed.[10] These changes, together with growth and decline of existing establishments, resulted in an increase in total manufacturing employees in the state of 6,178 or 0.7 per cent. Four thousand one hundred seventy nine of the increase could be attributed to 'net migration', or plants moving within *and* into the state; 743 was due to natural increase, or the difference between the employment of new manufacturing establishments and defunct establishments; and 1,256 was the 'residual growth', or the growth and decline of employment in non-mobile establishments plus the effects of relocation, births and deaths in small (4—20 persons) establishments. Dividing the state up into seven sub-regions, James and Hughes show (1973, p.411) that 'natural decline' and 'residual decline' were responsible for the major part (80 per cent) of the decline in the New Jersey parts of the New York inner core (Hudson County) and in Newark (Essex County), rather than relocation. Similarly, for the decline in Camden, Burlington and Gloucester counties, all New Jersey suburbs of Philadelphia. In the inner ring of the New Jersey portion of the New York metropolitan area, in Bergen, Passaic and Union counties, 'natural increase' and 'residual growth' accounted for 81 per cent of the employment growth. Only in the outer metropolitan ring, in Morris, Middlesex, Somerset, Monmouth, and Mercer counties was the influence of mobile industry dominant, accounting for 58 per cent of the growth. The changes are set out in Table 3.3.

As the James and Hughes analysis suggests (1973, p.408), small firms show a reluctance to move out of a metropolitan area. This is confirmed in UK studies which show a general (but not uniform) pattern of increase in employment size of establishment moved with distance moved. Keeble's study, for example, of 124 manufacturing concerns in North West London showed that whereas 78 per cent of moves of less than ten miles were by firms employing 11—100 workers, this group only accounted for 62 per cent of firms in the total

Table 3.3
Employment growth and locational change in manufacturing
industry in New Jersey, 1967–68

Counties	Total employment change[1]			No. of mobile plants	
	Net immi-gration	Natural increase	Resi-dent growth	Origins	Destina-tions[2]
1 Hudson, Essex	−1,359	−1,573	−3,700	100	84
2 Bergen, Passaic, Union	1,574	2,511	4,160	104	139
3 Morris, Middlesex, Somerset, Monmouth, Mercer	3,104	1,279	998	35	53
4 Hunterdon, Sussex Warren	0	−1,129	1,516	3	3
5 Cape May, Ocean, Atlantic	145	116	294	5	6
6 Salem, Cumberland	− 29	261	398	7	7
7 Camden, Burlington, Gloucester	744	− 744	−2,410	20	32
Total	4,179	743	1,256	274	324

[1]For definitions, see paragraph 17.

[2]Including 50 moves with origins outside the state.

Source: Adapted from F.J. James and J.W. Hughes (1973), The
process of employment location change: an empirical
analysis, *Land Economics*, 69 (4) Tables 2 and 6.

population of firms in the area studied. Conversely, 66 per cent of
moves over ten miles between 1940 and 1964 by firms in the area
were undertaken by larger, 100 plus employees, firms. These larger
firms only accounted for 38 per cent of all firms employing more than
eleven people in the area (Keeble, 1968).

More generally, Table 3.4 shows that of the 3,014 moves recorded
between fifty sub-regions of the United Kingdom 1945–65, those not
going to the peripheral areas[11] were smaller and moved on average

Table 3.4
Inter-subdivisional moves in Great Britain 1945—65

	Median distance moved (miles)	Branches as % all moves	Near employ- ment branches	end— 1966 transfers
Peripheral areas	approx. 150	83	395	310
Rest of Britain	approx. 50	52	285	175

Source: M.E.C. Sant, *Industrial Movement and Regional Development*, Pergamon, 1975, p.41.

only one-third the distance. Moves out from a given stock of metropolitan manufacturing establishments are subject to distance decay.[12] Keeble's figures for North West London (Keeble, 1968) show clearly how the proportion of the total number of moves in a given period falls off to destinations at increasing distances away from the city. This fall off is faster for small firms. These firms are typically more dependent upon the external economies offered by the metropolitan area of origin, and frequently, although forced or encouraged to decentralise by land and factory prices or by public policy, they wish to stay in close contact with the services and markets accessible from their original location after they have moved. This explains in part why transfer moves (which are anyway on average smaller than branch plant moves) tend to move shorter distances than branches.[13] For many branches, services and markets will be available within the structure of the parent company and local access outside customers and suppliers is less important. But this is only part of the explanation for the desire of many transfer moves to be over short distances only. Residential preferences of the owners or managers will be important. And, as we shall see in chapter 7, continuing access to the pool of specialist labour skills of the original area may also be important for some moves. For some, transfers permitting access to the pre-move employees of the firm may be critical, at least for a transitional period. A study of firms moving in South East England showed that the proportion of new employees recruited rose sharply with the distance of the move: firms moving over sixty miles recruited, on average, 86 per cent of their workforce in the new location, while firms moving less than five miles were able to retain nearly 90 per cent of their old workforce (Economic Consultants Ltd, 1971).

A further characteristic of decentralising industrial moves related to this theme of continuing access is that of radial patterns of movement. If linkages back to the area of origin are important, a move out along principal radial lines of communication makes a lot of sense: although such patterns may also reflect a sequence of search behaviour for the new site. Once again, London provides strong evidence for this characteristic documented by Keeble (1968) and by Economic Consultants Ltd (1971).

The pattern of progressive and radial decentralisation into a metropolitan hinterland but with a decay of distance is sharply modified in the United Kingdom by two elements of public policy. Firstly, the programme of new and expanded towns around the two major generator metropolitan areas for industrial movement — Greater London and the West Midlands conurbation — has meant that the volume of movement to those outer parts of the two regions has been higher than might have been expected on the basis of a regression model which takes account of distance decay (D. Keeble, 1971, p.63). New and expanded towns have modified the patterns of labour availability in the two regions, while industrial development has been encouraged with serviced industrial land, available buildings, and a generous application of the central government Industrial Development Certificate control (discussed later in this chapter under section headed 'The impact of policy').

The second modification is the impact that British regional development policy has had on movement patterns. Industrial movement out of the two largest conurbations has been either to the local regional hinterland or to those regions favoured by development incentives in the north and west of the county. Flows from these two conurbations to other regions, or flows between other regions, have been relatively insignificant. Flows originating in other regions have mainly been intra-urban and inter-regional decentralisation flows. The dominance, therefore, in the total movement pattern in between the fifty subdivisions of the country of intra-regional and assisted area moves, has given rise to what Keeble has called the 'dual population hypothesis' (1971, pp.42—53, 1976, pp.135—42).

Keeble argues that the shorter distance 'overspill' moves out of the main metropolitan areas have very different characteristics to the longer distance assisted area moves. The overspill moves are typically going to smaller towns, they are often smaller plants, complete transfer moves for which links to the origin area are important, and they contain a high proportion of establishments manufacturing relatively unstandardised products subject to rapid changes in production techniques or in demand. They tend to contain relatively high proportions of research staff and skilled workers and have been concentrated in the fast growing engineering and electrical goods sectors.

Conversely, the longer moves to the assisted areas of the UK are typically larger, they are branch plants, often going to large urban centres, they employ high proportions of unskilled or semi-skilled, often female workers and they frequently produce standardised goods by assembly-line or flow-line technologies. This dual-population view of inter-subdivision industrial movement is rather overly simplistic. Movement into and within some UK regions does not fit the characterisation;[14] and it does not distinguish between decentralisation moves to metropolitan satellites which are essentially extensions of the suburbs, and the longer distance but still intra-regional movement to small towns and the rural periphery. And the hypothesis suggests that the two types of reception area do not compete with each other for the flow of moves generated by the metropolitan areas. Recent regression evidence (Sant, 1975) however, implies that such competition does exist, the characteristics of the two groups of moves overlapping. There is no American evidence detailed enough to be able to judge whether this sharp contrast between intra-regional and inter-regional moves exists in the United States.

Keeble's contrast between intra-regional and inter-regional moves only partly holds up when one examines the reasons for movement. The decision to open a new plant in all types of destination is very much prompted by the same list of factors as that in Table 2.2 and discussed in section headed 'Pressures to move' chapter 2. The principal study in both the US and the UK which allows reasons for moving to be disaggregated by type of move is the 1964—67 British government 543 firm survey, and the published results of that survey only refer to reasons given by sub-category of move if the proportions are strongly high or low compared to the all-survey average (which is given in Table 2.2).[15] However from these results, it is possible to infer a different emphasis in the factors encouraging movement among short distance (but inter-subdivisional) moves by comparing branches and transfers (complete relocations), given that transfers are relatively more numerous among the short moves.

Transfers are less likely to want to move to permit an expansion of output than branch plant moves, but are more likely to do so because of inadequate existing premises or site. Branches are more likely to be 'pushed' by an unsatisfactory labour supply position at the existing site, or by the refusal or expected refusal of an Industrial Development Certificate. Transfers are more likely to move because of town planning difficulties, or because the lease on existing premises fell in (or a good offer for the property was received). Transfers are less likely than average to move because of regional development inducements offered, or to be closer to existing or potential markets or to be closer to sources of materials or components. The opportunity to purchase or rent premises or sites at the new location was relatively more important for transfers.

This survey makes no reference to the direct influence of the supply and price of land and premises in the metropolitan area. As Smith has stressed (1972, pp.33—9) this factor varies with the growth rate of the national economy as well as with planning controls over vacated premises and what is offered in the hinterland locations. And the survey makes no reference to the influence of local business and property taxation as a 'push' factor. This is taken up in the following section. The main contrast between the pressures to move in intra-regional and inter-regional movers seems to be that 'forced' moves (moves due to a lease falling in, old buildings, town planning difficulties) are more common in the first group and 'expansion' moves (needing space and/or labour and/or markets) are more common among the second.

In the United States evidence from Michigan suggests that labour costs and trade unionism and local taxes may be more significant 'push' factors in the UK, especially for transfer moves (E. Mueller and J.N. Morgan, 1962, p.212; Mandell, 1975).

As in the discussion of 'push' factors, the 1964—67 British government survey can be used as the basis for discussing the 'pull' factors for intra-regional moves. All of the 543 firms in the survey opened a plant in the four-year period in an area where each firm had not manufactured previously. Fifty-three per cent went to assisted area locations, 19 per cent to a new or expanded town outside an assisted area, and 28 per cent went to locations elsewhere in the UK (Department of Trade and Industry, 1973a, p.529). Because of the construction of the survey, this final group is largely synonymous with non-metropolitan destinations (other than new or expanded towns) of intra-regional moves. Table 3.5 lists the major factors determining the location in each group, as well as in complete relocations and in branch plant moves.

Table 3.5 suggests that the Keeble dichotomy does not hold up strongly in the relative importance of location factors between the inter-regional and intra-regional groups of movers.[16] Once one allows for the prime importance of inducements to the assisted area

Table 3.5
Having decided to open a new plant in a new location which factors determined the location you chose?

(Percentages of replies naming factors specified as major reasons.)

Factors	Assisted areas	New & expanded towns[3]	Rest of UK	Transfers	Branch plants	Total
1 Availability of labour at new location	80	61	66	64	79	72
2 Knowledge or expectation that IDCS obtainable or in future	50	58	38	48	47	48
3 Availability of government inducements	81	1	4	20	45	39
4 Assistance or encouragement from LAs[1] or promotional bodies	37	49	26	41	34	36
5 Access to specified transport facilities	33	39	25	32	25	31
6 Market forces	24	42	33	28	30	30
7 Good amenities & environment	27	39	27	39	24	29
8 Availability of suitable non-government factory	22	22	39	31	27	28
9 Managerial ties to an earlier location	12	46	29	35	24	24
10 Special characteristics of site	21	14	21	19	18	20
11 Supply forces	11	18	19	12	15	15
12 Available industrial and commercial services	2	7	3	5	0	3
13 Other	11	13	14	16	9	12

[1] Local authorities

[2] Not including branch plants of overseas origin

[3] Outside assisted area

Source: Department of Trade and Industry, Inquiry into Location

Attitudes and Experience, *Memorandum submitted to the Expenditure Committee (Trade and Industry Subcommittee) on Regional Development Incentives*, (Session 1973–74), p. 600.

movers, the rankings of the factors listed are remarkably similar in the two groups; with two exceptions. The availability of a non-government factory and managerial ties to the earlier location were both substantially more important to the intra-regional movers. The managerial ties were referred to as major factors by 63 per cent of moves under twenty miles and by 49 per cent of the moves between twenty and forty-nine miles. The availability of labour in the new location rose in importance with distance moved to all destinations, being cited by 52 per cent in moves under twenty miles to 88 per cent in moves over 250 miles. Unfortunately, this survey did not enquire about continuing access to an existing labour force in the old location (except indirectly in asking about managerial ties). Another large survey in the UK in the South East region (which includes the London metropolitan area), came to the following conclusion on location factors:

> On the basis of this rather limited evidence it would therefore seem that one of the major factors governing the choice of locations within the South East is the availability of suitable premises (and/or i.d.c.s.); and that in the conditions of the South East firms rank highly their preference to retain as much as possible of their existing labor force, and hence to move short distances (Economic Consultants Ltd., 1971, p.3).

This same survey could find no strong differences between the characteristics of long and short moves within the South East region:

> It might be inferred that the distance moved relected the ease with which suitable premises on sites will be found in the vicinity of the existing plant, rather than special locational requirements of certain types of establishments (Economic Consultants, 1971, p.5).

Further work by Hamilton (1978) however does provide a further contrast. He shows that between 1964 and 1972 in the UK the floor-space per worker in manufacturing increased most markedly in the 'green field' zones separating the major urban-industrial agglomerations or in the outer fringe areas surrounding them. He sees the decentralisation of the larger scale, capital intensive or assembly line industries to these areas in contrast to the decentralisation of smaller, lighter, more labour intensive units to the more rural areas without a growth in floorspace per worker.

One location theory and growth centre theory[7] both suggest may influence a decentralisation to be intra-regional rather than inter-regional is that of linkage. Both branch plants and transfers may require continuing links with previously established customers and suppliers of materials and components and of industrial and commercial services. This requirement would discourage movement far away from the metropolis of origin. However, the evidence suggests that for most sectors of manufacturing industry and especially for larger companies, local linkages are relatively unimportant, either in holding mobile plants close to the city or in influencing the choice of location in a new area. Table 3.5 shows the very low importance attributed by respondents to services as a location factor; and supply forces were a major factor for under one-fifth of the companies. Only market forces were of considerable significance, for one-third of the rest of UK moves.

The relative importance of local customers compared with local suppliers is reflected also in Table 3.6 from the South East planning team study. This table also shows how the importance of local (less than thirty miles) customers and suppliers is less for firms located away from the centre of London. This may imply that those firms for which these sort of local linkages are important have been held into the city, or it may imply that for those expanding firms investing in new plants and being encouraged to locate in the outer parts of the region by other factors (land prices, labour supply, etc.) local linkages are relatively unimportant. This latter implication is supported by evidence on the small proportions of inward migration plants (mainly from London) in East Anglia which seek to establish new local linkages within and close to their chosen communities (M.J. Moseley and P.M. Townroe, 1973, p.139).[18]

Hamer (1973, pp.8–12) quotes the results of a 1969 survey of the Boston economic development and industrial commission of 222 firms in the Boston metropolitan area. Proximity to customers was offered as a reason for *not* considering a move by only 13·1 per cent of firms in Boston and 7·4 per cent of firms in the suburbs. Proximity to supplies was even less important (3·2 per cent and 3·1 per cent). Of the firms in the suburbs 10·9 per cent said that proximity to customers was a reason for considering a move, but only by 1 per cent

Table 3.6
Distribution of sales and purchases of establishments moving to
locations within South-East England: by subregion

	Sales		Purchases	
Location	% within 30 miles	Rest of South-east	% within 30 miles	Rest of South-east
Inner London	45	15	27	14
Outer London	31	16	26	16
Outer metropolitan area	26	22	20	19
Outer South-East (North)	17	31	8	25
Outer South-East (South)	13	30	11	28
All areas	38	21	21	19

Source: Economic Consultants Ltd, *Strategic Plan for the South East:
Studies Volume 5*, 1971, HMSO, London.

of Boston firms. Of the Boston firms 3·9 per cent gave proximity to
supplies as a reason, compared to 8·3 per cent of suburban firms. The
relative unimportance of local (i.e. metropolitan) suppliers and
markets for these firms is summarised in Table 3.7.

Even within sectors traditionally highly dependent upon local
linkages there is evidence that for substantial subgroups of firms (or
processes) within these sectors the requirement of local proximity is
lessening. The Steed (1976) study of printing and apparel in Montreal
and Toronto finds this. And in New York, Segal (M. Segal, 1960, p.
148) has shown how within the printing and publishing industry in the
1950s those publishing activities and specialised printers for the
financial, advertising, and legal firms stayed and expanded within the
metropolitan area; but production of staple items, such as legers or
sales forms and printing and binding of books, moved further out to
low wage areas. He cites a similar movement in more routinised
processes of the garment industry to mining communities in Pennsylvania and the textile towns of New England all within contact of

Table 3.7

Origin of major deliveries and sales allocated to market areas for sampled firms in Boston, 1969 (percentages)

	Deliveries		Sales	
	Boston	Suburbs	Boston	Suburbs
Metropolitan area	41·4	28·2	12·3	8·2
New England	20·9	24·1	15·0	18·6
Rest of US	31·2	39·0	68·1	66·2
Foreign	6·5	8·7	4·6	7·0

Source: A.M. Hamer, *Industrial Exodus from the Central City*, Lexington Books, Lexington, Mass., 1973, p.11.

central New York overnight by truck.

Managerial ties between plants of a multi-branch company are another aspect of linkage which Table 3.5 suggests may be particularly important for intra-regional moves. Unfortunately the published results of that survey do not allow the labour transfer aspect of managerial ties to be distinguished in each of the three categories of area from the ongoing operational links. Overall, however, the particular factor of the need for managers to attend more than one plant was a major locational factor for 13 per cent of respondents and a minor factor for 12 per cent. And the need to maintain personal contacts rated 11 per cent and 12 per cent. Managerial and staffing ties rated 32 per cent, 16 per cent for smaller multi-plant companies, compared with 24/26 for the companies in the largest 500 nationally and 21/20 for single plant companies. This was a major factor for 63 per cent of companies moving 1—19 miles, and 49 per cent for moves of 20—49 miles, compared to 5 per cent of moves over 150 miles (Department of Trade and Industry, 1973a, p.600). Spooner (1972) has shown how the need for close managerial supervision gave rise to a progressive 'colonisation' of nearby centres with available pockets of labour by branch plants of a shoe company based in Somerset, England. Erickson (1976, p.257) in his survey of 112 establishments moving into non-metropolitan Wisconsin also discovered the importance of managerial ties for branch plants, usually to a corporate headquarters. One-fifth of his branch plants cited 'Proximity to other plants of the company or historical ties' as a 'Primary locational objective'.

Table 3.5 does not allow non-metropolitan transfers to be distinguished from non-metropolitan branch plants but it does seem safe to infer that complete relocations within a region rate questions of amenity and environment as a very important, if essentially supplementary, locational factor. It rated 39/42 in the British survey for all transfers and 24/39 for all branch moves. The greater importance of amenity for transfers is supported by the Erickson Wisconsin survey:

> The analysis provided evidence that branch operations chose to locate in non-metropolitan areas for a different set of reasons than new indigenous enterprises. Branch plants were typically less concerned with the aesthetic and less urbanized aspects of non-metropolitan locations, rather preferring an assured labor supply and organizational proximity. (R.A. Erickson, 1976, p. 258)

If companies move within a region to a non-metropolitan location to find labour, cheap sites and high amenity while retaining easy contact with the city, they are in fact encouraged to move there in both the United States and the United Kingdom directly and indirectly by the actions of public policy. The following section considers the British industrial plant licensing system, the influence of local business taxes in the United States, and the pressure of town planning controls in both countries.

The impact of policy

A Urban development restrictions

The direct significance of town planning policy as a factor stimulating industrial movement out of a metropolitan area beyond the suburbs is very difficult to assess. As Table 2.2 indicates, town planning difficulties were a major reason for opening a new plant in a new location for only 11 per cent of the 531 British firms, a minor reason for only 3 per cent, and the outstanding single reason for 4 per cent. Of the 11 per cent of firms for which this was a major reason, 7 per cent had premises which were to be demolished for road widening or other town planning schemes, and 4 per cent had been refused town planning permission for a planned development. Demolition was understandably a major reason for movement among non-expanding firms in the survey; and among firms based in the centre of metropolitan areas where considerable redevelopment was taking place. Such firms have frequently been bitter at the delays and uncertainties placed upon them by prospective compulsory purchase orders.[19]

Failure to give planning permission for suburban locations may operate, like exclusionary zoning, to force a company which is decentralising out of the central city for other reasons, to move out beyond those suburbs it would otherwise would have wished to consider as the site for its new plant. The effect of this pressure does not seem to have been great in the UK. Of possible greater significance is the supply of land zoned for manufacturing industry development on the fringes of the metropolitan area. Clearly a restricted supply will force up the price in the face of a strong demand by decentralising units, encouraging longer distance moves. There is, unfortunately, no evidence of the importance of such a restriction for the locational pattern of new industrial investments within a region.[20]

The United States has no central government (or even state government) control over the location of new industrial investment. The United Kingdom, however, has such a control through the industrial development certificate system. Since 1948, all industrial building projects above a minimum size (and this minimum has varied over the years) have to be granted a certificate by the responsible central government department (currently the Department of Industry) before planning permission may be obtained from the local land use planning authority.[21] This national control has been designed to steer industrial investment away from the more prosperous buoyant parts of the country to these areas suffering from high unemployment, high outward migration, low activity rates and low wages. It complements the financial incentives and the infrastructure programmes of regional development policy in the assisted areas, being the 'stick' behind the 'carrot'. The system is intended to be flexible and discretionary and the majority of IDC applications in all areas have been approved, especially in the 1970s[22] so that any possible discouragement to industrial investment overall is felt by most observers to have been small.[23] Indeed, in the early 1960s in the tight labour markets of the Midlands and the South East the costs incurred to firms refused an IDC were offset by savings to the firms which could now expand. The policy is also low in its cost to government relative to its achievements. The system has been

74

regarded as a cornerstone of British regional policy by successive governments, and there is little doubt that the control has generated significant intra-regional and inter-regional industrial mobility over and above that which would have occurred with incentives alone.[24] The 12 per cent of firms in the British government movement survey which cited 'refusal or expected refusal of IDC' as a major influence on the decision to move (see Table 2.2) may be an understatement of the full significance of the control for flows of mobile industry. Large multi-plant companies are in near continuous discussion and negotiation with the regional offices of the Department of Industry and they acquire a good sense of what is acceptable and what is not when the time comes for a formal application.

Evidence from the British government movement survey shows that for late 1960s movers, the IDC control was not too important for projects in which considerations of markets, labour force, or site requirements were to the fore. Engineering firms felt themselves to be particularly strongly influenced, especially twenty-four movers from the West Midlands conurbation, half of which cited refusal or expected refusal of an IDC as a major reason for considering a move. The control was in general a major push for 42 per cent of West Midlands conurbation firms, and 35 per cent of other Midlands firms, compared with only 8 per cent of Greater London moves and 16 per cent of moves originating in the South East outside Greater London. This contrast between the two regions responsible for generating the majority of inter-subregional industrial moves in the UK is difficult to explain, although it does imply a more vigorous prosecution of the policy as well as stronger ties of external economies for many firms to their West Midlands origins. Other non-IDC factors were pushing firms out of Greater London. There is no indication that the IDC control has been used to steer industrial projects within the assisted area regions.

The system has been the subject of a lot of criticism. The flexibility of 'each case on its merits' has been seen as a cover for an insufficient appreciation of the requirements of the applicant by the civil servants involved in administering the control. The control is therefore felt to be a threat to the long term health and growth of both individual companies and of local communities in the South East and the Midlands regions of the United Kingdom. The system has also been criticised for delays and bureaucratic inertia; even though it is clear that a compulsory consideration of a wider range of locational alternatives has been positively beneficial to some companies. Perhaps too many small projects were refused in the 1960s. The floorspace limits should have been higher. The system and these criticisms have been fully examined elsewhere.[25]

The influence of IDCs on the patterns of intra-regional industrial mobility in Britain has been threefold. The control has complemented town planning policies in restricting suburban growth around the two major donor conurbations of mobile industry. Relaxation of the control in the satellite new towns in the 1950s and (to a lesser extent) in the town expansions of the 1960s accelerated industrial development and hence the population growth in these towns. The control has also permitted industrial movement outside the development areas to small problem areas with high unemployment, such as Portsmouth and East Kent (Keeble, 1976, p.265). More recently the control has been relaxed to allow and encourage industrial development in depressed inner city areas of the two conurbations.

In 1965 Office Development Permits were introduced for new office construction in the South East and Midlands Regions. The minimum exemption limit and the areas included have changed several times; the control currently covers projects of over 30,000 square feet in the South East region. Again, appraisal of the full significance of this control has been difficult. It seems clear however that it has contributed substantially to intra-regional office decentralisation out of London, both directly and indirectly in forcing up office rents in central London by restricting the supply of new construction (at least up to 1974 P.W. Daniels, 1977, p.271). It has probably been less successful in encouraging inter-regional movement than its manufacturing industry counterpart (J.B. Goodard and D. Morris, 1976, p.78).

B Local business taxation

The only local business tax in the United Kingdom is a property tax on assessed rental values of industrial buildings: the rates. Derating of industrial property (by 75 per cent) has been used as an industrial incentive in Northern Ireland and in Scotland (by 50 per cent) although there is no evidence as to its effectiveness.[26] Elsewhere in the United Kingdom there is little indication that industrial rates have been a significant push or pull factor in the mobility of manufacturing industry. Although they form an industrial cost which varies with location, rates are a very minor element in total costs, and they have not been listed in any of the British location factor surveys as an influence on propensity to move or on the choice of a new site. The revenue from industrial rates has possibly been an influence on the willingness of metropolitan local governments to encourage the export of industry, and of would-be reception areas to actively seek new industry using such inducements as serviced land, industrial buildings, staff housing etc. (B.M.D. Smith, 1971, pp.53—9; M.M. Camina, 1974, pp.98—110).

The situation in the United States is rather different. Local counties and municipalities have the ability (this ability varies from state to state) to levy a range of different taxes on local businesses. These taxes come on top of state and federal business taxes. Reductions in these local taxes are one of the most common forms of locational incentives to industrial investment, and have had some influence on the choice of new locations at the inter-regional level, as we shall see in the next chapter. The burden of these local taxes on industry is widely seen as the key indicator of the business climate in a local community (A.K. Campbell, 1958, p.200). According to Weinstein and Firestine (1978, p.134), 45 states offer tax free state and local revenue bond financing to industry, 25 states do not collect sales taxes on newly purchased industrial equipment, and 38 do not levy inventory taxes on goods in transit.

The evidence of the impact of tax differentials between local communities in the United States is somewhat conflicting. In a review of existing studies published in 1961, Due concluded that:

> On the basis of available studies, it is obvious that relatively high business tax levels do not have the disastrous effects often claimed for them. However, without doubt, in some instances the tax almost plays the deciding role in determining the optimum location, since other factors balance. The tax climate factor without doubt causes some location decision making, by causing firms to exclude certain states and urban areas from consideration (J.F. Due, 1971, p.172).

Due refers to statistical studies, which could find no correlation between relative growth rates of industry in different communities and relative tax burdens, and to studies which show that the local tax burden is usually only a small percentage of the value of sales. Due also discounts the results of interview studies, claiming that the anti-tax attitude of businessmen conditions them to stress the tax factor when it is presented to them in a list. He found that only a minority of such studies mentioned tax as a location factor, and in those that did so, tax was found to be important for between 10 and 25 per cent of firms. Due also argues that firms with a high tax burden are more willing to cooperate in surveys and hence bias the sample. More recent evidence broadly agrees with Due. Cameron (1969, pp.5—8) for example, examines variations in business taxes in Franklin County, Ohio and finds that for hypothetical firms in selected industries the

77

tax differential between areas is always below 1·2 per cent of operating costs. She concludes that zoning laws are more effective than high taxes in keeping industry out of middle and upper income residential communities, and that tax differentials are too small to influence locational choices based upon forecasts of operating costs and assumed future tax rates. Both Due and Cameron stress how the net burden of a local tax differential is reduced by the deductibility of state and local taxes for federal tax purposes. Bryant (1971), Lewis (1968), and Weinstein and Firestine (1978), all writing about tax concessions, all agree that local taxes have a low impact on locational choice.

Not all authors agree with this verdict however. Mueller and Morgan (1962, p.212), in their study of 239 plants in Michigan, found that taxes were cited by 20 per cent of respondents (weighted for employment) considering relocation as a possible advantage of a new location, and by 8 per cent (again weighted for employment) of those considering expansion. And in reply to the question: 'Are there any minimum requirements which must be met for locating plants in this line of industry?' or in response to a list of twenty-one locational factors, 52 per cent of respondents (again weighted) picked taxes as important (op.cit., 1962, p.208). However, when asked specifically about reasons for location of a plant at a particular site, only 3 per cent of respondents cited 'Better tax situation'. Local taxes thus seem to generate a stronger reaction in interview studies when referred to generally rather than when linked to a specific locational choice. This conclusion is reinforced by the high rating of state and local business taxes as an important factor in plant location in Mandell's 1972 study. Fifty-nine per cent of his sample in Detroit rated this factor 'most important', 37 per cent in Atlanta, and 38 per cent in Chicago. These were not mobile or recently moved firms; and it must be remembered, as Due (1961), Cameron (1969), and Bryant (1971) stress, that low taxes may mean inadequate or poor quality services, therefore not proving so attractive once individual sites are investigated.

One American study which has asked the question of recently moved plants 'Why did you leave the city?' was the 1947—55 study of New York by the Regional Planning Association referred to by Campbell (1958, pp.195—218). Taxes were a primary reason for 14 per cent of firms leaving New York City and a secondary reason for a further 25 per cent. Campbell stresses the great variety of taxes then existing in the New York metropolitan region. In New York State the emphasis was on a corporate income tax, compared with a property emphasis in New Jersey, and a tax on gross receipts in New York City. [27] So the form as well as the level of local taxes is important; not just for the volume of necessary paper work, but also for the amount of discretion given to assessors in property taxes, and for the strength of the link with growth and profits of the total tax assessment in any given fiscal year.

Local taxes seem to be an influence on the choice of site within a local area only at the margin when other things are broadly equal, or they act as one element in the 'business climate' of an area, acting indirectly upon locational choice. One result may be to reinforce industrial movement into non-metropolitan areas.[28]

Intra-regional movement of offices

Both New York and London have been responsible for generating considerable volumes of decentralising movements of office employment, as described in the last chapter. In both cities, the major part of this flow has moved to destinations in the metropolitan rings surrounding the urban cores, rather than moving further beyond the suburbs to self standing towns in the outer metropolitan areas and the inter-regional hinterlands. However, there are indications from both countries that these more distant (from city centre) locations are proving to be increasingly attractive to metropolitan based office organisations.

As Table 2.5 shows, between 1963 and 1975, 27 per cent of the clients of the Location of Offices Bureau moved more than forty miles from central London, accounting for 39 per cent of the total employment in the moves. The average size of these moves increased from the edge of the Greater London Council area up to eighty miles out, confirming Wabe's (1966) finding on a smaller (114) group of central London outward migrants. For the office firms moving within a 100 miles or so radius of central London to a hinterland which may be taken to include the Outer South East region, East Anglia and the edge of the South West region, there were four types of destination:

(a)   Outer zone commuter towns, with a manufacturing base but with a large pool of office-type occupations among the daily out-commuters. Many of these commuters would be only too happy to work locally and so they form a very significant locational 'pull'. Those towns include Guildford, Horsham, East Grinstead, Reading, High Wycombe, Chelmsford and Tonbridge.
(b)   Seaside towns, which overlap with the previous group but are more distant, with a different environmental attraction. This group includes Southend (the largest single concentration of

79

these intra-regional office moves), Folkestone, Brighton and Worthing; and Southampton and Portsmouth, Poole and Bournemouth.

(c) New and expanding towns seeking to diversity their manufacturing base. The principal destinations have been Harlow, Basildon, and Hemel Hempstead of the London 'ring' of new towns; and Basingstoke, Swindon, Ashford, Aylesbury, King's Lynn and Bury St. Edmunds of the London sponsored town expansion schemes.

(d) More distant but high amenity sub-regional centres, all with good transportation links with central London. This group includes Chichester, Bath, Cheltenham, Oxford, Northampton and Peterborough (both designated new towns in the 1960s), Colchester, Ipswich and Norwich.

In all of these destinations, the new offices have established themselves both in the town centres (normal when renting floorspace) and in suburban 'park-like' surroundings (usually only by companies constructing their own buildings). Speculative office park developments, such as are found in the United States, are very rare in the United Kingdom. The flow of commercial concerns has been reinforced by the movement of parts of central government departments; such as the move of the Civil Service Department to Basingstoke, the Stationery Office to Norwich, the Customs and Exise to Southend, the Inland Revenue to Worthing, the Ministry of Defence to Bath, and the Ordnance Survey to Southampton.[29]

As suggested in chapter 2, information about the decentralisation of offices from New York is much less complete and there are no studies of other American cities. The office construction statistics in Table 2.7 give some indication of the existing decentralisation pressure in New York which reaches the intermediate ring rather than the outer ring. Quante (1976, p.136) judged that the decentralisation implied by the Regional Plan Association forecast will, in fact, be much greater, as firms move to the suburbs and the regional hinterland (and elsewhere in the nation) to find and attract appropriate labour. A number of the moves of the headquarters of the top 500 manufacturing concerns analysed by Quante (1976) were out beyond the suburbs but there was no analysis of why this small group should have moved further. Little is known about intra-regional mobility of offices elsewhere in the United States. The assumption in the literature is that office activities are typically heavily concentrated in the downtown areas of the major cities, and that when movement takes place it is to the suburbs rather than to non-metropolitan locations in the hinterland.

Two other sorts of service sector activity have moved out of the metropolitan areas in both countries in the recent past. The first is warehousing. Again, the statistics are poor but it seems that warehousing moves and expansions have been concentrated in suburban locations close to good transportation links. There is some indication in South East England of warehousing development away from the London metropolitan area. This is often associated with a local industry (such as food processing in King's Lynn); or with imports and exports, although the warehouse may be some distance from the seaport or airport.

The second is the movement of research and development units of large companies. When freestanding these have typically chosen high amenity suburban and semi-rural locations, in order to attract staff (J. Westaway, 1974, pp.66—7). The IBM choice of Hursley in Hampshire, England is a good example of this locational choice for a research laboratory. In the post World War II period, a number of large British manufacturing concerns moved their R and D units to old country mansions in the outer metropolitan areas of London and Birmingham. And the concentration of research concerns around the Boston route 128 or the PaloAlto area in California is matched in the UK by firms close to Cambridge or Edinburgh Universities. The majority of R and D is however undertaken within or close to production units of the parent company.

Experience with planned satellite dispersal

The intra-regional movement of industry in the United Kingdom has been very significantly affected over nearly thirty years by the programme of new towns and expanded towns.[30] A minority of the new towns were designated with a primary objective of stimulating regional economic development, but the majority of the new towns and all of the expanded towns were founded on the need for additional public housing to relieve the pressures of excess residential demand in the largest conurbations. A basic principle of the design of these towns was that jobs should accompany the houses. Since many of the towns chosen as the initial core for development were very small (and in the case of many expanding towns with a stagnant or declining economic base), a growth of jobs necessarily meant an inward migration of industry; principally, of plants from the same source conurbation as the new inward migrant inhabitants. Initially, therefore, all of these towns actively sought migrant manufacturing plants. In this they were assisted by the way in which the IDC policy was operated, by a buoyant economy and a strong demand for new sites and factories in the 1950s and 1960s, and by the advantage of being able to offer to both prospective companies and their employees houses associated with jobs.

The results of these two programmes have been fairly dramatic on the geographical distribution of new industry.[31] For example, as noted in chapter 1, the eight new and expanded towns[32] in the outer metropolitan area of London attracted firms resulting in a net increase of manufacturing jobs of 51,000 between 1959 and 1966. The movement of firms to the seven principal town expansion schemes in East Anglia[33] resulted in the creation of 11,000 manufacturing jobs in the same period.[34] By the end of 1977, the eight new towns of the London ring had constructed 919 factories, employing 109,000.[35] And the twenty-four smaller towns which had agreements with the Greater London Council had constructed 1,196 factories, employing over 80,000. The role of these schemes in other regions for intra-regional dispersal of industry has been less significant but still important. In the West Midlands for example, Telford and Redditch New Towns had attracted over 580 plants and 15,300 jobs in manufacturing by the end of 1977. Over the whole country Sant (1975, p.149) found that 'new town target population' was the most significant sub-regional variable to correlate with inward migration of manufacturing industry in each of three periods, 1952–59, 1960–65, and 1966–71, out of a set of seventeen variables.

The British government movement survey analysed plants moving to new and expanded towns outside the assisted areas as a separate subgroup, as shown in Table 3.5. The table shows that for these plants, availability of labour was relatively less important than for plants moving elsewhere; but that access to an IDC, good amenities and environment and assistance from public authorities were all more important than elsewhere. Also, the factors of markets, transportation facilities, and managerial ties to an earlier location were more important for these firms, all perhaps reflecting the siting of the schemes relative to their parent conurbations. Government inducements were of no importance, for in all of these non-assisted area locations, factories and sites are leased at commercial rates. Good amenities and environment were a minor factor in the locational choice of 45 per cent of firms in these towns as well as a major factor for 39 per cent. The commentary to the published results of this survey (Department of Industry, 1973, p.592) sees the choice of new and expanded town sites as one involving more factors than for moves to other areas. Very few respondents in these towns were prepared to choose an outstanding single factor. Access to a previous location and the efforts of a promotional body (most probably the New Town Development Corporation or the local council of the town expansion) seems to have been particularly important in tipping the balance for many. The access factor is reflected in the radial patterns of decentralising movement referred to earlier.

This movement of industry has had four consequences for these towns around London, as Keeble (1976, pp.252–5) suggests. The towns now have a much higher proportion of manufacturing jobs in their total employment structures than other centres of comparable size. Secondly, the towns have succeeded in attracting plants from the fastest growing sectors of manufacturing (electrical and mechanical engineering and vehicles). Thirdly, both the plant sizes and the company sizes are above average, although in time the larger units may be expected to attract and to spawn smaller units. And finally, the occupational structures within the firms attracted have been skewed towards skilled male workers and to female workers. While the higher average skill levels have meant higher than average wage levels, the lack of opportunity for semi-skilled and unskilled men has been a point of concern. [36]

The new town and town expansion machinery has made it easier for industrial firms to find sites in areas of good access, with adequate labour supplies, room for expansion and with a high level of amenities for all employees. Once a scheme is safely launched and is developing, an incoming company knows that it can find housing for existing employees, that necessary services and infrastructures are available, and that the size of the labour pool and the range of public and commercial services will both grow relatively quickly. The recent lowering of population forecasts, in the face of falling birth rates, has led to the cutting back of the target populations of a number of the larger and more recent new town schemes (e.g. Peterborough, Central Lancashire); while the exporting conurbation authorities have been reluctant to renew and increase their town expansion agreements. At the same time many of the London schemes are now reaching their initial target populations, and their development corporations are being wound up. They will therefore not be actively seeking migrant industry in the future, [37] and it seems unlikely that such large proportions of the total volume of inter-subregional industrial movement in the UK will now be directed towards new and expanding town sites.

The impact of mobile plants
on smaller communities

As mentioned in the introduction, this book does not include a detailed consideration of the literature on the impact of new industry in local communities in the United States and the United Kingdom. However, as a conclusion to this chapter on intra-regional movement, this section will briefly note the types of issue which arise when new industry moves into a community, particularly a smaller community. The literature on these issues is extensive, as a recent American survey (G.F. Summers, 1976) testifies.

The strongest impact an incoming industrial investment will have on a community will be felt through the labour market. We have already seen that a dominant reason for industry to move to urban centres in non-metropolitan areas is the availability of labour, often cheaper and non- or weakly unionised labour. The recruitment of a labour force for a new plant in these centres may upset existing employment patterns and wage differentials, especially among the scarcer more skilled occupations. A firm paying rather higher wages than the existing local rate will tend to widen already extensive commuting hinterlands (N.M. Hansen, 1976, chapter 7), slowing outward migration from smaller rural centres. In the medium term, this recruitment may also attract a return migration back to the non-metropolitan centres from the large cities, as Hansen has shown (1973, p.100 and pp.153—8) in areas of Tennessee and the Ozarks. The new firms appear to attract managers and skilled workers from metropolitan areas within the state or region, and more marginal workers from all over the country.[38] Something of the same phenomenon has been noticed and encouraged by the Development Board in the Highlands of Scotland.

In the longer term, it is to be expected that incoming industry leads to an upgrading of the incomes and skill levels of the local labour force. This is not disputed in any research in either country except perhaps in the case of rural blacks in the American South (N.M. Hansen, 1973, p.164). This upgrading is assisted by general public policies for industrial training in both counties, such as those operated under the provisions of the 1973 Comprehensive Employment and Training Act (CETA) in the United States and by the Training Services Agency in the United Kingdom. The average skill and income levels are enhanced by selective inward migration.[39]

More indirectly, the new jobs and higher incomes will have a local impact through local expenditures. These expenditures will transmit a multiplier effect, creating indirect jobs in the service sectors. This is one of the cornerstones of growth centre theory (N.M. Hansen, 1972). However, the relatively few detailed studies of this multiplier impact suggest that the effect is fairly small; and that spending 'trickles-up' to larger urban centres in the region and the nation rather than benefitting local services or 'trickling-down' to smaller centres. This limits the diffusion of urban and economic growth pressures resulting from the initial industrial investment.[40]

One reason for non-metropolitan communities seeking industrial development is the anticipation of local fiscal benefits. New industry is seen as enlarging the local tax base, a base that is perhaps being eroded by population losses and declines in economic activity. The value of land and buildings rises, local consumer incomes increase, retail sales rise, and new state and federal grants and transfers will be generated. The benefits from increased taxation revenues and other public monies have to be set off against those expenditures in incentives and in services necessary to attract the new industry. The net gain to the public community may be small, or even negative, as a number of studies have suggested. This contrasts sharply with large gains in the private sector.[41]

In terms of social attitudes and behaviour, the impact of new industry on smaller more rural communities is probably little different than the impact of that same industry in metropolitan suburbs. In both the United States and the United Kingdom, the small proportion of the labour force involved in agriculture, the coming of national television and national chain store shopping, the improvement and lengthening of education and relatively high rates of internal migration have all reduced the social differentials between city and country which existed as recently as twenty-five years ago. The idea of factory life introducing a foreign culture to a rural workforce is no longer tenable in either country. Studies have shown that the inhabitants of non-metropolitan areas generally welcome (non-polluting) industry and believe that industrial development benefits their community. General opinions and patterns of social participation do not vary markedly between general residents and inward migrants or employees of a new plant. Any problems of social integration and lack of neighbourliness soon disappear after a settling in period.[42] As the quotation from Freidmann and Miller at the beginning of this chapter suggested, specific urban fields are widening and becoming less focussed on an urban core. And attitudes, norms, and patterns of social behaviour which relate to earning a living, are becoming increasingly uniform geographically across both nations.

[1] Depending of course on the size of the city regions considered, which in turn depends upon the relative distances between metropolitan areas.

[2] As Friedman and Miller show for the 1950s (1965, p.314, map 2). Ledebur (1977) has recently summarised the changes in agricultural technology, the shifting pattern of demand.

[3] Op.cit., p.316. To which must be added a fifth use: energy extraction.

[4] Niles Hansen (1973, p.11) quotes a survey from the Commission on Population Growth and the American future which showed that while only 32 per cent of those sampled lived in rural areas and small towns, 53 per cent would prefer to live in such areas. See also Ledebur (1977). Fifty-two per cent thought that the Federal government should discourage further growth of large metropolitan areas, and 58 per cent thought that the government should try to encourage people and industry to move to smaller cities and towns.

[5] See P. Hall et al. (1973).

[6] Alternative regional delineations of the United States are reviewed by Hansen (1976, chapter 4). He also considers the 472 basic economic research areas used by the US Department of Agriculture, the 489 Rand McNally areas, the 507 economic subregions, and the 509 substate planning areas designated by state governors. There were 243 Standard Metropolitan Statistical Areas in 1970.

[7] A standard metropolitan labour area (SMLA) contains a *core* of a single or contiguous local government area with an employment density of over five workers per acre *or* a total employment of over 20,000 jobs, plus a hinterland of those contiguous areas from which more than 15 per cent of the working population commute to the core. This hinterland is termed the metropolitan ring. A SMLA normally has a minimum population of 70,000. A metropolitan economic labour area (MELA) is the SMLA plus further contiguous areas which send more workers to the given core than to any other core. These further areas make up the outer metropolitan ring.

[8] R. Drewett et al., figure 1, p.7.

[9] See also evidence for the New York metropolitan region (M. Segal, 1960, p.145), and for mobility in the city region of Amsterdam in the Netherlands (W.T.M. Molle, 1977).

[10] 163 of the intra-state relocatees employed 20–49 people, a higher proportion of the subgroup than the 26 inter-state relocators of this size. Inter-state (or inter-region) moves tend to be larger, a result confirmed in the UK (e.g. D.E. Keeble, 1968). Similarly, within the

state, inter-county moves tend to be larger than intra-county moves (F.J. James and J.W. Hughes, 1973, p.408).

[11] These areas being the focus of regional development policy.

[12] Keeble (1973, pp.15–20) has used a gravity model to examine this distance decay in the 1945–65 US moves.

[13] Keeble (1968, p.30) found that in moves of over 10 kilometres the proportion of transfers fell off in a very steady gradation with increasing distance. This finding came from an examination of 399 moves out of NW London.

[14] As Spooner (1972) has suggested from his study of movement in Devon and Cornwall.

[15] Departments of Trade and Industry (1973a, pp.544–71).

[16] Attributes of each of the factors listed here are discussed in section headed 'Attraction factors: the survey evidence', chapter 4.

[17] See chapter 4.

[18] Lever's very detailed study of six manufacturing industries in West Central Scotland in 1970 (glass products, engineers' small tools, paint, electrical switch gear, paper packaging, and light clothing) found that only one-fifth of all inputs by value originated within Scotland. Four-fifths of the inputs were received from other regions of the United Kingdom or from overseas (W.F. Lever, 1974, pp.318–19).

[19] P.M. Townroe, 1971, pp.39–40; G.C. Cameron and K.M. Johnson, 1969, p.269.

[20] See B.M.D. Smith (1972, pp.33–7) for a general discussion on the importance of town planning policies in influencing the supply and the price of industrial land in the West Midland conurbation.

[21] See p.12.

[22] The proportions of IDCs refused to those issued in those regions of the United Kingdom outside the development areas and Northern Ireland in the six years from 1970 to 1975 were (in percentages): 3·9, 4·5, 2·2, 3·8, 3·5, 1·7.

[23] A.J. Brown, 1972, p.303; G.C. Cameron, 1974, p.94.

[24] Rhodes and Moore (1976a) estimate that approximately 100,000 jobs were created in the assisted areas in new factories between 1960 and 1971 as a result of the stricter application of the IDC controls compared with the 1950s. They attribute one-third of the industrial moves to these areas in the period to the influence of the IDC system. This analysis assumes that the different elements of UK regional policy operate independently rather than as an independent package.

[25] E.g. A.J. Brown, 1972, pp.301–5; G.C. Cameron, 1974, pp.93–6; P.M. Townroe, 1977, pp.26–9; Hunt Report, 1969, pp.101–6.

[26] Prior to 1963 industrial derating still existed elsewhere in Great

Britain, a legacy of the 1930s economic recession.

[27] Other local taxes in the US include taxes on sales and inventories. A definition of what is to be included in assessed property varies widely.

[28] Y.P. Joun and C.R. Beaton, 1969, pp.67—75; W.V. Williams, 1967, pp.49—59. See also B.L. Weinstein and R.E. Firestine, 1978, chapter 5.

[29] Existing and proposed dispersals of civil service jobs from central London are listed in the Hardman Report (Hardman, 1973).

[30] New towns are developed by a corporation appointed by a central government minister under the 1946 New Town Act. The central government is the prime source of finance. Each development corporation recruits its own staff of architects, planners, surveyors, engineers, accountants, etc. Expanded towns are developed under the 1952 Town Expansion Act by the local municipal authority in partnership with a large exporting authority, such as the Greater London Council. Relevant expertise is drawn from both authorities and the sources of finance used are those available to all local governments. A full description of the history and the organisation of both types of town growth can be found in J.B. Cullingworth (1975, chapter 11).

[31] Even though these schemes have accounted for a relatively small percentage of the total number of houses constructed in the UK in the post World War II period.

[32] Crawley, Bracknell, Harlow, Basildon, Stevenage, Hemel Hempstead, Welwyn and Hatfield; and Aylesbury and Letchworth.

[33] King's Lynn, Bury St. Edmunds, Thetford, Haverhill, Huntingdon, Mildenhall, and St. Neots.

[34] See map in D. Keeble, 1976, p.249.

[35] *Town and Country Planning*, February 1978.

[36] See also I.K. Seeley, 1968.

[37] Although a number of these towns are seeking offices to balance up their employment structure.

[38] Studies which have considered the full impact of new industry on population growth and composition are reviewed in G.F. Summers et al., 1976, chapter 4.

[39] G.F. Summers et al., 1976, p.46. Chapter 5 reviews studies of the impact of new industry on an employment pattern and on incomes.

[40] Relevant studies are reviewed by M.J. Moseley, 1974 and A.R. Pred, 1976, pp.151—72. Low local multipliers have been identified both for consumers expenditures (or wage earners expenditures) and for the purchases of the new industrial firms themselves. Local

linkages of new industry in non-metropolitan areas seem relatively unimportant, failing to develop substantially over time (M.J. Moseley and P.M. Townroe, 1973, p.139). In the United States, both a cause and a result of this low industrial linkage may be reflected in the apparent permissive role of the interstate highway system in promoting non-metropolitan growth; although the evidence of a link between proximity to a multi-lane highway and population growth is confused by the strongest such link being found in non-metropolitan count close to metropolitan areas (N.M. Hansen, 1973, chapter 3).

[41] G.F. Summers, et al., 1976, chapter 6.

[42] The American literature is reviewed in G.F. Summers et al., 1976, chapter 7. See also C. Bell and H. Newby, 1975. And the most interesting twin studies of Banbury, a town expansion scheme, in the early 1950s and again in the late 1960s (M. Stacey, 1960; et al., 1975).

4 Inter-regional industrial movement

The central concern of this chapter is with the factors which influence owners and managers of industrial companies to choose one new site for a new manufacturing plant rather than another when the alternatives are well away from the headquarters or an existing factory of the company. Given the ambiguities of the term 'regional' as discussed in the last chapter, inter-regional industrial movement here refers to moves out of a city region or urban field to other cities and their non-metropolitan hinterlands, or to a non-metropolitan national periphery. These moves will in general be over distances in excess of 80–100 miles.

As in the previous two chapters, the first section describes the major changes in population and employment distribution, in this chapter between regions, before considering the flows of industrial moves between regions in the United Kingdom. There is no source which can give this overall picture of the geographical distribution of industrial moves in the United States. Discussion of these patterns will include examination of the major characteristics of the plants involved. This section concludes with reference to inter-regional location patterns in particular of offices, of science based industry and of corporate headquarters.

Section two brings together the evidence from interview and questionnaire surveys undertaken over the past twenty-five years in the two countries to gain further understanding as to which location factors are important for the choice of new sites for those longer distance moves. This section includes some discussion of the difficulties invoved in comparing the results of the various surveys. Each major location factor, except government inducements, is then analysed in turn. The section includes consideration of the general difficulty of ordering or ranking these factors, and with reference to some of the reasons given by companies for *not* choosing an area or site.

Direct multiple regression analysis of the variables which determine the destinations of industrial movement has not been attempted in the United States for the lack of a suitable data base. However, significant lessons may be drawn from regression and correlation analyses of output and employment growth at the state and county levels. The key results of three such analyses are set out in the third section of the chapter. In each, the authors were searching for significant locational variables. Better data in the United Kingdom has allowed direct regression analysis. The key results of the work of Sant and Keeble are presented; as well as the work of Rhodes and Moore which considers the specific impact of regional economic development policy on both the volume and the direction of industrial movement flows using a regression framework.

The summary of the Rhodes and Moore results leads to a wider and more detailed examination of the role of regional economic development incentives in the pattern of inter-regional industrial movement. The available literature relevant to this section from both the US and the UK is very extensive; therefore reference will, in the main, be restricted to those studies considering aspects of regional economic development policy which seek to attract new investment and job opportunities into a designated area. No attempt will be made to comprehensively review studies and discussions of policies seeking to develop economic activity from the base of existing companies in an area; or to consider further aspects of regional development such as the local impacts of new investments, the influences of and on population migration, or the inter-relationships with local community and national planning policies.

Patterns of inter-regional movement

Over the past twenty-five years, continuing a long established historical trend, the centre of gravity of the population of the United States has continued to move west. As noted in chapter 1, the growth in the West has been accompanied by growth in the South also, particularly in those 'Sunbelt' states which have attracted large flows of retirement migrants (Florida, New Mexico, Arizona, Southern California). The attraction of the West and South is shown in Table 4.1 which summarises the population changes in nine US regions 1950 to 1975. This table shows how the Southern regions in particular have accelerated in their population growth relative to the nation as a whole through the 1960s and early 1970s: and how the relatively faster growth of the Pacific states (principally California) has slowed in the early 1970s, although it is still faster than the national average.

These regional summary figures are of course disguised considerably because of region differences. For example, in New England, New Hampshire accelerated in the 1960s with a 21·5 per cent growth rate compared with 13·8 per cent in the 1950s, while

Table 4.1

Population by region in the United States 1950–75

Region	1950	1960	1970	1975(1)	Percentage change(2) (Thousands)		
					1950–60	1960–70	1970–75
New England	9,314	10,509	11,842	12,198	12·8	12·7	3·0
Middle Atlantic	30,164	34,168	37,199	37,263	13·3	8·9	0·1
East North Central	30,399	36,225	40,252	40,979	19·2	11·1	1·8
West North Central	14,061	15,394	16,319	16,690	9·5	6·0	2·2
South Atlantic	21,182	25,972	30,671	33,715	22·6	18·1	9·9
East South Central	11,477	20,050	12,803	13,544	5·0	6·3	5·7
West South Central	14,538	16,951	19,321	20,855	16·6	14·0	7·9
Moutain	5,075	6,855	8,282	9,644	35·1	20·8	16·3
Pacific	15,115	21,198	26,523	28,234	40·2	25·1	6·3
United States	151,326	179,323	203,210	213,121	18·5	13·3	4·8

(1) Preliminary figures for 1975.
(2) April 1 to April 1, except July 1 in 1975.

Source: *Statistical Abstract of the United States 1976*, Tables 10 and 11.

Maine fell back to 2·4 per cent compared with 6·4 per cent. West Virginia in the South Atlantic region lost population in both decades (minus 7·2 per cent and minus 6·2 per cent) before stabilising in the early 1970s: both North and South Dakota lost population in the 1960s. These figures also give no indication of the extent to which the population changes are job related. Certainly the 1·3 million migrants to Florida in the 1960s and the 1·4 million in the early 1970s contained many seeking retirement homes. Similarly among the 0·2 million and 0·3 million migrants to Arizona in the same periods. Many of these migrants came from the older industrial states, for example being part of the outflow of 0·3 million from New York State 1970 to 1975, or the 0·28 million from Ohio in the same period.

In the absence of comprehensive industrial movement figures, the changing population balance within the United States suggests two stages of inter-regional industrial mobility in the country over the past quarter of a century. The first stage is revealed in the turn-around in relative population growth between the 1950s and 1960s in the Southern Border states, such as Arkansas, Kentucky, Georgia and Tennesee. All of these states, often as a result of strenuous civic and state action, managed to attract numerous manufacturing plants, principally branch units, away from the metropolitan industrial centres of the North East and the North Central Mid-West. Industry also continued to flow to California, following the acceleration of the California economy and inward migration through the 1940s.

The second stage, from perhaps the mid-1960s to the present day, has probably involved less inter-regional industrial migration as rates of population change in most states have slowed and inter-regional growth in non-metropolitan areas has increased relative to the metropolitan centres. Indeed recent work has shown that the migration of firms has contributed only a very small percentage to employment growth in the South and West (and similarly a small percentage of employment losses in the North).

Allaman and Birch (1975) have shown that between 1969 and 1972, 64 per cent of the employment growth in the Sunbelt South was caused by the expansion of existing firms. Only 1·2 per cent resulted from inward migration to the region. Conversely, over 50 per cent of the employment losses in the New England, East North Central and Middle Atlantic regions (the 'Northern Industrial Tier') was attributable to the death of firms. Only 1·5 per cent was due to the outward migration of firms. Between 1969 and 1974 the net employment impact of birth and death processes among branch plants was a loss of 100,000 jobs in Ohio alone, although of the 143 firms relocating from the state, 42 per cent moved to the Sunbelt South

(Jusenius and Ledebur, 1977). A complementary detailed study by Rees (1978a) in the Dallas — Fort Worth area examined 551 new plants established beween 1967 and 1975. Sixty-one per cent of these were from births, the remaining 39 per cent being branch plants of multiplant companies, and only half the branch plants were established by firms with headquarters outside the SMSA.[1]

As is already evident from the earlier chapters, the inter-regional distribution of industrial movement in the United Kingdom has been recorded by the British government, and published figures are available for the 1945 to 1971 period. The main flows for the 1945 to 1965 period may be seen in Figures 4.1 and 4.2[2] (from M.E.C. Sant, 1975, pp.116—17). The pattern of movement 1966 to 1971 may be seen in Table 1.3 in chapter 1. These flows contributed to the population and employment changes between the UK regions summarised in Table 4.2.

The geographical pattern of industrial movement in the United Kingdom has followed five phases since 1945. In the immediate post World War II period, with building licences hard to obtain, many branch plants in manufacturing industry were established in old premises dating from the 1930s (and before) or in ex-munitions factories. These factory buildings, together with available labour at a time of very low unemployment, tended to be in peripheral locations, encouraging movement to regions such as Wales, Scotland and the North West (G. McCrone, 1969, pp.112—19; A.J. Brown, 1972, p.286; W.F. Luttrell, 1962, p.67). In the 1950s the rate of longer distance movement out of the South East and West Midlands regions fell as new plants were opened in the new towns ringing London and (later) Birmingham, encouraged by the IDC licensing policy and by the efforts of the municipal authorities in both cities to promote decentralisation of jobs together with housing to ease housing shortages and facilitate slum clearance.

By the end of the 1950s, it was evident that the prewar regional imbalances in the country which still existed in the late 1940s were not going to be reduced by rising prosperity in the nation as a whole and severe structural problems began to emerge, in the main associated with a limited number of declining and geographically concentrated industries: coal mining, ship building, textiles and iron and steel manufacture. As the dimensions of the regional problem began to be recognised and as associated political pressures mounted in the early 1960s, incentives were increased and the IDC stick was used more vigorously. With a fairly buoyant growth rate in the national economy, the flow of industrial moves, both transfers and branch plants, to the lagging regions (or 'assisted areas') responded. This is

94

Table 4.2

Population and employment in regions of the United Kingdom (mid-year estimates)

Regions	Resident population			Employees in employment[1]		
	1961	1975[1]	Percentage Growth	1965	1975	Percentage Growth
South East	16,071	16,936	5·4	7,461	7,319	− 1·9
East Anglia	1,489	1,780	19·5	590	671	13·7
South West	3,712	4,233	14·0	1,453	1,523	4·8
West Midlands	4,762	5,178	8·7	2,332	2,212	− 5·1
East Midlands	3,330	3,728	12·0	1,453	1,485	2·2
Yorkshire & Humberside	4,677	4,894	4·6	2,073	1,985	− 4·2
North West	6,407	6,577	2·7	2,845	2,675	− 6·0
Northern	3,113	3,126	0·4	1,270	1,266 ·	− 0·3
Wales	2,635	2,765	4·9	1,028	998	− 2·9
Scotland	5,184	5,206	0·4	2,116	2,076	− 1·9
Northern Ireland	1,427	1,537	7·7	460	494	7·4
United Kingdom	52,807	55,962	6·0	23,081	22,704	− 1·6

[1]Unemployment rate in second quarter of 1965 was 1·4 per cent and in 1975 was 3·6 per cent.

Sources: *Regional Statistics No.12*, Central Statistical Office, HMSO, London, Table 2.1.

Department of Employment Gazette, August 1976, pp.839–850.

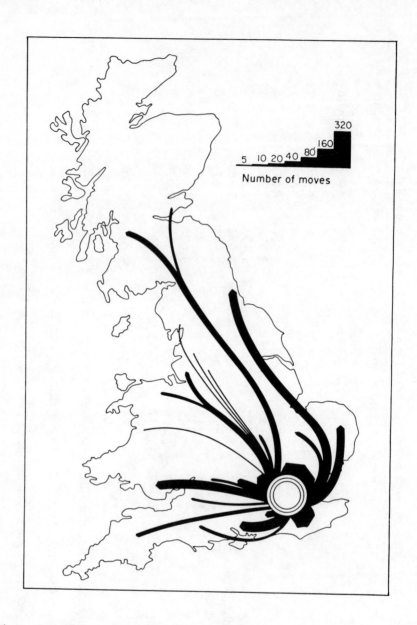

Figure 4.1 Flows of industrial movement from Greater London, 1945–65.

Source: M.E.C. Sant, *Industrial Movement and Regional Development*, Pergamon, 1975, p.116.

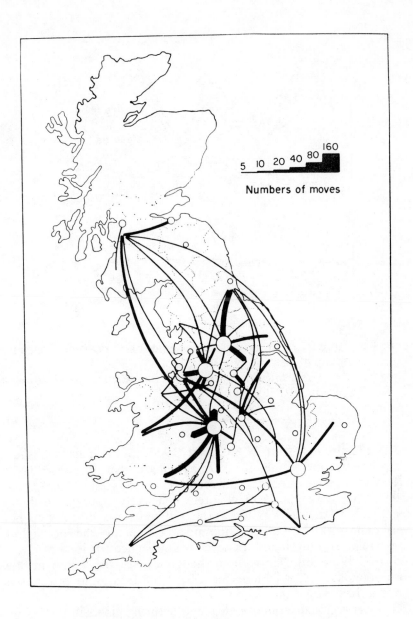

Figure 4.2 Major flows of industrial movement from provincial
          sources, 1945–65.

Source: M.E.C. Sant, *Industrial Movement and Regional Development*,
         Pergamon, 1975, p.117.

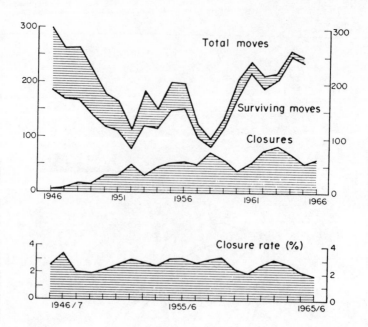

Figure 4.3 Time series of industrial movement and post-move closures
in Great Britain, 1946–66.

Source: M.E.C. Sant, *Industrial Movement and Regional Development,*
Pergamon, 1975, p.72.

shown in Figure 4.3 (from M.E.C. Sant, 1975, p.72). This high level
of response was maintained in the fourth phase, that of the late 1960s
by the very strong regional policy measures introduced in 1965, 1966
and 1967 (G. McCrone, 1969, chapter v). This response dropped
dramatically in the early 1970s, as the policy was eased back by a new
government in the face of an economic recession, and the total volume
of inter-regional movement has never again reached the level of the
1966 to 1969 period. Throughout the five phases, the dominant flow
of inter-regional industrial movement has been from more prosperous
regions to less prosperous regions.

The inter-regional flows of new manufacturing plants in the UK
have been of a larger average size of establishment and have contained
a higher proportion of branch plants as compared with transfers than
the shorter distance intra-regional movers as shown in Table 3.4. And
as Table 3.5 suggests these longer distance moves are of plants with
products and processes which do not require links with supplier and

customer. The majority of the branch plants are parts of large multi-plant and multi-subsidiary companies. Linkages have been internalised within the organisation. The dominant locational influences are labour availability, government incentives, and the availability of sites and buildings when required. The plants supply a national or international market, or perhaps just another unit of the same company, but not a regional or local market. And, a point of local concern, the inward migrant branch plant is subject to ultimate control from another region (or even another country). A high proportion of new plants have been seeking previously unemployed or under-employed female labour rather than the semi-skilled and skilled men made redundant by declining sectors. This has also been a worry for the reception regions.[3]

In both countries, as implied in the last two chapters, there has been a limited amount of inter-regional movement in the service sector (P.W. Daniels, 1975, chapter 6). Only 13 per cent of the moves of clients of the Location of Offices Bureau in London between 1963 and 1975 moved more than eighty miles, although these tended to be larger units of organisations, the total accounting for 19 per cent of the jobs moved in the period (Table 2.5). Inter-regional office movement in the United Kingdom has been further sustained by the longer distance dispersal of parts of central government departments from London. For example, the Post Office Giro Centre was established at Bootle in Lancashire, the Central Vehicle Licensing Centre, the Business Statistics Office and the Central Companies Records Office of the Department of Industry have all been moved to South Wales, national insurance cards are now all issued from Newcastle-upon-Tyne, and the National Savings Bank has been moved to Glasgow. The impact of one of these public sector moves — that of the Post Office Savings Department — has been analysed from both the point of view of the employees and the receiving city — Durham (E. Hammond, 1968).

Some similar inter-regional movement has occurred within the departments of the US federal government. For example, the Department of Health, Education and Welfare maintains regional offices across the country and the Internal Revenue Service has consolidated to regional offices. No attempt has been made to record the inter-regional movement of office jobs in the United States in the private sector, although it is clear that within both manufacturing and the major service employers (banking, insurance, finance etc.) very considerable movement is taking place all the time.[4] It is implied by the growth of the large organisations studied by Pred (1975, pp. 115—41) in eight West Coast SMSAs although Pred's figures all refer to one point in time only. Having divided the country into nine regions Semple (1973, pp.309—18) has considered the changes in the degree of dispersion of corporate headquarters in the United States between 1956 and 1971. He concludes that the distribution has become more even between the three major regions among the headquarters of the fifty largest corporations in each of six classes of activity (manufacturing, retailing, transportation, life insurance, banking and utilities); and also more even between all nine regions, except in the case of utilities, retailing and transportation. Once again movement of office activities is implied, and can be supported by individual examples (such as the move of the headquarters of the Richfield Corporation to New York and then to Los Angeles) but a full picture is not available.

Attraction factors: the survey evidence

There have been many industrial location surveys in each country over the past twenty-five years. Unfortunately, the vast majority have been restricted to a relatively small sample of firms, often located in one local area, state or region of the country. Many have not asked questions of recent movers, but have rather been more speculative, asking, 'If you were to consider relocating, then . . . .' type questions to existing established companies. Coupled with different phrasings to the questions and different approaches to scoring or ranking location factors (use of pre-listed factors or not, scoring on a scale etc.), it might be felt that the many structural differences in the surveys preclude much useful comparison of the results. Rather than discuss the strengths and weaknesses and results of the (ten) most important surveys from each country, or trying to force the results into a common table, this section will approach successively the major location factors revealed as being important in the choice of locality and site in the surveys, bringing in empirical results from the various surveys where they may seem relevant. Once again, the basic survey will be the British government survey of UK 1964 to 1967 moves used in the previous chapter, as this covers a large number of location decisions with more details from cross-classifications than is available in other studies.[5] The Economic Development Administration of the US Department of Commerce has also published the results of a very large survey of 2,616 companies in expanding sectors of US manufacturing industry on industrial location determinants (J.G. Hamrick, 1973). This survey provides results for firms in each of 223 product classes, but not by any other company or plant characteristic, even though a concurrent survey of plant characteristics was undertaken. This second survey was also published, broken down by product class. The questions on locational determinants were asked in late 1971, whether or not the firms had definite or tentative plans to expand existing facilities or establish plants at a new location between 1971 and 1975 (27 per cent only had such plans). So the majority of responses are expressions of locational preference by managers in companies not planning a move in the near future (although an unknown proportion may have moved in the recent past). This weakens the results.

The EDA study does raise general methodological questions of the most useful format of industrial movement surveys designed to assist in the preparation of public policies at both the local and national levels for the location of new plants. Before examining the various locational factors individually in the remainder of the section (and the factor of inducements or incentives offered by governments and public sector agencies will be left until the last section of this chapter), the next few paragraphs will therefore briefly discuss a number of survey methodology issues for industrial movement studies.

Nearly all surveys of recently moved plants include a question phrased something like: 'Why did you choose this location?'. The various factors itemised by respondents are then collated into a table with the factors ranked by the number of times mentioned or the percentage of the respondents offering the factor (rather as in the table reproduced as Table 3.5). There are four dangers for the interpretation of such results. The first is that the question is not being directed at the correct person within the plants or the company. The manager of the new plant in the new location may not have had any hand in the choice of that location and so can only work from intra-company documentation or hearsay. Or the respondent (especially perhaps to postal questionnaires) may be a second tier official of the company, only present on the fringe of the decision making process.

A second danger is present in any questioning of an important decision: post-hoc rationalisation by the respondent. An industrial manager, or perhaps especially an owner-manager, may not like to admit to an outside official or academic body that the choice was governed by personal residential preferences or by internal company politics. And memories fade, the answers perhaps reflecting an opinion of what *should* have been important in the light of subsequent experience at the new location.

The third danger is that individual factors on a prompt list or those offered without prompting mean slightly different things to different respondents. 'Available labour' for example might be interpreted as a pool of unemployed labour, or as a pool of relevant skilled employees which could be tempted away from other local companies. Or 'Favourable labour-management relations' may mean an absence of unions to one respondent, or absence of strike activity to another. Also factors overlap, such as 'Access to markets and supplies' and 'Access to specified transport facilities' (as in Table 3.5).

The ranking or ordering of the replies received to the 'Why did you choose this location?' question can also be misleading. Some respondents will check many reasons presented in a check list, or will offer many to an open question, or will agree to many in response to prompting in an interview: all without consideration of the relative importance of each factor in the final choice. Some surveys ask for a major factor/minor factor distinction, or an outstanding single factor, if relevant. Others have attempted a scoring, perhaps on each factor, over 5 or 10 steps from 'zero relevance' to 'crucial importance'. Again, there is the problem of different respondents perceiving the scales differently. Also, different combinations of factors may have been important to a single company in looking at alternative sites. So that the choice may have involved a trade-off decision between (say) better access, good local services but high taxes and wage rates against greater remoteness, a pleasant environment, investment inducements and lower wage rates. Location factors in an individual case therefore have to be seen in composite bundles. Weighting responses by the number of employees in the firm offering these responses seems particularly irrelevant. Perhaps surveys of this kind should always ask whether any specific factor was significantly against the location chosen.

The validity of sampling procedures among populations of firms or establishments is another methodological issue for location surveys. In local areas the total population may be small and any sampling combined with the low response rates (particularly with postal surveys)[6] would produce a final number of responses too small to allow any analysis of sub-groups of firms. For effective investigation of the factors of importance in location decisions, possibly the more important consideration is to focus the survey on those companies which have been involved in movement in the relatively recent past, before memories get blurred and/or experience in the new location colours the view of what was important in the locational choice. Identifying recently moved firms or establishments is a difficult task however for the research worker. Usual industrial directories are not too helpful. Sources which have been used include newspaper announcements, lists from local planning agencies or development promotion agencies (such as the Location of Offices Bureau in

102

London), lists from utility companies serving new industrial estates or parks. Identifying the most appropriate respondent and obtaining his cooperation is the next problem. All of these issues have been discussed in greater detail by this author (P.M.Townroe, 1971) and by others (M. Cooper, 1975; E. Mueller and E. Morgan, 1962 etc.).

One distinction that is not always made clear in the design of these surveys and the presentation of their results is that between the location factors which have influenced the management of a company in their choice of *regions* from those factors influencing the choice of *local community*, and those influencing the choice of a particular *site* or *building*. It may be felt that this distribution is self evident, a given factor operating clearly at one or other or at all three spatial levels. But this is not always the case. For example, a company may choose a local community on the grounds of good labour relations in spite of the region as a whole having a reputation for labour unrest. They may decide that a good transport link of specific relevance to the company outweighs generally poor transport access from the community; or the company may find a cheap secondhand building in an area otherwise known for rather high priced factory buildings. The extent to which companies search for a new location in phases, working down from the region to the site, will be examined in chapter 6.

In interpreting survey data it must be remembered that a firm may select a small number of areas as suitable from the point of view of its main needs, such as the availability of labour, and then come to its final decision on the basis of some quite different factor, such as the local tax base. Companies choosing a site in a new country will of course have an additional set of factors operating at the country wide level. These are not considered here.[7]

The individual location factors may now be considered in turn:

Labour

We have already seen (Table 2.2) how an unsatisfactory supply of labour at the existing plant location ranked third as a reason for considering a new location in the British government movement survey. It was a major reason for moving 40 per cent of the firms, a minor reason for 11 per cent, and the outstanding single reason for 16 per cent. It was a particularly important reason among the clothing, textile and footwear firms in the survey needing female workers. (Department of Trade and Industry, 1973, pp.537 and 548—9). Labour supply problems have ranked highly as a push factor in the majority of British movement surveys (e.g. J. Dunning, 1960; W.F. Luttrell, 1962; G.C. Cameron and B.D. Clark, 1966; D.E. Keeble,

1966; B.J. Loasby, 1967), although in some surveys labour supply pressures were analysed as synonymous with the pressures of growth and expansion (e.g. P.M. Townroe, 1971, p.38). The importance of labour supply and high labour costs as push factors is further supported by American surveys (e.g. in the Michigan studies: G. Katona and J.M. Morgan, 1952, p.76; E. Mueller and J.M. Morgan, 1962, p.212).

Labour supply will be even more important as a pull factor than a push factor. This is reflected in Table 3.5. As that table shows, access to labour was the dominant locational factor for all the moves in the British government survey and was a major factor for 80 per cent of those firms choosing an assisted area location. The further the distance of the move, the greater the percentage of respondents listing labour as a major locational factor, from 52 per cent of firms moving less than 20 miles to 88 per cent of those moving more than 250 miles. It was particularly important in the textile (90 per cent) and clothing (97 per cent) industries; and it was more important for branch plant moves (79 per cent) than for transfer moves (64 per cent). The prime importance of the availability of labour for longer distance moves in the United Kingdom is supported by the results of a number of other surveys. For example P.D. McGovern, (1965, p.30), D. Law, (1964, p. 136) and A.S. Murie et al. (1974, p.70) studying moves to Northern Ireland; or G.C. Cameron and B.D. Clark (1966, p.164) studying moves to assisted areas between 1958 and 1963.

The importance of labour as a locational factor is also implied by many American studies, although these have not been based or analysed on surveys of long distance moves alone. For example, Logan's study of 271 manufacturing establishments in Wisconsin reports the labour group of factors ranked most important by 17·5 per cent of the firms. In the second Michigan study, labour costs and the availability of labour were ranked first and third in importance as locational factors (E. Mueller and J.M. Morgan, 1962, p.208). Schriver's (1971, p.63) study of 307 manufacturing firms employing 25 or more, locating in Tennessee between 1955 and 1965, showed 202 or 65 per cent, of the firms indicated that the low cost and availability of labour was important. Nearly twice as many firms indicated this as the important factor rather than the second and third ranking factor (low cost of electric power and favourable labour-management relations) from a list of twenty-one factors. However, overall, labour as a location factor does not have the same universal dominance in the American studies as in the British survey results.[8] In the EDA survey referred to in paragraph sixteen above, pools of trained or unskilled workers were felt to be 'critical' community

104

attributes by only 18 and 17 per cent of respondents, although 35 and 29 per cent rated the existence of such pools as 'of significant value' and a further 35 per cent for each factor rated them as of 'average value' (J. Hamrick, 1973).

Markets and personal reasons were ranked higher as the most important location factors (36 per cent and 18 per cent) in Logan's Wisconsin survey. Garwood's study of 116 firms establishing in Utah and Colorado between 1946 and 1951 places the labour factor third, behind markets and materials as influences on location (J.D. Garwood, 1953, p.83). A study quoted by Weinstein and Firestine (1978, p. 138), of 318 companies in New York State found the supply of skilled labour to be far and away the most important location factor cited, scoring nearly twice the next factor, markets.

Most industrial location surveys do not break down the labour factor into a series of sub-questions or factors. However, there are some exceptions. The British government survey found little difference in the importance attributed to the availability of male as opposed to female labour, but did find, perhaps surprisingly, that the availability of skilled labour was a major factor for only 21 per cent of cases. The report suggests that this might be because most firms fully expect to compete for skilled labour wherever they locate, or because they expect, or hope, to transfer the necessary skilled people, or because skilled labour is often not required, at least initially, in a new branch plant. (Department of Industry, 1973, p.575). The split between labour costs and labour availability in the Michigan surveys has already been noted, although in general the suggestion in the results of all these surveys, that companies may be attracted to a location to exploit a weak labour market in order to reduce the cost of labour is carefully avoided. Even in the US where there are sharp inter-regional wage differentials, these are not reflected in location survey results.[9] The Shively study of 330 manufacturing plants locating in Nebraska distinguished labour availability from labour quality and, using a weighting for degrees of importance, scored labour quality as the most important of 43 location factors; labour availability coming third and wage rates sixth (Table 4.3). The Fantus Company report for the Appalachian Regional Commission drawing upon the company files, also scores labour cost advantage relatively highly (Table 4.4).

Perhaps because of very high levels of union membership across all sectors of British manufacturing industry, the question of the presence of union representation in the labour force of a local area is not felt by industrial management to be significant for the choice of location and so trade unions are not listed as a location factor in the various British

Table 4.3

Ranked location factors cited by 330 manufacturing plants in Nebraska

Rank	Factor	Points(1)	Rank	Factor	Points
1	Labor quality	645	22	Quality of local schools	428
2	Highway transportation	640	23	Groundwater	420
3	Labor availability	637	24	Amount of unionization	417
4	Available site	604	25	Proximity to raw materials	416
5	Reliability of electric service	585	26	Construction costs	401
6	Wage rates	582	27	Housing for plant workers	385
7	Proximity to market	582	28	Housing for executives	372
8	People who started plant lived here	537	29	Caliber of local ID group	347
9	Natural gas availability	529	30	Local financial institutions	327
10	Right-to-work law	520	31–32	Recreational opportunities	298
11	Taxes	519	31–32	Vocational training programs	298
12	Electric rates	514	33	Air freight transportation	293
13	Rail transportation	511	34	Nearness to colleges and universities	288
14	Community attitude toward industry	505	35	Hotel, motel and meeting facilities	271
15	Friendliness of people	490	36	Air passenger transportation	267
16	Natural gas rates	480	37	Supporting industries	264
17	Attractiveness of community	474	38	Local investors	230
18	City water at site	473	39	LDC financing	166
19–20	Health facilities and services	465	40	Local subsidies	159
19–20	City sewer at site	465	41	SBA financing	133
21	Available building	435	42	Industrial revenue bonds	126
			43	Recommendation of consultant	120

(Table 4.3 continued)
[1]Three points were awarded each time a factor was noted 'very important', two points for 'important', one point for 'minor importance', and no points for 'not important at all'.

Source: R.W. Shively,

Table 4.4
Industrial location factor scores

Location factor	Weighted score	Critical importance industries
Transportation:		
Services	53	8
Costs	41	8
Proximity to customers	46	8
State manpower training assistance	31	2
Labor cost advantage	24	2
Low cost electric power	24	2
Urban orientation	24	1
Proximity to raw materials	11	2

Source: Based on Fantus report, *The Appalachian Location Research Studies Program: Summary Report and Recommendations,* (New York, December 1966). Table 3, pp.12–13.

surveys. The quality of labour relations, however, which may or may not be linked with union representation as perceived by a management, has been seen as significant in several studies, particularly in the choice of general area or region. In this author's 1969 survey (P.M. Townroe, 1971, p.66 and pp.78–9) adverse hearsay evidence on the quality of labour relations in particular regions of the country seemed to be used as one way of initially limiting the range of possible areas in which to search for a new site. Labour problems were an important factor in the rejection of Northern Ireland by a sub-group of firms moving to UK Development Areas 1965 to 1969 (A.S. Murie et al., 1974, p.77); and 'labour difficulties', which included problems of supply and estimations of attitudes, were given by 29 per cent of respondents in the British government survey (Department of Trade and Industry, 1973, p.610) as the reason for not settling in other locations in the region chosen for the new plant.[10]

In the United States the question of trade union strength in an area has assumed greater prominence in the choice of location of new plants and has been suggested as one reason for firms from the Northern cities seeking Southern small town sites (W. Thompson, 1975, p.190). As suggested by Table 4.3, the existence of a right-to-work law in a given state will increase the attractiveness of that state to new industrial investment. In some states, and in particular in the non-metropolitan areas, union organisation has been discouraged as part of local efforts to attract new industry. Hansen (1973, pp.96–7 and 106) cites a number of new plants in Tennessee and Mississippi which are not unionised, as examples of local inter-state variations in union-strength.

In the South it seems that many inward migrant plants are attracted to pools of non-union white labour in the smaller towns from which black labour is often forced to leave and to migrate to Northern cities or increasingly to larger Southern centres. Areas with a high proportion of blacks in the non-metropolitan South have not attracted industrial investment as successfully as the predominantly white areas, perhaps because, as Hansen suggests (1973, p.164): 'many employers believe that blacks are less productive and more inclined towards organisation by unions'. There has been no research to discover how far these employers act on the basis of detailed investigation into educational attainment, health standards, productivity in existing plants etc., or whether, as in the British case, hearsay and subjective judgement form the basis for this implicit racial discrimination.

In both countries, the evidence seems to suggest that the size of the labour pool and relative rates of unemployment among skilled and/or trainable labour together form a leading location factor for the majority of long distance moves. The quality of the labour recruited, the attitudes and (possibly) the degree of unionisation (but see chapter 7) are all factors which do more to explain the profitability and subsequent growth of the new plant rather than the choice of location; although the two sets of factors perhaps inevitably get confused in the different wordings of the questions in different surveys, and confused in the minds of managers questioned some time after the process of choosing the location when current labour issues dominate.

Transport and access to
markets and suppliers

Again, some ambiguity arises in the responses to location survey questions about transportation and access to markets and suppliers. An industrial move may be undertaken to make possible the serving of a particular market or the contact with a particular supplier which would not otherwise be possible. But much more likely is a move to improve the accessibility to existing and potential markets and/or suppliers, and this may be reflected in positive responses to location factors such as 'Improvement in transport efficiency' or 'Access to specified facilities'. The means and the end are rarely distinguished in the location surveys. One exception is the EDA survey of potential location decision makers (J.M. Hamrick, 1973). When asked to choose up to three locational objectives to be achieved in making a move, 59 per cent of respondents chose 'Ability to serve new and/or expanded markets', 49 per cent chose 'Closer proximity to distributors and/or customers', 31 per cent chose 'Improvement in transportation efficiency or economy'. Then among plant site features in the same survey, 'Being within thirty minutes of a major highway interchange' was of critical value for 37 per cent, of significant value for 39 per cent, and of value for 17 per cent, and of no value for 3 per cent. A scheduled rail service rated 23, 17, 22 and 34 per cents; a scheduled air freight service 12, 25, 31 and 28 per cents; and water transportation 3, 5, 9 and 79 per cents.

In a somewhat similar way, the British government survey (see Table 3.5) distinguished between ends and means; although the overall pattern of findings is that issues of transport and access are of much less importance to British long distance industrial moves than to their American counterparts (as may be expected a priori, given the continental scale of American moves). Accessibility to markets was of major importance to 30 per cent of respondents in this survey, and of minor importance to a further 14 per cent. Accessibility to supplies was of major importance to only 15 per cent, and of minor importance to 14 per cent. Both factors were less important to firms moving to the assisted areas than to old firms. The supply factor was more important for firms moving less than 150 miles than for long distance moves (perhaps implying that the retention of existing or pre-move supply linkages was what was important). The market access factor

109

was significantly more important for moves between 100 and 150 miles than for either longer or shorter moves. There was little difference in the importance of three aspects of market attraction distinguished in the survey: access to prospective home markets, access to existing home markets away from the previous plant location and access to existing home markets new to the previous plant location. Similarly there was little difference in the importance of two aspects to access to suppliers improving existing access, and preventing the deterioration of existing access. In response to the question about the means of access, access to four specified transport facilities (motorway within ten miles, port, airport and rail freight depot) was of major importance to 31 per cent and of minor importance to 20 per cent of respondents. Ports are perhaps more important in the UK than in the US given that half of the output of UK manufacturing industry is sold overseas.

The same British government survey also shows how transport and accessibility factors are often the main reasons given by companies for rejecting a region as an area in which to search for a new site or factory having actively considered it. For example, 38 of 88 firms in the survey considering but eventually rejecting Scotland did so because of 'remoteness/transport/communication problems' and 33 did so because of 'uneconomic distance from markets/supplies'. Twenty-three did so because of 'labour difficulties'. Comparable figures among 68 firms considering but rejecting Northern Ireland are 52, 26 and 22; for 92 firms in South East England only 10 and 5 quoted the access reasons while 34 quoted the labour factor in deciding to locate elsewhere (Department of Trade and Industry, 1973, p.607).

Other surveys which have given strong prominence to accessibility include Logan (1970, p.326) in Wisconsin and Cameron and Clark (1966, p.163) in the assisted areas of the United Kingdom. In both countries however, the importance of this location factor may be reducing over time as transportation technology improves, and the real costs of distance fall.[11] The completion of basic networks of freeway standard highways (the American interstate system and the British motorway system) has greatly increased the ability of much of manufacturing industry in both countries to be relatively 'footloose' in its choice of location in both countries. However, in examining these survey results it is important to remember that there are great differences between industrial sectors in the importance of transportation costs in the overall costs of production. Distribution costs are likely to be dominant in the choice of plant location in both countries in industries such as drinks, bricks, cardboard and metal containers,

110

etc. Value, bulk, weight and fragility will all be important attributes of the product (W.F. Lever, 1974).

The majority of longer distance inter-regional industrial moves involve the establishment of a branch plant of a company, frequently by a company which already has a number of other branch plants or subsidiary production units in other locations. Therefore, ease of access between the plants of the company may be more important than good access to a diffused market or to suppliers. This is suggested in Table 3.5 as being a major factor for 32 per cent of the British government survey firms, although it is grouped in with the further factor of the ties of management and staff to an earlier location. The need for managers to attend more than one plant was a major factor for 13 per cent of firms and a minor factor for a further 12 per cent.

Site and buildings

Table 4.3 ranks 'available site' fourth and 'available building' twenty-first. Table 3.5 shows 'Availability of suitable non-government factory' as a major factor for 28 per cent of respondents, and 'Special characteristics of site' as a major factor for 20 per cent. Industrial sites for small and medium sized plants without specialist requirements of excessive local bearing capacity of the ground, or of extreme levels of water purity, or the need to be adjacent to a highway interchange and so forth are now available in the vast majority of communities in both countries from perhaps 5,000 population and upwards. Provision of land or of serviced sites is one of the most common services or inducements offered by local government or promotional agencies to attract industry to an area (M.M. Camina, 1975; and Committee for Economic Development, 1966). The price of the site seems to be not important for a significant minority of mobile firms, perhaps because it is a low proportion of the total costs of a project or because the location search quickly gives an industrial manager a feel for the land markets and the price is only noted as significant when relatively high or low compared with the going rate. Price of the site is more important for small companies than large and for companies with a non-urgent move than those in a hurry to get established (P.M. Townroe, 1971, p.85).

The availability of an existing building seems to be relatively unimportant for most longer distance moves, although the advance factory programme of the British Government has met a clear demand for a minority of firms in a great hurry to get into production in the new location (D.E. Keeble, 1976, pp.225—6). The availability of a

111

building, new or secondhand, has been more important to shorter distance moves in the West Midlands or South East regions of the UK where permissions to build new factories have been difficult to obtain (D.E. Keeble, 1976, p.260). For small companies or for companies with small experimental projects a short term lease on a trading estate may be a way of keeping the initial capital commitment low. Taking a lease rather than buying a freehold ties up fewer of the assets of a company in an investment which is only indirectly productive. However, 41 per cent of mobile companies in one UK survey purchased freehold land. These were larger companies with larger projects and included many fast growing concerns (P.M. Townroe, 1971, p.87). There are no comparative US figures available. Respondents in the Townroe survey saw a freehold purchase as a long term investment, as an insurance, and as a security to set against future loans and borrowings.

One final site characteristic which seems to be of near universal importance to moving companies is room for further expansion (e.g. T.E. McMillan, 1965, p.244). Sometimes this involves purchasing a site larger than required immediately; an option is taken out on adjacent land (P.M. Townroe, 1971, p.88). Over half (53 per cent) of the firms in the EDA study preferred a plant site of between five and twenty acres.

Amenity and environment

If transport is becoming less important as an industrial location factor, whether in obtaining supplies or in meeting markets, and labour and site conditions can be met in many centres, then questions of amenity and environment will assume greater prominence in the decision of location. It was suggested in the last chapter that an improved environment was one of the factors encouraging firms to decentralise from large cities out to non-metropolitan hinterlands. The high degree of 'foot looseness' from traditional economic location factors means that the locational choices on inter-regional industrial moves may also be strongly influenced by environmental pressures; in a number of different ways.

Many location surveys, particularly those including smaller firms and short distance moves, discover a high proportion of respondents giving a high ranking to location factors such as 'personal reasons' (see G. Katona and J.N. Morgan, 1952, p.75; and E. Mueller and J.N. Morgan, 1962, p.209) or 'people who started plant lived here' (see

112

Table 4.3) or 'Home area, personal' (M.I. Logan, 1970, p.326). These sorts of replies, understandably, most frequently come from owner-managers or proprietors. In larger companies, where a salaried manager is frequently making a location choice for someone else to live with, the issue of amenity is approached rather differently. He too will be concerned with the quality of life in the chosen community as suggested by various of the more indefinable factors in Table 4.3: 'Attractiveness of community', 'Friendliness of people' or 'Communities attitude towards industry'. Or as suggested, by the quality of local school, health facilities or housing. The prime consideration here will be the success in transferring and recruiting labour (including executives) into the community.[12] So these factors tend to work negatively (W.F. Luttrell, 1962, p.65). They also link in with the important consideration of climate, which has already been suggested above as an important influence in recent trends in industrial location in the United States.

Amenity and environment in a local community also includes the availability, reliability and price of local services, principally the utilities, the sort of services which are suggested in Table 4.3. Proximity to colleges and universities also has been important for many science based industries, as Shimshoni (1971, pp.108–36) has shown in the Boston and San Francisco areas; and available college training programmes might attract a firm to an area (P.A. Montello, 1972, p.352). Although a British study found a fair degree of ignorance of new inward migrant companies of the training facilities available in the study area (H.C. Baker et al., 1969).

The influence of amenity considerations is seen in the responses to questions of preferred size of community for a new industrial site. In the EDA study for example, 73 per cent of the firms questioned would have wanted to locate in a community of less than 250,000 people. Twenty per cent preferred a community of less than 25,000 population but at that size the pool of suitable labour is very small. Overall, however, and on average, amenity and environment factors are not ranked very highly in industrial location surveys in either country; although this may be due to a reluctance to admit to more subjective elements in the decision or a failure by the investigator to pose relevant questions.

Attraction factors: the regression evidence

From the survey evidence of the factors which determine industrial locational choice, we may turn to five statistical studies using

113

correlation and regression analysis: three American and two British. [13] The American studies examine patterns of industrial locational change rather than undertaking direct analysis of flows of industrial moves. The strength of the conclusions to be drawn from the relationships discovered is therefore somewhat weakened for the purposes of analysing the forces influencing the distribution of industrial moves. The British studies use data on inter-subregional flows of industrial movement to test hypotheses of locational choice behaviour more directly, allowing the introduction of variables which measure the impact of the various relevant public policy measures.

The Burrows, Metcalf and Kaler study.   This study, for the Economic Development Administration, developed an econometric model to forecast the future industrial structure of the 3,097 counties in the United States upon the level and mix of existing industry and on a limited number of relevant and easily obtainable socio-economic variables (J.C. Burrows et al., 1971). The model was designed to obtain ten year projections, and the estimated equations relate 1960 employment to 1950 socio-economic data in order to give expected 1970 employment from 1960 socio-economic data. The aggregated (national) county projections were then scaled to be made consistent with a national inter-industry model, using twenty-two industrial categories. There were numerous statistical problems as well as a general data handling problem.

Ignoring the county by county and industry by industry pattern of results, the significant variables from the very wide number (168) used to explain employment growth in this study give one empirical base for suggesting important socio-economic influences on the choice of new location by mobile industry. The most effective variable in explaining employment growth was population growth. Population density (measured by distance from the nearest SMSA) was also significant in more than half the sector-by-sector equations, but its effect was stronger for the smaller SMSAs, suggesting urban external economies which diminish with increasing city size. [14] These external economies may be on both the demand and the factor input sides of the growing industry. The proportion employed in mining was significant in a negative direction, acting as a proxy for a wide group of socio-economic characteristics of many mining areas which discourage industrial growth. [15] The sizes of the local population and of the industrial employment were also important variables. No strong pattern emerged from the other variables. 'Economies of scale and external economies therefore appear to be key factors in industrial growth'(J.C. Burrows, et al., 1971, p.78).

The Harris and Hopkins study. These two research workers present '. . . an inter-regional, multi-industry model designed to explain industrial location' (C.C. Harris and F.E. Hopkins, 1972, p.xiii). In particular the study was designed to examine two groups of influences on the location of industry: regional factor prices and the effects of agglomeration, using regression analysis. The model is based upon the University of Maryland national inter-industry model. Location equations are developed for eighty-four industrial sectors using data from the 3,112 county-type areas defined by the US Bureau of Census, with county output estimates for each industry in 1965 and 1966 being the dependent variable, expressed as the change in the value of the output between two years.

Methodologically, the most significant element of this study is the use of marginal costs (where possible) rather than average costs of the inputs. (The model cannot account for regional variation in factory prices of the output.) This recognises that in locational decisions profit maximising firms will examine differences in cost structures at the margin, and therefore regional (or county) changes in output should be responsive to differences in input prices and externalities at the margin. Shadow prices from a linear programming transportation algorism are used to estimate the marginal costs of shipping both outputs and inputs. These are the costs to individual firms with the greatest regional variation (C.C. Harris and F.E. Hopkins, 1972, pp.14 −19).

The postulated model was successful in explaining a sizeable proportion of the variance in the change in output by country for most industries. The variables used included: transport costs of inputs and outputs, annual earnings per worker, land value per acre, the value of gross investment in equipment, the level of output, population density, and the presence of major buying and supplying sectors. All of the variables played some part in the estimated equations, although different variables were significant for different industries. One of the transportation variables was significant for 61 of the 84 industries, and output was significant for 76 (although with both positive and negative signs). Earnings were only significant in 16 industries, the value of land and gross equipment investment in 30 industries each. Population was highly collinear with the value of land but was significant in seventeen industries for which the value of land variable was absent. The growth of output in two groups of thirty-two industries was significantly influenced by the presence of buying and supplying industries or sectors (including personal consumption and exports overseas). For mobile industry, one implication of this study is to play down the significance of the labour supply factor. This conflicts with the survey evidence and may perhaps be attributed to the absence here of a suitable labour supply variable (such as unemployment rates or pool or female activity rates) to use to test for significance.

The Wheat study. This study examines the forces influencing the absolute, *per capita* and percentage growth in manufacturing employment between 1947 and 1963 in the contiguous states of the US (L.F. Wheat, 1973). Simple, partial and multiple correlation analysis is undertaken to identify dominant influences from a wide range of explanatory variables. These included many variables (roots, ratios, etc.) derived from a basic list of thirteen. The variables used reflected: demand and supply sides of markets; the forces of agglomeration and of relative urbanisation; wages, unionisation and labour supply; climate, and a weighting for temperature and distance.

The findings cover four chapters and 130 pages of text, and from this it is difficult to find unambiguous relationships to explain the regional growth of manufacturing employment. Conclusions are made more difficult to reach because of the level of spatial disaggregation (states) is fairly crude and because the level of spatial disaggregation some of the variables (for example, agglomeration is measured by dummy variables reflecting membership of two alternative groupings of North Eastern states). However, these considerations do not stop Wheat making strong claims for the findings.

> The findings leave no doubt that markets and climate are far ahead as the leading influences affecting manufacturing growth in the United States. Labour and thresholds follow as secondary influences. Resources and urban attraction might best be labelled tertiary influences, although one could easily quarrel about where resources belong. Agglomeration has no measurable effect on Manufacturing Belt growth (L.F. Wheat, 1973, p.183).

All three of these studies support the view that for non-resource based industries the dominant influence on the spatial distribution of the growth in manufacturing industries at the regional level in the United States has been the distribution of the markets on those industries and the cost and the ease of transporting goods to these markets. In this, these studies support the statistical work of Thompson and Mattila (1959) and of Perloff et al. (1960); but not of Fuchs (1961) who attributes one-third of employment shifts between census regions 1929 to 1954 to abundant, low cost, non-union labour in the South. However, Fuch's methodology may be criticised (e.g. L.

116

F. Wheat, 1973, p.15) and anyway conditions in many parts of the South have changed since 1954. The other factors examined in the three studies, such as labour supply and agglomeration economies, for the United States are probably more important as determinants of locational choice within regions rather than between regions.

The two British studies are focused more directly upon the choice of location for a plant near to a firm by examining the spatial pattern of industrial movement rather than of industrial growth. The use of data collected from individual moves allows the introduction of an origin-to-destination distance variable.

The Keeble Study. Using the employment at the end of 1966 in manufacturing plants moving between fifty sub-regions of the UK in the period 1945 to 1965, Keeble started his analysis by testing the predictions of a simple gravity model against the observed movement. The distance and attractiveness variables were subsequently incorporated into multiple regression equations. These were used to evaluate the role of distance and of labour availability in determining the choice of peripheral region[16] for moves from the South East and West Midlands regions, the two dominant 'supplier regions' which together accounted for 66 per cent of the employment generated by inter-regional migrant firms going to the peripheral areas (D. Keeble, 1972, pp.3–25).

Using the results of earlier micro-survey studies[17] which had suggested that the two most important influences on the choice of peripheral area locations were incentives and the availability of labour, the gravity model used the road distance to each of eighteen sub-regions in the peripheral areas from the centre of the two 'donor' regions and a weighted index of the number of unemployed workers in each sub-region in three years in the 1945–65 period. The government incentives (with the exception of Northern Ireland) were invariant between the sub-regions, and the hypothesis that distance and labour availability would dominate the choice between the sub-regions was strongly supported by high coefficients of determination between the actual employment created by migrant firms and the predictions of the gravity model.[18]

The variables were then set into the framework of a regression equation, with the end-1966 employment in migrant firms in moves from the South East and West Midlands regions and their central conurbations as four dependent variables, and the index of labour availability and the road distances as the explanatory variables. Again significant results were obtained. As Keeble suggests (1972, p.23), the distance variable may be acting as a proxy for a market proximity variable. Distance was inversely related to the volume of movement,

117

suggesting that companies in the UK in this period, forced to locate new plant away from the home base by the exercise of the industrial development certificate control, chose the peripheral area at the shortest distance, compatable with a satisfactory pool of labour. Keeble argued that his results supported the case for regional development inducements to be graded by distance from the economic core of the country.

The Sant study. Sant's work of the inter-subregional industrial movement statistics collected by the British Government is the most detailed yet undertaken in the UK and covers the period 1945—1971 (M.E.C. Sant, 1975). He used both time series and cross section regression analysis and, like Keeble, also experimented with a gravity model.

The time series analysis examines the determinants of the year to year fluctuation of moves into the ten regions of Great Britain over the period 1945 to 1965 (M.E.C. Sant, 1975, pp.81—101). The explanatory variables considered fall into two groups. The economic variables are four indicators of changing economic conditions over the period, only one of which, numbers unemployed, varies by region, as shown in Table 4.5. The structural variables are primarily concerned with variations over time in the activity of relevant public policy: of incentives and of the rate of house construction in new towns. In the 1950s the relative fall off in the number of migrant firms attracted to the development areas was due primarily to the low priority given to regional policy. The incentives were not generous. The growth of the London ring of eight new towns was a further factor. Industrial development certificates could be obtained for sites in the towns by firms facing refusals to expand elsewhere in the South East region. Therefore any time series model has to take account of the influence of this variable, both as attraction factor within the region concerned and as a competing attraction in other regions. Variable 8 was used as an indicator of the proportion of each region which was included as an assisted area in each year. In some regions this changed within the time period. Variable 10 was relevant for East Anglia only, the proportion or total construction accounted for by town expansion schemes in other regions being extremely small (M.E. Sant, 1975, pp. 84—8).

The region by region results of the regression models formed with these variables are given in Table 4.6. All the independent variables are lagged by one year against the dependent variable. This improves the equations and is justified *a priori* by the time lag between decision to search and actual move, shown by a survey study to average between

118

Table 4.5

Independent variables used in time-series analysis of industrial movement, 1945–65

(i)   Economic variables

V_1 Percentage change in manufacturing output[a] 1964 prices

V_2 Bank rate (annual average)[a]

V_3 Undistributed company earnings (£m)[a] 1964 prices

V_4 Numbers unemployed (June plus December average) ((000)[b]
V_{4a} Region i V_{4b} Great Britain less region i

(ii) V_5 Government expenditure on DAs: total (£m)[c] 1964 prices

V_6 Government expenditure in DAs: factory buildings and industrial estates (£m)[c] 1964 prices

V_7 Government expenditure in DAs: loans and grants (£m)[c] 1964 prices

V_8 Employment in DAs ('000)[b]
V_{8a} Region i V_{8b} Great Britain less region i

V_9 Houses constructed in new towns ('000)[a]
V_{9a} Region i V_{9b} Great Britain less region i

V_{10} Town expansion schemes in operation (East Anglia only)

---

[a] Annual abstract of statistics.

[b] Employment and productivity gazette (formerly Ministry of Labour Gazette).

[c] Annual reports on the Local Employment Acts.

Source: M.E.C. Sant, *Industrial Movement and Regional Development*, Pergamon, 1975, p.85.

119

Table 4.6
Best lagged regression equations (standardised) for time series of movement: standard regions, 1945—65

Region	Independent variables				r^2
	(i)	(ii)	(iii)	(iv)	
Northern England	−0·59V8b (4·7)	+0·36V4a (3·5)	+0·42V1 (2·6)		0·76
Wales	−1·07V9b (5·3)	+0·39V6 (3·2)	+0·49V9a (2·8)	+0·19V1 (2·0)	0·91
Scotland	−0·98V9b (7·0)	+0·71V9a (5·3)	+0·29V4b (2·7)	+0·29V1 (2·6)	0·92
North West	+0·94V3 (4·3)	−0·91V9b (4·2)	+0·37V4a (2·2)		0·61
South West	−1·00V9b (4·3)	+0·64V8a (4·5)	+9·30V2 (3·8)		0·78
South East	+0·48V9a (2·3)				0·23
East Anglia	+0·83V11 (10·8)	+0·31V8a (4·0)			0·92
Yorkshire & Humberside	−0·84V9b (6·2)	+0·29V8a (2·0)			0·71
East Midlands	−1·82V9b (3·9)	+1·13V9a (2·7)	+0·72V3 (2·0)	−0·62V1 (1·8)	0·67
West Midlands	−0·76V4a (2·8)	−0·72V8b (2·7)	+0·69V3 (2·4)	+0·62V4b (2·4)	0·45

Note: figures in brackets refer to values of Student's t.

Source: M.E.C. Sant, *Industrial Movement and Regional Development*, Pergamon, 1975, p.99.

six and twelve months if a factory is available and a further six to twelve months if a building is to be constructed (P.M. Townroe, 1971, pp.59–61). The equations presented in Table 4.6 were developed using a step-wise regression procedure to select the most appropriate variables, resulting in some strange combinations. One dominant feature, however, is the negative importance of new towns outside the region for all regions containing assisted areas (the first five regions in the table), except the Northern region. This was especially important for Wales, the assisted area region closest to the main areas generating industrial moves. All of the equations for these same regions contain at least one positive variable indicating the state of the national economy, confirming the dependence of a regional development policy based upon industrial migration on the national economic growth rate.[19] The volume of moves into the South East and East Anglia can be seen to be very dependent upon the build up of the new and expanding towns in these regions. The influence of the new towns programme was again strong for Yorkshire and for the East Midlands but the West Midlands ability to attract migrant firms was reduced by the extension of the development areas and in the years of high unemployment in the region; also the need for firms to move at all either intra-regionally or inter-regionally was reduced either because local labour was available or the economy was depressed and companies were not expanding.

The list of variables examined in the cross-sectional regression equations in the Sant study is longer than in the time series models, as shown in Table 4.7. Here the aim was to see how the geographical pattern of movement responded to disparities in the character of regions and the implementation of regional policy (M.E. Sant, 1975, chapter 4). This response was examined in each of four separate time periods between 1945 and 1971 (see Table 4.9). In each period, Sant argues (1975, p.123) that the probability of a move terminating in a given region depends on four sets of factors: (i) the distance between the region and the source of the move; (ii) the size of the region; (iii) factors which tend to attract moves; and (iv) factors which tend to repel moves. These four sets are reflected in the list of Table 4.7.[20] Fourteen variables are used to examine the geographical pattern of the generation of moves, and these, together with four additional variables which included a gravity measure, were used also to examine the pattern of attraction.

Table 4.8 shows the movement generation models for each of the four time periods. The dominant variable is then offset in influence by other variables which reflect the form and character of the sub-regions. In particular, by the degree to which a sub-region is urban

121

Table 4.7
Independent variables used in the analysis of movement
generation and attraction

A. Generation

(i) Mass factor
X_1 Numbers employed in manufacturing, 1951, 1961, 1966 ('000)

(ii) Areal spatial structure
X_2 Urban employment density, 1951, 1961, 1966 (employees per urban acre)
X_3 Per cent of region with urban status, 1951, 1961, 1966
X_4 Size of region (estimated radius, miles)

(iii) Labor factors
X_5 Female activity rates, 1951, 1961, 1966
X_6 Male earnings (average), manual workers, 1968
X_7 Female earnings (average), manual workers, 1968
X_8 Male unemployment, 1951, 1961, 1966–70 (average June + December)
X_9 Female unemployment, 1951, 1961, 1966–70 (average June + December)
X_{10} Total unemployment, 1951, 1961, 1966–70 (average June + December)

(iv) Regional policy factors
X_{11} Per cent employment in assisted areas
X_{12} Target population of new towns and town expansion schemes as per cent of base year population

(v) Others
X_{13} Industrial composition, 1951, 1961 (estimated)
X_{14} Employment change, 1951–61 (used only in moves in period 1960–65)

B. Attraction
Variables as above, except:

X_{1a} Total numbers unemployed, 1951, 1961, 1966–70 (average June + December)
X_{15} Total employment in development areas

122

Table 4.7 continued

X_{16} Total target population in new towns and town
    expansion schemes
X_{17} Modified gravity measure

Source: M.E.C. Sant, *Industrial Movement and Regional Development*,
        Pergamon, 1975, p.138.

(variable X_3), by the influence of regional policy (X_{11} and X_{12}) in the
first three periods (but not in the fourth when regional policy was most
active, demonstrating the imperfect measure of regional policy used
here), and by two of the labour factors X_5 and X_6. The lack of
significance of the unemployment variables is perhaps surprising, but
they are overshadowed by the mass factor, X, and enter three of the
equations when the mass factor is removed (M.E.C. Sant, 1975, p.147).

The movement attraction models in Table 4.9 do not reach such a
good level of explanation as the generation models,[21] but the two
important attraction variables X_{15} and X_{16} were omitted, even
though shown to be highly significant when tested on their own as a
pair (M.E.C. Sant, 1975, p.153). Over the four periods there is
considerable consistency in the set of significant variables. The total
numbers unemployed, a variation on the mass factor X_1, was
dominant in all periods except in the 1950s when it was supplanted by
the new towns factor, X_{12}. The gravity measure was consistently
positive and significant, X_{17}. The regional policy weight, X_{11}, was
only significant in the first and last periods, periods of high levels of
regional policy activity. This confirms the time series finding. 'Thus
in these we have the main elements of locational attraction at the
regional level, namely labor availability, regional incentives and land
availability and cost (the last being implied by urban employment
density), and the ability to satisfy the preference for short distance
movement'. (M.E.C. Sant, 1975, p.151)

**The role of regional
development incentives**

All of the five statistical exercises discussed in the previous section paid
relatively little attention to isolating the significance of incentives and

Table 4.8

Movement generation models: 1945—71

1945—51			1952—59			1960—65			1966—71		
(i)	(ii)	(iii)	(i)	(ii)	(iii)	(i)	(ii)	(iii)	(i)	(ii)	(iii)
$+1\cdot47\ X_1$	10.0	***	$+1\cdot32\ X_1$	9·7	***	$+1\cdot26\ X_1$	9·7	***	$+1\cdot14\ X_1$	10·2	***
$-0\cdot49\ X_3$	4·1	***	$-0\cdot19\ X_{11}$	3·1	***	$-0\cdot38\ X_3$	2·8	***	$-0\cdot15\ X_5$	1·8	*
$-0\cdot21\ X_{11}$	3·8	***	$-0\cdot39\ X_3$	2·9	***	$-0\cdot17\ X_{12}$	2·7	**	$-0\cdot15\ X_3$	1·5	*
$-0\cdot17\ X_2$	2·1	**	$-0\cdot16\ X_5$	2·1	**	$-0\cdot17\ X_8$	2·4	**	$-0\cdot11\ X_6$	1·5	*
$-0\cdot16\ X_{13}$	1·7	*	$-0\cdot09\ X_{12}$	1·5	*	$+0\cdot15\ X_{13}$	2·1	**	$-0\cdot11\ X_4$	1·3	*
						$+0\cdot13\ X_1$	1·7	*			

$r^2 = 0·89$ $r^2 = 0·85$ $r^2 = 0·86$ $r^2 = 0·82$

$X_1 - X_{13}$ as in Table 3.3.

Column (i) regression coefficients; (ii) value of Student's   (iii) significance level: 90% *; 95% **; 99% ***.

Source: M.E.C. Sant, *Industrial Movement and Regional Development*, Pergamon, 1975, p.146.

Table 4.9
Movement attraction models: 1945–71

1945–51			1952–59			1960–65			1966–71		
(i)	(ii)	(iii)	(i)	(ii)	(iii)	(i)	(ii)	(iii)	(i)	(ii)	(iii)
$+0{\cdot}60\ X_{12}$	5·4	***	$+0{\cdot}50\ X_{12}$	6·1	***	$+0{\cdot}90\ X$	6·8	***	$+0{\cdot}54\ X$	4·3	***
$+0{\cdot}42\ X_{1}$	4·4	***	$+0{\cdot}56\ X_{17}$	6·1	***	$-0{\cdot}41\ X_{3}$	3·7	***	$+0{\cdot}50\ X_{17}$	3·8	***
$-0{\cdot}39\ X_{2}$	4·2	***	$+0{\cdot}30\ X_{10}$	3·2	***	$+0{\cdot}38\ X_{12}$	3·7	***	$+0{\cdot}47\ X_{11}$	3·5	***
$+0{\cdot}28\ X_{17}$	2·8	***	$+0{\cdot}18\ X_{10}$	2·0	**	$-0{\cdot}29\ X_{2}$	2·4	**	$+0{\cdot}19\ X_{12}$	2·1	**
$+0{\cdot}18\ X_{12}$	2·0	**	$-0{\cdot}17\ X_{8}$	1·9	*	$+0{\cdot}21\ X_{17}$	2·0	**	$-0{\cdot}30\ X_{2}$	2·0	**
									$+0{\cdot}20\ X_{4}$	1·7	*
									$-0{\cdot}22\ X_{5}$	1·6	

$r^2 = 0{\cdot}76$ $r^2 = 0{\cdot}80$ $r^2 = 0{\cdot}69$ $r^2 = 0{\cdot}60$

Source: M.E.C. Sant, *Industrial Movement and Regional Development*, Pergamon, 1975, p.152.

125

controls for the choice of location by industry. The most satisfactory treatment was in the Sant time series model in which regional policy expenditure figures were included, but the model suggested that these expenditures were very much overshadowed in their impact by the new towns programme. However, Sant did not extend his analysis to the period from 1966 on in which British regional policy expenditure significantly increased; and he did not try to include a variable to measure the intensity of the central government industrial develop-ment certificate control. In this section, we begin by describing one further statistical analysis which was specifically designed to isolate the impact of regional incentives and controls on inter-regional industrial movement to the British development areas; before moving on to consider both the British and American literature on regional industrial incentives more generally.

Rhodes and Moore (1976a) use the same data source as Keeble and Sant to examine moves to the British development areas between 1951 and 1971. The basic equation used is:

$$MDA_t = a_1 + a_2 MU_t + a_3 I I_{t-1} + a_4 IDC_{t-1} + a_5 REP_{t-1} + u_t$$

where MDA is the number of moves to development areas; MU is the male unemployment rate used as an indicator of the overall national pressure of demand (and hence of industrial growth and pressure to move due to shortages of labour and factory space in the more prosperous regions); I I is the discounted present value of regionally differentiated investment incentives per £100 of capital expenditure; IDC is the percentage refusal rate for industrial development certificates in the Midlands and South East regions; and REP is an index number reflecting the changing real value of the regional employment premium labour subsidy. Further adjustments had to be made to these basic variables to reflect the introduction of special development areas in 1967 and changes in the geographical designation of development areas.

Using the equation, Rhodes and Moore find that all of the policy variables are statistically significant, and using the estimated coefficie-nts they are able to suggest both the number of moves and the employment generated by these moves attributable to the influence of each separate arm of regional policy. As Table 4.10 shows, they suggest that British regional policy induced about 165,000 jobs by 1971 from the operation of the policy from 1960, and that the con-trols in the more prosperous areas of the country were the most important elements of the policy.[22] This analysis has recently been extended to 1973 (B. Moore et al., 1977), showing how the impact of

126

Table 4.10
Employment creation in development areas by regional
policy — induced moves

		Annual average per annum	Total in the period 1960—71
1	The IDC policy (12 years)	8,325	100,000
2	Investment incentives (8 years)	5,875	47,000
3	Regional employment premium (4 years)	3,500 — 5,250	14,000 — 21,000
4	Special development areas (4 years)	0 — 2,500	0 — 10,000
	Total		161,000 — 168,000

Source: J. Rhodes and B. Moore, Regional economic policy and the movement of manufacturing firms to Development Areas, *Economica*, 43, 1976a, p.27.

regional policy declined in the UK in the early 1970s. The analysis suggests that the recent abolition of the regional development premium will lead to the loss of between 28,000 and 55,000 jobs in the development areas between 1976 and 1980. The Rhodes and Moore specification of the movement equation has been strongly challenged by Ashcroft and Taylor (1977), who argue for the inclusion of terms representing investment demand to replace the male unemployment rate used as a proxy for the pressure of demand, and then use the policy variable to distribute the movement generated between development areas and the rest of the country. These revisions lead Ashcroft and Taylor to a lower estimate of approximately 90,000 jobs created in the development areas by regional policy between 1961 and 1971. They argue that the location controls generated more industrial movement than in the absence of policy, while the role of capital subsidies was to divert that movement towards the development areas.

Even with the strong data base of inter-regional industrial movement statistics available in the United Kingdom, it has proved difficult to evaluate the influence of regional policy instruments on movement with enough detail to reach judgements on cost-effectiveness or on the ideal mix of instruments.[23] The Rhodes and Moore studies and the Ashcroft and Taylor study, are the best assessments to date using aggregate statistics. Earlier evaluations have considered industry by industry differential growth rates comparing the assisted regions with a national average to distinguish the total impact of regional policy on job creation in both mobile and indigenous plants (A.J. Brown, 1972, pp.317—18; J. Rhodes and B. Moore, 1973, pp.87—110). The impact of policy has also been seen in terms of changes in the differentials in key regional economic indicators such as unemployment, migration, the growth rate of industrial production, incomes, productivity, etc. (e.g. in G. McCrone, 1969, chapter 6). The desirability of individual instruments has been discussed in more general terms, drawing upon relevant research item by item (G. McCrone, 1969, chapter 8; A.J. Brown, 1972, pp.305—17; G.C. Cameron, 1974, pp.81—90).[24]

Away from aggregate statistics, a further method of evaluating the significance of policy instruments for firms choosing new locations is to ask the relevant managers and entrepreneurs directly. Table 4.11 sets out the pattern of responses in the British government survey, showing that the cash payment of an investment grant was the most important inducement to choose a given location for this group of firms. This table gives no indication of the importance or relevance of the more indirect forms of regional policy instrument such as infra-structure, expenditures on roads, schools, health services, housing or amenities; but the high ranking given to assistance in the training of labour does again confirm the stress on labour supply as a location factor as discussed earlier. Because the table is derived from questions to firms that did move, it may be misleading in reflecting the amount of attention given to regional incentives in the planning of investment by industrial managers in general. Morley, for example, found that 47 of 106 companies in the Northern region said that they did not take account of incentives in planning. Only a minority knew how long the incentives would be in force, and 66 per cent claimed that the absence of incentives would not have curtailed their investment plans (R. Morley, 1976, pp.172—4).

In the United States, the most important public policy influence on inter-regional industrial movement is the tax concession, backed by loan and loan guarantee programmes.[25] As suggested in the last chapter at the intra-regional level, the evidence on the effects and effectiveness of these incentives is very mixed. Thompson and Matilla,

Table 4.11
'Which government inducements were important to your case?'

		Percentage of eligible cases			
		All locations		AA locations[1]	
		Major factor	Minor factor	Major factor	Minor factor
	Government inducements as a whole	39	7	81	13
1	Investment grant differential (1 January 1966 onwards)	46	9	71	14
2	Plant and machinery grant (4/63 − 1/66)	32	12	62	21
3	Building grant	24	7	49	13
4	Free depreciation (4/63 − 1/66)	15	13	28	25
5	Assistance in training of labour	14	14	29	29
6	Government factory to rent	9	1	18	2
7	Government factory immediately available	9	1	18	1
8	Grants under Section 4 LEA	7	7	15	13
9	Loans	7	3	15	7
10	Assistance towards transfer of key workers	4	10	9	21
11	Government factory for purchase	1	1	3	2

(1) Assisted area locations

Source: *Department of Trade and Industry,* Inquiry into Location Attitudes and Experience. *Memorandum submitted to the Expenditure Committee (Trade and Industry Subcommittee) on Regional Development Incentives,* (Session 1973−74), 1973a, p.579, HC 85−1, HMSO, London.

for example, in their econometric study (1959, p.106) do not find any significant negative correlation between state and local taxes as a percentage of local income or state and local non-agricultural business taxes per employee and absolute or percentage growth in any industry or for all industries combined. Questionnaire evidence has ranked taxes well behind other location factors: for example eleventh in Shively's Nebraska study (see Table 4.3) or sixth in Schriver's study of 327 plants in Tennessee, (W.R. Schriver, 1974, p.60); although in the EDA's general survey of potential moves, 38 per cent agreed that taxes incentives or tax holidays were of significant value in considering plant locations, while they were of critical value for 8 per cent, and of minimal value for 19 per cent (J.G. Hamrick, 1973). As Hunker suggests, the businessman will always tend to emphasise taxes in general terms, given the opportunity. This is not the same as saying, or agreeing, that taxes were a specific important factor for a given decision. Hunker, a knowledgeable expert in this field, concludes that despite numerous state tax concession programmes, '. . . almost every reliable source argues that taxes are not significant to industrial location decisions and the many surveys of such decisions support this contention'. (H.L. Hunker, 1974, p.139.)[26] 'There are remarkably few documented examples in which state or local taxes were *compelling* factors in either attracting industry to a region or influencing its decision to leave', (op. cit., p.136).

Hunker's claims are given detailed empirical support in the case of one state, Minnesota. W.V. Williams (1967) compared costs in 1958 in average establishments in specific manufacturing industries before and after the inclusion of state and local taxes. Minnesota is one of the highest taxing states and Williams (1967, p.56) finds that: 'Production costs . . . vary spatially by amounts sufficiently large in most cases so that general tax abatement — especially any small reduction which might easily be accomplished — will not result in major changes in Minnesota's relative cost position'. However, Williams is cautious in his conclusions, especially in using evidence from average existing establishments to draw inferences for newly located or prospective plants. He states:

> The businessman's interpretation of high taxes as an expression of the community's hostility could be more significant to the location decision than the dollar magnitudes suggest. Adequate cost and tax information often are not available at the time a location decision must be made; therefore, the belief that taxes are relatively high may inflate their importance in the location decision (W.V. Williams, 1967, p.57).

McClure (1970) has used a neoclassical production model to demonstrate how the locational effects of differential taxation may be expected to depend upon: the kind of tax employed; the ease of substitution between the factors of production and between products in consumption; and the mobility of the taxed and untaxed factors. These considerations offer additional qualifications to attempts to evaluate tax concession programmes in a benefit cost framework (J.R. Rinehart, 1963; W.E. Morgan and M.M. Hackbart, 1974; D.A. Hellman et al., 1976, chapter 4). A benefit cost framework has also been used to examine the social return to state industrial development loans (G.W. Sazama, 1970a). Sazama questioned 185 firms in receipt of loans in five states, concluding that the loan was a crucial factor in attracting the project to the state in about half of all the cases (1970b, p.173).[27] The interest subsidy element in most of these programmes was very small, but under certain assumptions state loans induce a net increase in state income (1970a, p.394).[28] Formulae to calculate the net present values of different kinds of subsidy have been developed in both the UK and the US to demonstrate the impact of subsidies on relative costs and rates of return of the individual firm. For example, C.L. Melliss and P.W. Richardson (1976) in the UK; and W.J. Stober and L.H. Falk (1969) and D.A. Hellman et al. (1976, chapter 3) in the US. The degree to which subsidies to capital induce relative capital intensity in the choice of technique in new plants in the British assisted areas has also received empirical attention, using a direct regression approach (Hunt Report, 1969, Appendix J; M. Chisholm, 1970) and estimates of the elasticity of substitution (R.J. Dixon and A.P. Thirlwall, 1975, chapter 7; M.J. Tooze, 1976; and T.W. Buck and M.H. Atkins, 1976).

One major issue for the administration of programmes of incentives to influence industrial movement is the visibility of those incentives to the industrial managers responsible for making the choice of the new plant site. As suggested above in the reference to the Morley (1976) survey, the information levels of these managers may be low, despite extensive publicity by relevant government departments. This suggestion finds support in the research of Green (1977, pp.7–18). Green examined the information levels of two groups of industrialists: one group of 100 firms in the South East and West Midlands regions of the UK which were not involved in migration, and a second group of 82 firms which had moved between 1967 and 1970 to one of six assisted areas. Considerable uncertainty existed as to the extent of the assisted areas and the form and intensity of the different regional policy instruments. As expected the moves learnt by their experience and were better informed than the firms not involved in migration.

This confirms earlier survey findings that public incentives are very rarely a factor prompting an initial search for a new location, even when the total value of the incentives is significant in relation to total costs. Some movers may be eager to demonstrate that they should not be thought of as exploiting a social or political situation in receiving public money (P.M. Townroe, 1971. p.83; G. McCrone, 1969, p.195). This is a sensitivity which has been heightened by the publicity given to the closure of new plants after a very short life in an assisted area location in spite of the receipt of public subsidy.

Finally, in comparing the influence of industrial development incentives on inter-regional industrial movement between the two countries, it must be remembered that there are many more agencies, public and private, in the United States seeking to influence industrial locations than there are in the United Kingdom. Estimates of the number of agencies involved in industrial development in the US range from 14,000 to 20,000, all seeking to influence the new plant investment by 1,500 or so firms each year (H.L. Hunker, 1974, p. 189). Prime responsibility for regional industrial development in the United States rests with the Economic Development Administration of the US Department of Commerce as outlined in chapter 1; but other federal agencies also have an interest in and can provide funds for industrial development. These include the Department of Agriculture, [29] the Department of the Interior, and the Department of Housing and Urban Development. All states[30] and most counties devote some funds to industrial development, and many counties and municipalities are involved in development agencies, or local redevelopment and urban agencies which seek to promote economic development as part of their activities. Often a local non-profit industrial development or community development corporation is formed, with powers to accept funds, issue stock, borrow funds, and to buy, sell or lease industrial property.[31] Industrial development bonds are a form of financing for these activities which grew spectacularly in the late 1960s. Their tax exempt status proved a major attraction, an attraction which has now somewhat waned following more restrictive tax and legal changes (D.A. Hellman, 1976, pp.6–12). This form of financing is not used in the United Kingdom. Other public agencies involved in industrial development include the port authorities and tourist promotion agencies, while private bodies include industrial and land development companies, chambers of commerce, banks and, of significant historical importance, the railroads and the utility companies (H.L. Hunker, 1974, chapter 7).

In the United Kingdom the numbers of agencies involved are fewer. Local public agencies have less power to borrow or issue stock to finance industrial development and local activity is normally restricted to promotion; although a significant minority of local authorities can offer serviced industrial land, factory buildings and/or industrial mortgages as inducements (M.M. Camina, 1974, chapter 3).

[32] There are a certain number of regionally based industrial promotion organisations, funded from both public and private sources (for example, the North of England Development Council and the North West Industrial Development Association). Local chambers of commerce are sometimes active but not always, and banks, the utilities and British Rail are only involved in industrial development indirectly. The promotion of regional industrial growth by central government is concentrated within the Department of Industry, although many other departments are involved indirectly (Environment, the Scottish and Welsh Offices, Energy, etc.). There are also a number of central government agencies with funds available for industrial development, such as the Development Commissioners, the Highlands and Islands Development Board, and the Scottish and Welsh Development Agencies.

Notes

[1] The general trends are discussed by Jusenius and Ledebur (1976).

[2] See also map 1.3.

[3] These concerns with inter-regional flows of branch plant units are examined in P.M. Townroe (1975a, pp.49—57).

[4] Some of the difficulties involved in studying the employment trends in large multi-locational organisations in the United States are discussed by Allan Pred (1975, pp.115—41).

[5] Although the published results of this survey do not distinguish inter-regional moves from other more local moves as such. Assisted area destinations are distinguished (47 per cent of the total in the survey) and these will be synonymous with inter-regional moves in the British case (i.e. across the boundaries of the eleven standard regions) although up to 21 per cent of the 47 per cent may have originated within the same region as their destination. (Department of Trade and Industry, 1973, pp.528—9)

[6] The British government survey obtained an 80 per cent (usable) response rate to a short postal questionnaire sent to 787 firms; and a 69 per cent response to a request for a subsequent interview. Other recorded response rates include 79 per cent by Townroe (1971, p.30), 59 per cent by Cameron and Clark (1966, p.24), 73 per cent by Shively (1974, p.89), 61 per cent by Logan (1970, p.326), and 61 per cent by Murie et al. (1974, p.60).

[7]   See P.M. Townroe, 1976, chapter 10.

[8]   Labour availability was also the first ranking factor for the choice of location among 377 new establishments in Eire 1960—70. It was the main reason for choice for 35 per cent of the firms, ahead of transportation costs and facilities (23 per cent) and market and supply factors (23 per cent) (P.O. hUiginn, 1972, p.40).

[9]   As long ago as 1951, De Vyver was claiming for the South that 'Wage differentials are no longer a strong factor in pulling industry to this area. Differentials have been growing smaller and many industries bring their Northern wage scales with them'. (De Vyver, 1951, p.203) Although, see N.M. Hansen (1973, p.81—2) and his comments on Arkansas;and T. Till (1973).

[10] The percentage of respondent firms rejecting different UK regions because of 'labour difficulties' varied greatly region by region, from 22 per cent for Northern Ireland (where transport reasons were far more important) to 53 per cent for Yorkshire and Humberside. (Department of Trade and Industry, 1973, p.607)

[11] This trend may reverse if the real price of oil based fuels rises steeply in the medium term future. See also Chisholm (1971) and Kraft et al. (1971).

[12] Twenty-seven per cent of firms in the Cameron and Clark survey (1966, p.163) mentioned 'Attractiveness for local environment for transferred key workers and executives'.

[13] Pre-1970 American studies, examining patterns and causations is in inter-regional employment growth, using secondary data rather than interview data, are reviewed in the introductory chapter to one of the studies reviewed here (L. Wheat, 1973, chapter 1). These studies include the work of Thompson and Mattila (1959), Perloff et al. (1960), and Fuchs (1961).

[14] The Fuchs study (1961) of regional patterns of manufacturing employment growth 1929—54, using shift-share analysis, also found population density significant.

[15] Rice has provided evidence that a high incidence of poverty acts as a significant hindrance to attempts by a state to follow national industrial growth trends, (G.R. Rice, 1973).

[16] The 'peripheral regions' used by Keeble are those distinguished by R.S. Howard (1968, p.50) and comprise Northern Ireland, Scotland, Wales, the Northern Region, Merseyside and South West Lancashire, and Devon and Cornwall. These areas closely correspond with the areas in which companies were eligible for regional development incentives in the period (1945 to 1965) studied.

[17] Such as G.C. Cameron and B.D. Clark, 1966; D.E. Keeble, 1968; D. Law, 1964; B.J. Loasby, 1967; W.F. Luttrell, 1962; P.D. McGovern,

1965.

[18] Keeble's results are much stronger statistically than an earlier attempt by A. Beacham and W.T. Osborn (1970, pp.41–7) to explain geographical variations in the volume of movement. A.R. Townsend and F.D. Gault (1972, pp.92–8) have extended Keeble's gravity model to cover all moves nationally between the fifty sub-regions, using alternative parameters for both the mass and distance terms.

[19] See also P.M. Townroe, 1973, p.376.

[20] Sant acknowledges the weaknesses in the data used for some of the variables. Inability to obtain relevant figures may result in partial mis-specification of the models (M.E.C. Sant, 1975, pp.124–36). For example, it was not possible to obtain figures for expenditure on regional policy incentives broken down by region.

[21] Sant (1975, pp.151–9) examines the pattern of residuals from both the generation and attraction models and discusses other possible influences on movement behaviour, such as industrial linkage.

[22] The full employment creation impact of regional policy in the UK between 1960 and 1971 would be greater than this figure of 165,000 suggests. Moves to Northern Ireland, moves to the service and government sectors and multiplier effects are not included. Regional policy also induces faster growth in companies already located in the development areas, and these areas have benefitted from differentially favourable public expenditures on social and economic infrastructure. (See J. Rhodes and B. Moore, 1973, pp.87–110.)

[23] J.A. Schofield (1976) has attempted a cost-benefit assessment of industrial incentives within British regional policy for the period 1960 to 1966. He concludes (1976, p.190) that the real resource gains of the policy are smaller than previously supposed.

[24] The full range of available regional economic policy instruments designed to influence the locational behaviour of firms has been reviewed in general terms by this author (P.M. Townroe, 1978).

[25] The extent of state tax concession and loan programmes in the United States is examined in D.A. Hellman et al. (1976, chapter 2).

[26] For example, J.E. Moes (1962, p.125). Moes found that the provision of land and the servicing of land was regarded as far more important in the attraction of industry by his 384 Chambers of Commerce than the offering of tax exemptions. Also J.S. Floyd (1952, pp.16–23) considered interstate tax differentials and concluded there was little impact on location decisions. He points out (1952, p.20) that heavier taxes may mean better facilities.

[27] '. . . 28 per cent of respondents felt the loan was important in their choice of state, 35 per cent felt the loan played a role in their

decision to invest at all, and 65 per cent believed that the loan had some influence on the size of their investment; 38 per cent felt that without a loan their investment would have been more than 40 per cent smaller.' (G.W. Sazama, 1970b, p.176)

[28] D.A. Hellman et al. (1976, p.96) concludes that in the three state programmes examined the Kentucky revenue bond programme had the highest ratio of benefits to costs. The Pennsylvannia loan programme also yielded a positive return, although expensive in interest subsidy. The small costs of the Connecticut loan programme exceeded even smaller benefits. For further non-empirical discussion of local industrial subsidies, see J.H. Cumberland and F. van Meek (1967), and J.R. Rinehart and W.E. Laird (1972).

[29] Under the Rural Development Act 1972.

[30] D.A. Hellman et al. (1976, chapter 2) offer an overview of state financial incentive programmes.

[31] See D.R. Gilmore (1960) and the five local case studies in Committee for Economic Development (1966).

[32] A local authority in the United Kingdom may pass a special Act of Parliament to grant it additional powers, as for example in the case of the Tyne-Wear County Council (P. Rodgers and C.R. Smith, 1977).

5 Industrial movement and theories of industrial location

It is sometimes felt that a theory of industrial location must be primarily about the choice of a site for a new plant somewhere within a defined geographical area. One implication of this view would be that theories of industrial location can provide us with a clear framework within which to analyse industrial movement, offering hypotheses to test and criteria for evaluation. This view of the subject matter of industrial location theory is in fact only partially true. Among the theories which have been developed, there is a concern with all the locational influences upon industrial plants and not just those operating at the time of choosing a new site for a new plant. The implication assumed is not justified by past experience in the use of theories of industrial location. The relevance and the utility of the theories for the analysis of industrial movement has been weak, or unclear.

It is not the purpose of this chapter to present a systematic review of the various theories of industrial location. Excellent reviews are available elsewhere.[1] Rather this chapter will consider why it is that the body of location theory is not more useful in interpreting the growing volume of empirical results on industrial movement, much of which has been referred to in the previous three chapters. Since this book is designed to review the literature on industrial movement and migration and not the wider literature on industrial location, this chapter will be relatively brief. The first section considers the principle geographical and economic theories of industrial location. The second section considers the so-called 'behavioural' approach to industrial location, which has received a lot of attention in the literature and was largely prompted by studies of industrial migration and associated policy concerns. This approach has included models of the location decision making process as well as studies of organisational determinants and constraints on locational choice. Section three reviews those frameworks which are more directly concerned with aggregate patterns of industrial movement linking origins and destinations, rather than with the location problem for the individual firm or plant. The chapter concludes with the description of a matrix of locational probabilities which could form the basis for an empirically based theory of industrial movement.

Theories of industrial location

The theory of industrial location has been developed by both geographers and economists. As Smith suggests (1971, p.95) the geographers have been more concerned at arriving at generalisations from empirical studies, often (at least until fairly recently) without a clear theoretical framework or conceptual base, while economists have been more concerned to develop formal equilibrium models, often at a high degree of abstraction and with little empirical content. For both groups of theorists, locational choice for the individual firm has been abstracted away from its context within other associated decisions of the firm and has been seen as a decision taken under conditions of certainty and adequate knowledge. The emphasis has been on the influence of the parameter of space on the choice of location, forcing, rather understandably, transportation cost considerations to the centre of the theoretical stage; to be joined, at the cost of the loss of simplicity, by spatial variations in other costs and in revenues. Further complicating factors, known intuitively or from empirical work to influence locational choices, were resisted in the interests of elegance and mathematical tractability. This has severely weakened the subsequent use of the resulting theoretical models for empirical study and policy analysis.

The development of theories of industrial location has contained a number of distinct traditions, themes, or frameworks. These traditions are usually identified by key contributions to the literature. The first, which is the most widely used and taught, is in the partial equilibrium comparative statics tradition of micro-economics, concerned with the specification of the optimum locations of agricultural products and individual industrial plants. This tradition comes through from Von Thunen and Launhardt in the last century to the critically important work of Weber.[2] The early emphasis was on minimising cost factors over space under conditions in which the location and size of the place of consumption are fixed, the locations of raw materials are given, and labour is in full elastic supply with a given geographical distribution of wages. The usual assumptions of neoclassical economics applied in respect of the profit maximisation goal, perfect knowledge and instantaneous response.

Weber saw his theory as a positive theory, describing why it was that industries located where they did. But since the location problem for management (and for governments seeking to influence managements) is the best site at which to locate or relocate a plant and the theory is framed in terms of the determination of an optimum location, this tradition can also pose the choice of location as a normative issue. In the frequently quoted words of Losch (1954, p.4), 'The real duty of the economist is not to explain our sorry reality, but to improve it. The question of the best location is far more dignified than determination of the actual one.' Losch in fact developed the Weberian approach, introducing a demand element allowing spatial variations in revenue to be set against costs. The concern became the optimal pattern of factories in a market area. Isard then brought together the market areas of Losch, the concentric rings of agricultural land use of Von Thunen, and Palander's development of classical Weberian theory, using the principle of substitution to develop an economic landscape which links in with economic production theory.

The classical tradition therefore developed towards a more general equilibrium view of the space economy and a search for rules to explain its structure, a second tradition. The application of the general equilibrium theory of economics to the location of economic activities poses severe problems however, problems which may only be overcome by severe abstraction.[3] The general equilibrium approach has been developed using programming models, particularly by Koopmans and Beckman (1957), Lefeber (1958), Bos (1965) and Serck-Hanssen (1970). Programming models have also been developed for direct application by companies, often using approximate or heuristic methods, and always greatly simplifying the problem, usually by abstracting away from demand, other than considering the transportation cost of distribution.[4]

Both of the traditions referred to regarded the economic agents invovled as responding to locational forces passively without anticipation of concurrent or subsequent actions of their competitors. However, interdependence was early recognised as being particularly important in an evolving pattern of industrial locations, usually in terms of market area competition between firms rather than interdependence in an industrial linkage sense (D.M. Smith, 1971, pp.137–43). Greenhut (1956, 1963) attempted to integrate the least cost and locational interdependence approaches, using maximisation of total profits as the corporate objective and laying heavy stress on the demand factor. He has since developed this integation to theories of the spatial equilibrium of oligopolists and of spatial pricing (M. Greenhut, 1970 and 1975).[5]

Greenhut has also been one of the few theorists to lay considerable stress on the role of personal factors in locational choice, and although reluctant to leave economic man in his theorising he was very clear from his own empirical studies that personal considerations providing a psychic income may strongly influence an entrepreneur in his choice of site (1956, pp.277–9 and 282–3). The acknowledgement of psychic income does not have to imply a move away from rationality in decision making nor does it imply an environment of uncertainty. But it may imply a choice that is not money profit maximising. Over time however, under conditions of perfect competition, the plant at the sub-optimal location will be subject to numerous locational forces and the economic system will adopt those plants which adapt to the forces of competition. In eventual equilibrium, therefore, random or non-economic elements in locational choices are subsumed (C.M. Tiebout, 1957).

An element of randomness is introduced into determinate location models if the existence and the cost of uncertainty is acknowledged. As Webber (1972, p.273) has suggested and analysed, uncertainty affects all three major variables explaining the location of firms: distance costs, external economies and economies of scale within the firm. There will also be considerable uncertainty for many firms as to the size and location of the market; and as to the number and beha- viour of rival companies.[6] Webber suggests (1972, p.276) that these uncertainties encourage firms to make defensive decisions, as demonstrated by game theory models, decisions which may therefore be optimal for the firm but sub-optimal from the point of view of society.[7] A further reaction of theory to uncertainty may be to relax the objective of a single optimum location but rather to think in terms of spatial margins to profitability, as suggested by Smith (1966, p.96 and 1971, chapter 10).[8]

Smith develops an approach which stresses the economic limitations imposed on the freedom of locational choice of the individual company, rather than searching for a profit maximising optimum. The emphasis therefore shifts from models for direct prediction or prescri- ption towards a theory which seeks greater understanding of industrial locational behaviour as observed and of the circumstances surrounding the location decision. This is a theme which will be taken up in the next section of this chapter.

The literature on theories of the location of economic activity is very extensive.[9] Why has this literature not made closer connections with the literature on industrial movement? One reason must be a lack of research investment in making such connections. The research work on industrial movement, as seen in the previous three chapters, has been heavily empirical, often with a strong policy content. The potential role and contribution of a body of formal theory has not been obvious. The normative, deterministic and abstracted orientation of the theory may find little sympathy from research workers looking for positivistic answers in a complex, stochastic environment. Empirically, transportation costs have been discovered to be relatively unimportant in the total cost structure of industry. [10] There is also a lack of priority given to transportation issues by firms choosing to undertake a move and then in choosing a new site as revealed in many questionnaire surveys (as seen in earlier chapters). And there is some evidence that many firms are unaware of the true costs of transportation to themselves (W.M. Cook, 1967). All of these findings might appear to reduce the direct relevance of theories so strongly focussed on a transportation cost variable. But such empirical worries again raise the question of the purposes of a theory, and of whether location theory should concern itself with the single firm or with the spatial distribution of many firms, and of whether '. . . reality is not to be used to check whether theory is "right", but theory is to be used to check whether reality is rational and to point out where and why it is not'. So that '. . . where the real world diverges from the normative prescription a case can be made for the use of legislation or other devices to bring reality into line with the prescription' (M. Chisholm, 1971, p.130).

If there is a confusion over purposes in discussions on location theory, there has also been a growing empirically based realisation of the complexity of the location decision for many firms. The choice of location is inter-twined with many other decisions within the firm: whether to invest in a new plant or expand an old one, the scale of the investment, the pricing strategy to be followed, the present and future size and locations of other units (both production and administration and sales) of the firm, the existing and potential influence of governmental policies and rulings, the overall trade off between short run profit and longer term gains. All of this complexity [11] Pred (1967, p.84) would argue, categorically prevents the attainment of an individual real-world unambiguous optimum location. Therefore a greater understanding of the forces involved in locational choice and in patterns of industrial movement may be obtained by greater attention to behaviour and decision making processes and to the internal and external constraints on behaviour rather than by further modelling on the basis of severe assumptions.

The behavioural approach

The so-called 'behavioural approach' to industrial location has received much attention over the past ten years or so, and although it has yet to provide us with models capable of more than loose prediction or of evaluation in social welfare terms, the approach has led to a much greater understanding of locational behaviour in

141

industry and has led the way to significant new avenues of research. The approach has therefore contributed to the understanding of the choice of new locations of mobile companies, and has in particular offered some guidance on the impact of incentives and controls. This continues to be an area for further research.

At the risk of some over-simplification and ambiguity for the term 'behavioural' has meant different things to different people, we may identify five strands within this approach, each of which has been developed referring back to the basic economic models of location:

(a) Goals and maximisation

This first strand picks up a theme which has been extensively discussed in micro-economics: a questioning of the relevance of non-profit goals, such as growth, psychic income, stability, or prestige; and a suspicion, now empirically confirmed,[12] that full costings of alternative locations are not undertaken by mobile firms and that a satisfactory location rather than an optimum location is frequently the one chosen. Both of these factors will work in favour of the more indirect elements of a policy to influence industrial mobility and against the efficiency of financial subsidies. Satisficing allows room for uncertainty and non-profit objectives increase the role of personal discretion, judgement and prejudice. Both would reduce the determinancy of any locational models, adding randomness to patterns of industrial migration unless clear patterns of non-profit goals and of the mechanisms of satisficing could be empirically established and used to modify conclusions drawn from standard economic models.

(b) Models of decision making

The second strand involves the study of locational decision making procedures, usually within a framework of a model such as that illustrated in Figure 5.1. This strand has not advanced much beyond detailed empirical description, based on surveys of recently moved plants. The results of these surveys will be examined in the next chapter. There is no doubt that introduction of the concepts of context, of sequence and of sources of uncertainty into discussions of locational choice has added richness and texture, even if the principal returns to the research investment have been to improve pedagogy and provide caveats for more formal modellers (H.A. Stafford, 1972, pp. 207–13).

142

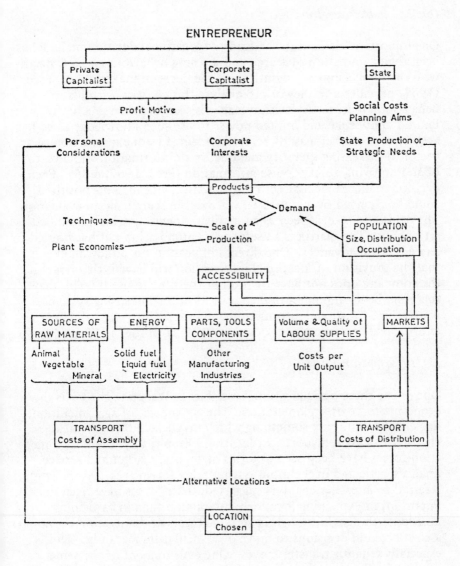

Figure 5.1: A Model of the Factors Influencing Industrial Location
Decisions

Source: F.E.I. Hamilton, Model of Industrial Location in R.J. Chorley
and P. Haggett (eds) *Socio-Economic Models in Geography*,
Methuen, London 1967, p.365.

143

(c) The behavioural matrix

One important element in the study of locational decision making has
been the examination of search and learning behaviour and a concern
with the dimensions of cognititon of the decision makers.[13] Pred
(1967) provides a framework to analyse this concern with his
behavioural matrix. A decision maker is seen as possessing both
limited knowledge and limited power to use such knowledge as he has
acquired. A matrix may therefore be formed by the interaction of a
vector of increasing quantity and quality of information and a vector
of an improving ability to use information (Pred, 1967, p.25). Each
decision maker is located within this matrix, although his position
could be changed over time by investment in search and in evaluation.
The decision maker is seen as a satisficer, operating within bounded
rationality. The matrix is a useful conceptualisation but has not led to
any empirical advances. One direct implication for policy making is
that the provision of locational information will have little impact if
the company does not have the skill or the time to use it. This may
therefore be an argument in favour of locational licensing systems
which force locational information and criteria into what the firm sees
as principally an investment decision (P.M. Townroe, 1976, pp.26—9).

(d) Information flows

One of the three basic locational variables in Weberian theory is the
economic force of agglomeration. The advantages of agglomeration,
like cheap labour, are something which may lead a factory not to
choose the least-transport cost location. Empirically, these agglomeration forces have been seen in terms of supply, market and service
linkages, reflected in the input-output table for an area. As the studies
referred to in earlier chapters suggested, these forces have been more
important in explaining locational interaction than in explaining
locational choices, although in certain sectors agglomeration economies
are reflected in decisions to move over small distances only. This is
especially true for transfer moves. One development of the same
concept has been to view flows of information as having a similar
friction of distance. Certain forms of interpersonal communication
require regular face-to-face contact between employees of the same
multiplant company or between the company and other companies
and agencies; certain contacts are intermittent but require to be face-
to-face when they do take place. Certain individuals, functions, or
occupations, in any organisation therefore benefit by being located
close to good (fast, efficient, cheap) modes of communication.

Conversely certain locations may be identified as having high 'contact potential' while others may be very low. The inspiration for this fourth strand of the behavioural approach comes from Sweden (G. Tornqvist, 1970 and 1973; B. Thorngren, 1970) where the identification of contact networks has been used in policy formation for transportation, communications infrastructure, regional development and urban expansion. Comparable work has also been undertaken on the office sector in London and on a sample of offices decentralising from London, already referred to in chapter 2 (J.B. Goddard, 1973; and J.B. Goddard and D. Morris, 1976).

(e) Organisational constraints

The emphasis in the location decision studies on the context of the structure of the company, and of associated decisions, has linked to the evidence from the contact studies on information flows within companies, to provide the final strand of the behavioural approach. The major part of employment created by mobile industry will be in plants belonging to large multiplant, multiproduct, multilocation companies. The corporate strategies and the internal managerial structures of these companies exercise an influence on locational choice over and above the standard economic variables (G. Krumme, 1969; P. Dicken, 1971).[14] The resulting spatial structure of the company in turn influences urban growth (A. Pred, 1973, 1975 and 1976). The importance of these considerations for the extent and pattern of industrial mobility and for the effectiveness of public policy is suggested by the evidence given by leading British companies to a House of Commons select committee examining regional development incentives. This will continue to be an area for further research. The organisational structure of the firm will also influence the location decision making procedure and hence the output of that decision, as we shall see in the next chapter.

The behavioural approach has focussed attention on the individual firm, studying industrial location and movement at the micro level. A further approach is to consider patterns of industrial movement, within the wider context of the space economy.

Theories of industrial migration flows

Attempts to provide a theoretical framework or explanation for the flows of mobile industry (as defined for this review) in general or across the landscape of the UK and the US are few and far between.

In the last chapter we reviewed a series of regression models. None of these models was grounded explicitly in a theory of movement, many of the explanatory variables used being included on intuitive grounds or on the basis of industrial location surveys. There was little theoretical input, useful though the results were as a possible input themselves into a theory of movement.

One group of regression models contains an implicit theory of industrial movement. In a gravity model of industrial migration it is assumed that distance imposes a friction to migrants and that the volume of movement is positively associated with the size of the areas (variously defined) of origin and destination. Thus, at a given level of national aggregate demand, reflected in pressures in local markets for jobs and for factory space as companies do or do not wish to expand, there will be a certain dispersion of mobile plants between urban centres. If the demand pressures affect the larger urban centres more quickly than the small centres (as well they might, if the larger centres are the prime locations of the fastest growing sectors of industry and contain the socio economic environment most conducive to innovation, risk taking and investment), then there will be a flow of mobile plants from larger centres to smaller centres proportional to the sizes of the centres involved and a declining function of the distance between the centres. Alternatively, pressures of high aggregate demand, inducing industrial movement, may affect some larger centres in the country before others. This has been the situation in the United Kingdom, where the prime source areas of inter-regional and inter-subregional moves have been the Greater London and West Midlands conurbation areas. In this situation, the estimated gravity function has to be source region specific rather than a general national function (D.E. Keeble, 1972, pp.15—20; A.R. Townsend and F.D. Gault, 1972). [15]

The particular skewed pattern of industrial movement in the United Kingdom led Keeble (1971, pp.42—53) to make a further theoretical generalisation: his so-called dual population hypothesis, as referred to in chapter 3. At a sub-regional level (and therefore ignoring the intra-urban pattern of movement), most migration of manufacturing industry in the United Kingdom can be classified into two distinct spatial types. One is short distance intra-regional movement from the major cities out to surrounding towns, notably from London and the West Midlands conurbation. The other is long distance movement, almost all originate in these prime source areas and move to the assisted areas of the country. These two flows of movement have different characteristics, as listed in chapter 3 (D. Keeble, 1976, pp. 135—42). As suggested there, this dual population view of inter-

146

subdivision industrial movement is rather simplistic. It does not fit all regions in the UK, and the hypothesis does imply an absence of competition between the two groups of reception area for migrant plants. This is not supported by Sant's (1975) regression evidence.

Keeble's generalisation is a deduction from an examination of detailed British evidence. But in its general characterisation it bears a remarkable similarity to another theory of industrial movement, essentially inductively arrived at from American experience. It is surprising that no-one in either country has thought to put the two together. Wilbur Thompson (1968 and 1969) calls his theory a 'filter down theory' of industrial location. It was proposed within a wider characterisation, a theory of urban-regional growth. Thompson's core idea is that the larger urban areas are more than proportionately sources of creative entrepreneurship and innovation.[17] These larger areas tend to combine a mix of fast-growing industries with a steadily declining share of these growth industries. The near average growth rates of these centres result from a successive spinning-off of these industries. This spin-off, or decentralisation, comes about in an industrial sector as the product ages and the technology matures. Mass-production becomes possible and skill requirements fall. The aging industry seeks pools of available cheaper labour and so plants filter down the skill and wage hierarchy of urban areas, from the large cities to the small non-metropolitan towns. 'The smaller, less industrially advanced area struggles to achieve an average rate of growth out of enlarging shares of slow growth industries, originating as a by-product of the area's low wage rate attraction', while 'The larger, more sophisticated urban economies can continue to earn high wage rates only by continually performing the more difficult work' (W.R. Thompson, 1968, p.56). The intermediate areas will tend to have an above average growth rate, having growing shares of slow growing industries.

Thompson's thesis is supported by American evidence. Berry's overview of growth patterns in the daily urban systems (DUS) of the United States demonstrated a median growth rate of population increasing progressively with size of the DUS up to a population of one million and then stabilising at about the national growth rate (B.J. L. Berry, 1973, p.22). As earnings in manufacturing increase, the DUS growth rate tends to rise to stabilise at the national average rate. In greater local detail, Hansen (1973, p.48) shows how, in his six study regions, the apparel sector was important in the manufacturing growth in his 'turnaround-reversal' rural counties: counties which lost population in the 1950s and gained in the 1960s. The apparel sector is a low wage, low national growth sector of industry nationally. A more general pattern, consistent with the Thompson filter down thesis, was found in the Ozarks and the Tennessee Valley (N.M. Hansen, 1973, p.85).[18]   Further support comes from the Erickson (1976) study of branch plant mobility in non-metropolitan Wisconsin.

A matrix of locational choice

One central lesson to be gleaned from both the empirical studies of industrial movement reviewed in chapters 2, 3 and 4 and the theoretical writings on industrial location referred to in this chapter is that great heterogeneity of locational experience must be expected within any substantially sized cohort of migrating plants. The many differing characteristics of the alternative locational opportunities facing the management of a company interact with the many different characteristics of the firm and the proposed plant, and with the reasons for undertaking a move at all. This interaction produces a set of parameters which, especially in the face of uncertainty and in the absence of a striving for optimality, may resolve the collective locational problem in a variety of ways. There will be differing degrees of probability with which any one particular prospectively mobile plant will be located in any one particular potential location. A positive theory of industrial movement, when applied at the microlevel, has to view locational choice in these terms with different solutions proving equally satisfactory given the levels of uncertainty involved. Yet within this variety, certain relationships between the parameters of the company and the prospective locations do hold. These relationships have been discussed in reviewing the empirical evidence available, and they allow the suggestion, on an informed but subjective basis, of differing probabilities that particular corporate attributes will result in particular locational choices. An exercise of this kind has produced the matrix presented in Table 5.1.

As will be seen in the table, some of the company and plant characteristics seem to be important for some of the alternative locations and their attributes and not others. For other potentially important relationships, the research is ambiguous and the probability has been assigned without great confidence. For the rest, a simple 1, 2, 3 scoring has been used based upon the available empirical evidence. [19]

A matrix such as Table 5.1 acknowledges the complexity of locational choices for many manufacturing companies. A more normative theory which desired to provide evaluative guidance as to where an individual firm should move, can also use such a matrix, on

Table 5.1

Probabilities of locational choice for prospectively mobile plants, based on surveys of migrant firms in manufacturing in the UK and US

Company & plant characteristics	Alternative locations, which are:				with:					
	Close by existing	Sub-urban	Non-metro-politan region	New region	Large labour pool	Good transport access	Finan-cial in-centives	Avail-able build-ings	High residen-tial amenity	Same industry already present
1 Company										
Public	1	1	2	3	3	3	3	2	( )	—
Private	2	2	3	2	2	2	1	3	3	—
Single plant	2	2	3	2	2	2	1	3	3	—
Multiplant	1	1	2	3	3	3	3	2	1	—
2 Plant										
Transfer	3	2	3	1	2	2	1	3	3	—
Production unit	1	1	2	3	3	3	3	3	1	—
Subsidiary comp'y.	1	1	1	3	2	2	3	2	( )	—
<50 employees	3	3	2	1	2	2	1	3	3	—
50–500	1	2	3	2	3	2	2	3	2	—
>500 employees	1	1	2	3	3	3	3	1	1	—
Urgent	3	3	2	2	2	2	1	3	3	—
Non-urgent	1	2	3	3	2	3	2	2	3	—

3 Process

	1	2	3	4	5	6	7	8
New technology	1	3	3	2	3	2	1	2
Old technology	2	1	2	3	2	3	3	1
High skill level	2	3	2	1	2	2	1	2
Low skill level	—	1	3	3	2	3	3	1
Capital intensive	2	1	1	3	3	1	3	1
Labour intensive	—	2	3	3	2	3	3	2
Need to retain existing local linkages	—	1	2	1	3	1	1	3
Need new local linkages	3	1	2	( )	3	( )	2	1

4 Product

	1	2	3	4	5	6	7	8
New market sought	—	1	2	1	3	2	3	1
High trans. cost	2	1	1	2	3	2	3	1
Made to order	3	2	2	1	2	2	1	3
Batch production	—	2	2	2	3	2	2	2
Mass production	—	1	1	3	3	3	3	1

5 Reasons for moving

	1	2	3	4	5	6	7	8
Need more space	—	2	3	2	2	1	2	2
Compet. for labour	2	1	2	3	1	2	3	1
Gov. restrictions	—	2	3	3	2	2	3	1
Compul. purchase	—	2	3	1	1	1	1	3
Review of locational costs	—	3	2	3	3	2	3	1
Des. to impr. envir.	—	3	2	1	2	1	3	1

Table 5.1 continued

3 = high
2 = average
1 = low
( ) = uncertainty about judgement
— = no relevant link seen

Source: Author.

the reasoning that most industry is relatively locationally footloose and there is safety in following the satisfactory experience of other similar plants. A wider evaluation on the economic efficiency of given flows of industrial moves is still only possible within the framework of models constructed with severe abstractions from experience in the real world. A theory to provide a framework for such an evaluation would need to be more eclectic than those hitherto and would presuppose extensive agreement or prespecification of objectives and/or policy interventions in other related areas of the space economy. In industrial movement studies, theories of the middle range seem likely to provide more significant hypotheses and predictions than attempts at constructing general theories.

Notes

[1] See especially D.M. Smith (1971), but also F.E.I. Hamilton (1967); or recent texts in economics and geography such as H.W. Richardson (1978), P.E. Lloyd and P. Dicken (1972, Parts One and Two), and R. Thoman et al. (1968). Also the important collection of readings of G. Karaska and D.F. Bramhall (1969).
[2] The history of this tradition is reviewed by Isard (1956, chapter 2).
[3] These problems are discussed by H.W. Richardson (1978).
[4] See L. Cooper (1967), H.W. Kuhn and R.E. Kuenne (1962); R.E. Kuenne (1968). Or in a recent business text T.A.J. Nicholson (1971, chapter 7). R.C. Vergin and J.D. Rodgers (1967) review techniques for solving location problems, including those at the intra-firm and intra-plant level.
[5] The notion of interdependence is also involved in game theory approaches to the location problem. Isard and Smith for example have developed a Weberian locational game (1967, pp.45—80). More

generally, Isard (1969).

[6] 'Uncertainty is a logical outcome of the imperfection of knowledge implied by the friction of space . . . ' (M. Chisholm, 1971, p.123).

[7] Webber (1972, chapter 7) develops a model of town formation, with successive firms choosing locations within the market area under conditions of uncertainty, recognising locational interdependence.

[8] Taylor (1973) has investigated the spatial margins of the iron founding industry in the UK.

[9] See B.H. Stevens and C.A. Brackett (1967).

[10] See M. Chisholm (1971). In Great Britain the proportion of net production costs incurred in transport is about 5 per cent across manufacturing industry. Among the more mobile sectors of industry it is considerably less.

[11] The extent of this complexity is summarised in a series of diagrams in P.M. Townroe (1969).

[12] The failure to undertake comparative costs analyses in locational choice was found by G.E. McLaughlin and S. Robock (1949, chapters 2 and 3) and R.T. Klemme (1959, pp.71–7) in the US and by W.F. Luttrell (1962, p.79), P.M. Townroe (1971, p.69) and G.C. Cameron and B.D. Clark (1966, p.116) in the UK. Both Townroe (1971, pp.89–90) and M. Cooper (1975, p.89) in their British studies find a search and choice behaviour by mobile firms which suggests a satisficing approach to the choice rather than a search for an optimum. The larger the firm, the less likely either of these propositions is to hold.

[13] See, for example, R.D. Golledge and L.A. Brown (1967), and the review by M. Cooper (1975, pp.14–25).

[14] A general discussion of the influence on local employment structures of corporate strategies and product changes is discussed by G. Krumme and R. Hayter (1975), with a case study of Boeing in Seattle.

[15] The gravity measure used by Sant (1975, p.140) in his regressions and referred to in Tables 4.7 and 4.9 is a modified measure which is really only a distance decay function of a given total volume of moves, and is not a gravity model in the usual sense of the term.

[16] The pressures of the Industrial Development Certificate system encourage larger firms undertaking large investments to disregard potential intra-regional locations but to focus on the assisted areas.

[17] This view of the city sees the large cities as the central modes of interurban information exchange. '. . . a disproportionately large percentage of non-local specialized information flows within a system of cities must inevitably have their origin or destination in major metropolitan centers' (A.R. Pred, 1973, p.46). The Thompson filter theory therefore has a direct link to the geographic theories of city

system development, based upon the notions and empirical study of innovation generation and information flow.

[18] The filtering has implications for public policy: ' . . . there are indications that despite deficiencies in public policies and programs the process of industrial filtering does eventually lead to the upgrading of both manpower qualifications, types of industry and incomes. These phenomena are clearly in evidence in the South. The industrialization of the South was initiated in large measure by the movement of textile mills from New England and other northern areas into the Piedmont region of the central Carolinas. The textile mills in turn generated other activities . . . . The growth of manufacturing in the Carolinas, especially North Carolina, was followed by similar expansion into Georgia. Decentralization next spread to the Tennesee Valley, which has managed to achieve a higher degree of industrial diversification than either the Carolinas or Georgia. More recently, the states of Mississippi and Arkansas have entered the lower rungs of the filtering process . . . . Although Georgia is actively recruiting northern industrial firms, it is not attempting to "sell" the state on the basis of a labor force willing to work for low wages; that era has passed. Tennessee officials take a certain pride in the fact that they no longer need to tempt firms with the subsidies available in Arkansas and Mississippi. Arkansas and Mississippi are gratified with industrial growth based on low wage, slow growth industries, though stirrings for something better are apparent and probably will be realised.' (N.M. Hansen, 1973, pp.163–4.)

[19] This is a development of the idea of the industrial development screening matrix (D.C. Sweet, 1970).

6 Location decision making procedures

In the next three chapters the perspective is strictly that of the individual company. The available literature on each of the three topic areas under consideration is limited in both the United States and the United Kingdom. This is especially true for chapters 7 and 8. For the general topic of this chapter, location decision making, it is less true. There is a wide literature of handbooks, text books and books of a prescriptive nature suggesting how companies should choose new plant locations and suggesting relevant analytical techniques to assist in this process. This literature will not be examined here. Material on how companies in fact choose new plant locations is less frequently available and this will be reviewed here. There is also quite a wide literature on decision models applied to location, discussing location and decision procedures in general terms without an empirical foundation. This literature will not be systematically reviewed but will be referred to in the context of the empirical findings.

As a framework for the subsequent discussion, the first section of this chapter briefly outlines a decision making model, proposed elsewhere by this author in the context of locational choice.[1] The following three sections discuss the empirical studies on how a commitment to undertake a move is reached in the firm, how the locational search is undertaken and relevant information acquired, and how alternatives are evaluated. The inter-relationship between location decision making procedures and the outcome of the decision and the method of achieving a final choice is then examined at the end of the chapter.

A decision making model

An industrial company reacts to information imposed upon it or to information sought and collected from its external environment. It also reacts to information generated internally by the operation of current policies and by thinking about future strategies and developments. Much of this information flow will have an implicit or explicit spatial component. Both internal and external forces build up the need for the company to make a locational choice for a new plant.

154

Similar forces provide both the opportunities and the constraints in the decision. We may therefore view the company as an open ended system reacting to external pressures and as a group of sub-systems reacting to each other internally.[2] Systems and sub-systems evolve over time, creating problems or situations which require a response, within the context of the goals and objectives of the company.

The process of choosing a new location may therefore be seen as similar to other decisions the management of a company are required to make. There is a three step process of selecting a response to a situation created either by the community at large or by the company at large. These three steps are shown in Figure 6.1. The initial understanding of the problem or situation and the range of probable options open to the management involves the *perception of the decision field*. Possible responses then have to be evolved, leading to the *formulation and comparison of possible actions*. This step may involve some feedback to a redefinition of the basic parameters of the decision. A decision is then reached, *a choice of action*, leading to an output as a formal commitment is made and resources are assigned.

Overlaying the simple sequence are two important elements of complexity, both shown in Figure 6.1. The first is the context existing for the decision because the company concerned has a particular organisational form, a particular mode of operation and a particular set of corporate values. This context changes over time but will always influence all three stages of the decision: by producing a view of how situations should be classified (and hence approached as a managerial task of problem solving), by relating current operational policies to potential future developments, and by the specification of objectives and the awareness of constraints. The second element of complexity, uncertainty, may be increased or decreased by the ways in which the contexts relate to the decision stages. The problem of finding a new plant location will frequently involve the company (or important parts of the company) in an extensive review of operations, and, since it is a problem which occurs so rarely for many companies and even more rarely for given individual managers, the uncertainty surrounding this decision may be considerably higher than that normally experienced by the managers. As suggested in Figure 6.1, three kinds of uncertainty may be distinguished: uncertainty about the external environment of the firm may lead to demands for further gathering and interpretation of information relevant to the problem; [3] uncertainty about appropriate value judgements can lead to demands for policy guidance; and uncertainty about the influence of the decision on related decision areas in the firm may be especially important in the choice of a plant site, where the area and site chosen

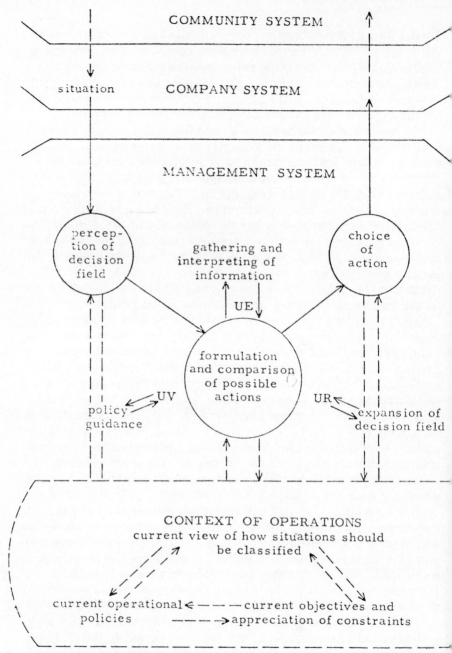

COMMUNITY SYSTEM

COMPANY SYSTEM

situation

MANAGEMENT SYSTEM

percep-
tion of
decision
field

gathering and
interpreting of
information

choice
of
action

UE

formulation
and comparison
of possible
actions

policy
guidance

UV

UR

expansion of
decision field

CONTEXT OF OPERATIONS
current view of how situations should
be classified

current operational
policies

current objectives and
appreciation of constraints

Figure 6.1: Uncertainty and context in the choice of industrial
location.
Source: P.M. Townroe, *Industrial Location Decisions: A Study in
Management Behaviour,* Occasional Paper No.15, Centre for
Urban and Regional Studies, Univeristy of Birmingham, 1971
p.13.

156

may affect many other areas of policy and operations within the firm.

In viewing locational choice in an industrial company in these terms, it has to be remembered that the decision involved is a strategic or planning decision rather than an operational decision. As such it is concerned with the development of the organisation rather than with the internal workings and efficiency of the organisation and with routine relations with the environment.[4] Unlike many other decisions in the firm, a plant site decision is taken so rarely in all but the largest companies,[5] that there will be no agreed system for approaching the problem by the management. There is a lack of precedence and experience to fall back upon. One of the key attributes of the location decision making process in many companies is therefore likely to be managerial inexperience.[6] Because the whole process of establishing a plant in a new location is something out of the ordinary and non-routine, it will hold certain temptations for industrial managers. The problem challenges the full range of managerial skills, requiring creative thought and allowing the industrial executive to demonstrate his energy, drive, skill and decisiveness. But enthusiasm for the challenge can lead to an insufficient appreciation of the limits of skill and knowledge possessed by those involved, and to an urgency which leads to a glossing over of important but time consuming points of detail. The dominant influence of the various kinds of uncertainty in the decision may receive insufficient attention. Evidence of this inexperience has been found in the studies of location decision making procedures.

The model of Figure 6.1 is only one of the many which have been proposed as a framework for interpreting corporate decisions and which link problem solving processes in general to the specific problem of locational choice.[7] The three prime concepts of the model, process, context and uncertainty, flow through the four stages of a decision process:[8] (i) policy and process initiation, which includes the perception of the new situation and an appreciation of the dimensions of the problem, (ii) the search for alternative solutions, (iii) the evaluation of the consequences of each alternative, and (iv) choice and commitment to action. A location decision may, therefore, be seen as having distinct stages within the process.

Although no two locational choices by mobile companies are ever arrived at in exactly the same way, there are a number of attributes of the decision process which can be viewed within a general framework. [9] A locational choice comes out of an investment policy of the firm, which in turn comes out of a more general managerial policy towards the growth and development of the company. This general policy reflects agreed, but perhaps not fully explicit, goals and motivations. It also reflects responsibilities to the owners of the enterprise and to the work force. It will be modified by external pressures. From these internal and external forces pressures will arise for changes in floor space requirements and in external locational advantages for a given plant of the firm. These pressures lead to a review of the present site(s) of the company, of space requirements and locational costs, and of the cost and willingness to go through with a move. If the output of this review is a decision to move, then a further decision is required as to whether a branch plant or a complete relocation (transfer) is required. Once a commitment to obtaining a new site is made, then a period of search and information processing is undertaken, responding to the various locational influences suggested in earlier chapters. From this process alternatives may be proposed, costings and other forms of evaluation may take place, and a new site is chosen. A further sequence of managerial activity then commences through to the commissioning of the new plant.

The time span for the full decision making sequence, from the time the firm first became aware of the problem (or opportunity) which involved the choice of a new location through to implementation at the new site, varies greatly between companies. In Cooper's study (1975, pp.79–80) of 87 firms, 2 took less than six months, 15 took six months to one year, 21 took one to two years, 35 took between two and five years, and 14 took over five years. Variations in size of the firm made little difference to the time spent, smaller firms being somewhat faster on average. Cooper's findings broadly agree with those of this author (P.M. Townroe, 1971, pp.59–60), who found also that the movers to the assisted areas in the UK took less time to choose a new site than other moves, and that fast growing companies took less time than slow growing companies if the move was to an assisted area but not otherwise.[10] As may be expected, moves requiring purpose built premises took longer than those able to use secondhand or advance built factory units. Smaller companies took longer to search for a new site than larger companies in the Townroe survey. In Cincinnati Schmenner (1978, pp.4–129) found a median search time of six months for plants employing less than forty and ten months for larger units. To this must be added an average of six months in deciding whether to move at all or whether or not to establish a new branch plant, and then in larger plants a further six months, on average, planning the move-in.

The commitment to move

The first stage of the location decision making process involves reaching a commitment to undertake some form of move. The evidence on the pressures encouraging a move was discussed in the section headed 'Intra-urban patterns of movement in manufacturing industry' of chapter 2. Pressures of the need for more space and more labour to permit an expansion of output are the dominant reasons for moving. Growth in the size of the operations of the company was found to be four times as important as the level of profitability in the planning of the project in this author's 1969 survey (P.M. Townroe, 1971, pp.40–1). A change in the locational efficiency of the firm, the spatial pattern of costs and revenues, will rarely be sufficient to encourage a move, without a direct push (such as a lease falling due) or a strong growth motivation. The concept of a threshold of locational stress proposed by some authors (P.E. Lloyd and P. Dicken, 1971, p.148 and M.J.M. Cooper, 1975, p.52) must not be taken to mean that a firm only moves in response to exogenous pressures, or in response to pressures which build up slowly over time. Very often the commitment to move is reached rapidly, usually at the very top level of management (R.W. Schmenner, 1978, pp.4–122). Indeed, a detailed consideration of *not* moving was only undertaken by half the firms in this author's survey (P.M. Townroe, 1971, p.64), and only six (of fifty-nine) included the not moving alternative among a detailed costing of alternatives. The case for not moving was more likely to be considered in those firms in which a case had to be made to a board of directors or senior management to release the resources necessary to undertake the search for a new site. In a few cases, the not moving option was only considered in detail after an initial selection of sites and factories had been visited and the full realisation of what was involved in a move began to hit the management.

There are alternatives to moving for most companies, even rapidly growing companies.[11] These include delay (an option which few firms cost out), a partial move to a pilot plant only or a staged move to an extendable new plant, or the extension of existing premises even if at first sight this seems to be ruled out on cost grounds; or the company can purchase another company, perhaps a smaller unit suitable for expansion with the injection of new capital. The takeover option can avoid many of the problems associated with a move, particularly in the areas of labour relations, interruptions to cash flow and the transfer of management personnel. Finally, through shift working, investment in new equipment, or the greater use of sub-contractors or out-workers, etc., the desired increase in output might be obtained from existing premises and the capital outlay on a new plant may be deferred.

A decision to undertake a move will involve a choice between a complete relocation and a branch plant unit, either a production unit alone or a full subsidiary division of the company. For most companies when opening a branch the real possibility of transferring the operations of the parent plant as well as opening the branch is something that seems obviously and intuitively impossible. Only 13 of the 38 branch moves in the author's study (P.M. Townroe, 1971, p.48) considered a transfer. For the majority of these moves, especially those moving for other than market or labour supply reasons, the best site for the new branch would have been alongside the parent plant. So the branch was located at a distance with some reluctance and a transfer was not considered, even though a complete move offers many advantages (W.F. Luttrell, 1961, pp.102–4).[12] Only 5 of the 21 transfer moves considered a branch move, mainly because the transfer moves were typically small firms and/or were forced moves in the face of a lease falling due, compulsory purchase, etc.

Schmenner's survey yielded returns from 21 plants in Cincinnati and 46 plants in New England which were new branches in a multiplant company. Using probit analysis, he could compare the characteristics of these new plants with the existing plants (R.W. Schmenner, 1978, pp.4–107–4–116). He found that the new branch plants were typically smaller and of simpler organisation (fewer products, more likely to lease space, less apt to be unionised and to operate multiple shifts, warehousing on-site). The plants were dependent on other plants within the company for both components and services, often manufacturing mature and technically well established products as spin-offs from a parent plant. The new branches tended to use more modern facilities and technolofy than comparable non-mover plants.

Schmenner found that a base plant is more likely to open a branch plant if:

1 the plant is already part of a multiplant operation,
2 the capital-labour ratio of the plant is high,
3 sales have been increasing,
4 new product development has been frequent,
5 employment is high,
6 the number of products produced at the plant are few,
7 the range of corporate functions performed on-site is extensive,
8 proximity to suppliers is valued, and
9 labour skills at the plant are low.

160

These factors typically contribute to a product-plant strategy of multi-plant development of the company. This contrasts with the consolidation function, as part of a corporate retrenchment, Schmenner found as a rationale in many of his transfer moves (1978, p.4—114).

In listing the pros and cons of branch plant versus relocation, Schmenner (1978, Table 3.3) uses his survey findings to suggest that a branch plant location strategy will be preferred if the problems of the parent plant are those of product proliferation, labour availability and of meeting expected future growth. Alternatively, relocation will be preferred if the problems are concerned with plant layout, materials, handling, new technology in the production process, production and inventory control, and lack of depth of managerial personnel to run plants at two sites.

The choice of location for a new branch plant will also depend upon the nature of the strategy being followed by the company concerned in opening new plants. In his survey of corporate headquarters of multi-plant firms, Schmenner (1978, pp.3—10) found that 48 per cent of both his Cincinnati and his New England sample were pursuing what could be termed a 'product plant' strategy, in which a single plant was responsible for serving the entire market on a single product or related group of products. This compares with 37 per cent of the Cincinnati firms and 27 per cent of the New England firms which were pursuing a 'market area' strategy opening new plants to serve each region of the country. A further 22 per cent of firms in each area followed a mixed product and market area strategy, while a fourth strategy was to assign separate plants to each stage in the production process (typical in the automobile industry). A fifth strategy is to open 'general purpose' plants to retain maximum flexibility. Clearly the strategy chosen must depend very much on the nature of the processes and the products involved as well as the distribution of the markets.

The extent and urgency of the commitment to move in a firm will also be reflected in the way in which the decision making process is organised. In smaller privately owned companies, the decision may be expected to rest with the chairman or managing director (and usually principal share holders). In only 7 of the 28 private companies of the Townroe survey was there a detailed discussion at senior management or boardroom level on the initial decision to search for a new location, and in 13 firms the decision was taken without reference to other staff. In the 31 public companies usually undertaking larger projects, the board of directors was consulted in 23 cases, but in the remaining cases the senior executive had a dominant role and in a few cases the board did not hear of the project until the new location was chosen. The board was only brought in when formal permission was required to

161

spend the capital. Schmenner (1978, p.4—124) found in his study of New England movers that on average only two managers in single plant companies were involved in the decision, and only 3 in multiplant transfer moves and 4 in new branch plants. In larger firms there are often two stages and levels of decision making. The expenditure of management time to go ahead with the preliminary planning and building up of a case for the project is authorised by the board of the subsidiary company or division involved. The parent board is then only involved in the authorisation of the capital expenditure (P.M. Townroe, 1971, pp.43—4).

Of the 59 firms in the Townroe survey, 36 claimed that speed was important for the project, and yet the majority of firms, including all the smaller companies, did not feel able to allocate one or more senior managers to the planning of the project full time. Cooper found that in the majority of his firms, executives involved in decision making spent less than 10 per cent of their time on the decision; ' . . . even in the case of an important decision such as that relating to location, decision making is usually incorporated into ongoing tasks as circumstances and time permit' (1975, p.81).

Search procedures and information sources

Once a commitment has been made to the need for a new location, the management of a company may take one of two broad approaches to the task of selecting a new location: (a) first drawing up a list of desirable locational attributes for the specific projects and then searching for sites which possess those attributes, or (b) proceeding by listing a number of locations which seem attractive at first sight and then eliminating those which fail to meet requirements. In the British government survey, 50 per cent of the 466 respondents adopted the first course, 32 per cent the second (and 18 per cent couldn't say); although among those searching for new and expanding town locations, the second method was more popular (Department of Trade and Industry, 1973, p.611). In the Townroe survey, 76 per cent of the firms said that they tried to establish a set of criteria to work to before possible sites and buildings were visited, but of these 45 firms only 23 formally wrote down a search specification (the remainder being mostly small companies in which a single person was involved in the decision). Seventeen firms said that the search criteria changed as the search process progressed and additional knowledge was gained [13] (P.M. Townroe, 1971, p.65).

The sequence of searching for a new site by British companies

seems to follow two alternatives.[14]   Firstly a local move is planned
and the search extends in successive concentric circles away from the
existing or parent plant or, for a plant based in a major city, the search
extends out of the city radially along prime routes of communication
(as suggested in the section headed 'Dispersal patterns' of chapter 2).
This was the pattern followed by the movers in New England and
Cincinnati (Schmenner 1978, p.4–129). Secondly, because of industrial
development certificate pressures or knowledge of the regional development incentives, the search moves directly to alternative assisted area
regions. For a few firms a search is not necessary. The company
(perhaps through a subsidiary) may already own land or the availability
of a site to purchase may have been a key factor in suggesting a move
initially. But the majority of firms seek alternatives (86 per cent in the
British government survey), and a majority of British firms consider
more than one region (58 per cent). Twenty-three per cent considered
four or more regions, being mainly larger UK based companies or overseas owned firms (Department of Trade and Industry, 1973, p.602). In
terms of individual locations and sites, in this author's 1969 study of 59
firms 17 considered only one location, 13 considered 2 to 4, 13 considered 5 to 7 and 16 more than 7. And 5 firms considered only 1 site, 13
considered 2 to 4, 10 considered 5 to 7 and 31 eight or more. Firms
which were in a hurry considered (although perhaps briefly) more
alternatives than firms for which the project was not urgent. Moves to
the assisted areas considered proportionally more alternative locations
but fewer alternative sites than other moves (P.M. Townroe, 1971, pp.
56–7).

Search involves visits of assessment, usually after an initial viewing of
areas and correspondence with public agencies and private landowners
or property agents. In 39 of the 59 Townroe companies the chief
executive saw it as his responsibility to go on the visits and he was
accompanied by other directors or executives in half of these cases.
Visits were, in all cases, a necessary condition of the initial acceptance
of the site or building, even when some urgency was involved in
obtaining a site, as was the case in thirty-six of the firms.

The sources of information used in the locational search process by
mobile companies are many and varied, reflecting the different kinds of
information required to reach a judgement on a new site. Table 6.1
shows the range of quantitative information used by 542 British firms.
To this list must be added further more qualitative items of information, such as the quality of local labour relations or the reliability of
local transport services. Both sorts of information are obtained from
many different sources, as shown in Table 6.2, which has been compiled
from American sources.[15]

In both countries information about sites and location in designated

Table 6.1
Data taken into account when choosing a location[1]

		Percentage of all firms replying affirmatively
(a)	Details of government inducements	65
(b)	Details of factories and sites available in new towns	41
(c)	Details of a range of factories and sites available elsewhere	69
(d)	Statistical data on labour supply	73
(e)	Statistical data on wage rates	47
(f)	Rail transport charges and frequency	21
(g)	Road transport charges	40
(h)	Air transport charges	9
(i)	Dock and shipping charges and ship frequency	18
(j)	Statistical data on the distribution of your actual market	45
(k)	Statistical data on the distribution of your potential market	38
(l)	Statistical data on the sources of your supplies actual or potential	41
(m)	Details of telecommunications services and costs	21

[1] 542 firms replying

Source: *Department of Trade and Industry*, Inquiry into Location Attitudes and Experience, *Memorandum submitted to the Expenditure Committee (Trade and Industry Subcommittee) on Regional Development Incentives*, 1973, p.612, HC 85-1, HMSO, London.

Table 6.2

Provision of locational information by public sources

Type of information

Source	General community information	Prevailing economic structure (competition)	Market growth & potential	Labour characteristics & costs	Transportation freight rates, schedules	Energy & power supplies & costs	Taxes, local & state	Housing
Federal/national Govt. agencies, departments	1	1		1		1	1	
State/local development agencies	1	1	1	1	1	1	1	1
Municipal officials	1			1			1	1
Banks	1		1					
Chambers of Commerce	1		1			1	1	
Agricultural/industrial/ commercial associations	1	1						
Unions				1				
Real estate firms	1			1				
Local newspapers	1							1
Specialised journals		1	1	1	1	1	1	1
Transportation agencies					1			
Utilities	1					1		

aincludes general amenities, educational facilities, community attitudes, political climate.

165

Table 6.2 continued

Source: Compiled by P.E. Lloyd and P. Dicken in 1972 from information in M.C. Neuhoff (1953), Techniques of Plant Location, Washington DC, US GPO; H.F. Lionberger (1960), Adoption of New Ideas and Practices, Ames; Iowa State University Press; J.M. Thompson (1961), Methods of Plant Site Selection Available to Small Manufacturing Firms, Morgantown: West Virginia University Press; E. Mueller, A. Wilken and M. Wood (1961), Location Decisions and Industry Mobility in Michigan, Ann Arbor: Institute for Social Research, University of Michigan.

development areas is more likely to come from public bodies. This is seen in the Townroe survey where the central government, development associations and local authorities ranked 1, 2, 3 as information sources for moves to the assisted areas, but personal sighting, estate agents and newspapers ranked 1, 2, 3 for the remainder (P.M. Townroe, 1971, p. 56). Real estate agents were second only to 'Own Research' in Schmenner's New England survey (1978, p.4—124). The importance of public agencies in providing information is further confirmed by Cameron and Clark (1966, chapter 6), Murie et al. (1974, p.75), and by the Schmenner study.[16] Public agencies are also important sources of advice (W.F. Luttrell, 1962, p.73). Because of the industrial development certificate procedure and the strong regional development programme in the UK, the regional offices of the Department of Industry play, at least in part, a role which in the United States is much more likely to be taken by private location consultants. The use of location consultants is rare in the UK.[17]

Evaluation procedures

The process of evaluating alternative locations and sites may be seen as a three stage sifting sequence. Not all companies will pass through all stages: for some companies the choice of the new location will seem obvious to them, without the need for searching for or evaluating alternatives. For the majority, however, there will be three stages. In the first stage, many areas are ruled out of consideration as impracticable. The reasons may be direct functional ones, such as transport costs, links with the parent company, supplies of available labour; or more subjective reasons, such as quality of the labour force or quality of the residential environment. This first stage 'sift' may be quick and without analysis, or slower and more considered. In the second stage, a more detailed look at a limited number of areas is undertaken, usually with visits and correspondence to relevant bodies. Then in the third stage, a short list of likely alternatives is subjected to detailed evaluation, often with other members of the management of the company not involved hitherto now taking part or with outside specialist advisers.

A priori, it might be expected that the eventual choice of location from the short list of the third stage would be on the basis of a comparative cost analysis. In fact, the survey evidence suggests that this is not the case in many, if not the majority of companies. Among Cooper's ninety-eight firms for example, 71 per cent 'selected their location on the basis of whether or not the site and/or buildings were suitable for the proposed project. Only 29 per cent made comparisons of costs, labor supplies, accessibility, or similar factors.' (M.J.M. Cooper, 1975, p.88). Only 3 of 22 firms moving to two town expansion schemes in the UK undertook cost analyses (I.M. Seeley, 1967, p. 188). In 22 per cent of the Townroe sample, no costing or financial evaluation was performed at all, and of the remaining 46 firms, only 20 undertook comparative costings, the other 26 costing out the final site only, 8 admitting to a lease costing only (P.M. Townroe, 1971, pp.69). Only 29 per cent of Cameron and Clark's 59 firms undertook comparative cost surveys (1966, p.116). [18]   In Schmenner's study, even in multiplant companies involving a plant size in excess of 100 employees, over 40 per cent of both transfer and branch moves were not costed out (1978, p.4—130). And it seems even more rare for cost factors to be set against non-costable items:

> We should have liked to have given an example of a classic case of locational choice in which operating-cost estimates were made for two or more possible places, all imponderables or non-cost factor assessed and then a way found of comparing the good and bad points of one place with those of the other. Unfortunately, we have not been able to find such a case (W.F. Lutrell, 1962, p.78).

Clearly for many companies, costings may offer spurious accuracy, and the most relevant variations between sites may be in the quantifiable considerations which enter only indirectly into costs (such as the available pool of labour) or in the more qualitative considerations which require high levels of judgement. Indeed, the most important cost item, the variation in the achieved levels of labour productivity, is nearly impossible for the firm to predict in advance. Thirty-two firms in the Townroe survey used an approach to the financial appraisal of the project which was different from that usually followed for an investment in new equipment.

The felt absence of need to undertake comparative costings is in part due to the high level of uncertainty surrounding the forecast performance of a project in a location new to the management of the company. One way of reducing the uncertainty is to draw upon the experience of other companies which have moved into the area some time before.[19] Sixty-three per cent of Cameron and Clark's moves to assisted areas undertook such consultations (1966, p.116), as did 67 per cent of the Townroe assisted area moves, although this was complemented by 81 per cent of non-assisted area moves not having such consultations (1971, p.68), reflecting the value of such talks to firms establishing new plants in an area new to their experience.[20]

The importance of non-quantifiable or subjective factors in the location decision, suggested in the model in the first section of this chapter, comes about because of uncertainty about the economic or financial parameters of the decision and because of uncertainty (due to lack of precedent, experience and example) about the most relevant procedure to follow in reaching the decision. The relative importance of these factors in the evaluation process is difficult to determine. The survey evidence referred to in chapter 4 gives relatively low priority to factors such as amenity; less than half of the companies in the Townroe survey looked seriously at the amenities and social facilities in alternative locations while even fewer claimed that the attitudes of the staff had been directly considered (P.M. Townroe, 1971, p.67). Perhaps the prime area for subjective evaluation in the location decision making process is in stage one. Hearsay evidence on labour attitudes or misleading (or outdated) ideas on communications can lead the 'mental map' of the industrial manager to be considerably distorted and the perception of viable opportunities to be somewhat myopic.[21] This may result in areas or regions being ruled out of consideration on very thin evidence, enabling the decision making problem for the manager to be immediately simplified.

The evidence as to why companies reject a region or a location within a region, having considered it, shows the room for the play of subjective evaluation.[22] The British government survey, for example (Department of Trade and Industry, 1973, p.607) shows that, as might be expected, the assisted area regions were largely rejected on the grounds of remoteness, communication problems and uneconomic distance from markets and supplies. But 'labour difficulties' were also important as reasons for rejecting regions both assisted areas and the remainder from 53 per cent of those considering Yorkshire and Humberside to 22 per cent of those considering Northern Ireland. The 'difficulties' included estimations of attitude as well as problems of insufficient labour. 'The citing of this reason fairly clearly hinged on subjective assessments and on the particular situations met in individual localities considered.' (op.cit. p.608). As Table 6.3 shows, labour difficulties remain important at the intra-regional level, although at that stage of the search, the lack of suitable sites or buildings becomes more important as a reason for rejecting locations.

The final choice

The discussion of the procedures followed in locational decision making in this chapter has implied throughout that the path taken by the management of a company to choose a new site will influence the location (and perhaps the nature of the site or building) chosen. Although this implication has been discussed and commented upon in the literature on industrial locations decisions, there have been few attempts to empirically isolate the influence.[23] One such attempt was made by this author (P.M. Townroe, 1972, pp.261—72). This study found, as might be expected in the face of a relatively small sample of decisions (fifty-nine) undertaken within companies which varied enormously in size, complexity and sophistication, that the great heterogeneity of locational behaviour made the isolation of any distinct patterns very difficult. The study did reveal, however, that certain elements of behaviour do tend to be found together in those firms which undertake a considerable investment of resources in finding the most appropriate new location. These elements, together can be said to represent a 'scenario of righteous behaviour':

The well managed company will first consider in detail whether a move is strictly necessary and whether there is not an alternative course of action which may reach the same ends. This will involve writing down the objectives of the move and deciding what the key factors in such a move will be before a search process is initiated. Then the requirements of the search for a new location are specified and a planned sequence is set out for the search in terms of areas and types of building or site to consider. The search itself involves many locations, many sites and many visits in order to gather the maximum amount of information. This may involve the use of consultants and will certainly involve consultation with trade unions and other companies in the new locations. The attitudes of existing staff will be given due consideration and staff facilities in the new locations will be an important factor in the assessment. This may involve direct consultation with existing employees. Since good management is receptive to new ideas, the original list of key factors may change. This will not, however, prevent alternatives being costed, preferably with the use of

Table 6.3

Reasons for not settling in other locations in the region chosen

	United Kingdom	Development areas and Northern Ireland	New and expanded Towns outside development areas	Rest of Great Britain
Number of firms responding	242	124	52	66
	Percentage of firms mentioning reason			
Distance/transport/access difficulties	16	16	17	14
Labour difficulties	29	36	13	29
Refusal of planning permission	2	1	0	5
Refusal (or expected refusal) of IDC	7	3	10	11
Poor amenities/environment	9	10	12	6
Local authority indifference	6	7	6	5
No suitable sites	26	23	27	32
No suitable buildings	30	28	23	38
Unsatisfactory public utilities	2	1	6	0
Other reasons	23	23	33	15

Source: Department of Trade and Industry, Inquiry into Location Attitudes and Experience, *Memorandum submitted to the Expenditure Committee (Trade and Industry Subcommittee) on Regional Development Incentives*, 1973, p.612, HC 85-1, HMSO, London.

Discounted Cash Flow techniques and with tighter financial standards than for smaller investment projects. The management will be aware that the search process itself has a real cost. The well managed company may prefer not to leave the decision to a single individual so that the eventual choice evolves from experience rather than being imposed by one man, and the final range of options will be formally presented to the Board of Directors rather than left as an executive decision (P.M. Townroe, 1972, p.263).

The pattern of inter-relationship of the individual behaviour elements referred to in the above quotation is weakened by small companies and those undertaking only short distance moves; but a leading indicator emerges which strongly associates with other elements. This is whether objectives were written down for formal consideration. Other important elements which each associate with a large number of other elements were: the specification of search requirements, consultation with trade unions, costing of alternative sites, consideration of the cost of the search and the formal presentation of the scheme to the board of directors for a decision.

The location decision making behaviour variables in this study were then linked to various characteristics of the companies and their moves: the category of move, the size and status of the company and the project, the decision makers involved, the factors encouraging movement and factors of attraction to locations. From a principal components analysis of all of these variables, five reasonably distinct groups of companies were identified (P.M. Townroe, 1972, p.269).

1 Group A: large privately owned and smaller publicly owned, all moving to the assisted area, with an individualistic pattern of decision making.
2 Group B: large publicly owned long distance moves, scoring highly on the elements of managerial performance.
3 Group C: a small group similar to B but exhibiting less managerial autonomy in decision making.
4 Group D: larger private and small public companies establishing branch plants, with mixed managerial performances reflecting ' . . . their collective image of the rather slow growing family firm.'
5 Group E: small private companies involved in local reactive moves, the decision being dominated by the owner of the company.

The study allows a number of distinct hypotheses to be proposed, most of which suggest avenues for further research. The hypotheses are split into five groups. The first group relate to the category of move:

171

1 That the goals and objectives for a branch plant are more explicit, and the change less, than for a transfer.
2 That the longer the distance of the proposed move the more consideration is given to not moving at all.
3 That development area moves consider a smaller number of alternatives than non-development area moves.
4 That assistance by official and semi-official bodies tends to increase the rigour with which the location problem is approached.

The second group relate to the structure of the company:

1 That the larger the proposed new plant, the more detailed the decision process, and the more 'economically rational' the final choice.
2 That the cost of gathering information does not explicitly limit the search.
3 That privately owned concerns are more open to subjective pressures than publicly owned companies.

The third group relate to the decision makers:

1 That decisions undertaken and arrived at by single individuals involve less formal commitment to specific goals and less formal appraisal of alternatives.
2 That individual decisions are less likely to involve a change of criteria during the decision making process.
3 That dependence upon external finance does not result in externally imposed conditions.
4 That companies seek a feasible alternative rather than the optimal alternative.
5 That, where growth is the main reason for movement, the location problem will be approached with greater rigour than when movement is for other reasons.

The fourth group relate to the factors encouraging movement:

1 That labour supply difficulties lead to a distinctive pattern of search and choice.
2 That difficulties in obtaining local industrial development certificates result in factor supplies being of central importance in the new location.
3 That forced move companies are more likely to accept a sub-optimum choice of site.

The fifth group relate to factors of attraction to locations and sites:

1 That the greater the technological requirement of the new site, the more important is the detailed specification of requirements and the evaluation of alternatives and the less important is the cost of the search.
2 That where the tie with the parent plant is important, a more extensive search procedure is undertaken.
3 That when a company is planning to construct a purpose built factory, requirements will be more closely specified and the search process will take longer than for the purchase or lease of an existing building.

One hypothesis in the third group suggests that companies seek a feasible rather than an optimal alternative in choosing a new location. This was also suggested in the discussion of the decision making model in the first section of this chapter. Evidence from two surveys supports the hypothesis. In Cooper's survey (1975, p.87) 55 per cent of the firms selected the first satisfactory site they discovered, while only a minority looked further. The larger the firm, the more likely it was to compare alternative satisfactory sites. In the Townroe survey (1971, p. 89), 17 of the 57 firms agreed that the site chosen was the first possible answer for their particular situation. A further twenty-three took the first satisfactory site (i.e. passed over other sites which would have been possible but had certain undesirable features), making a 'sub-optimum' rather than a 'minimum needs' choice. Only the final seventeen firms continued to consider alternatives before coming back to a site considered earlier. These firms might be thought of as exhibiting optimising behaviour in continuing to search until diminishing returns were identified.

If complexity and uncertainty are the prime reasons for satisficing behaviour, rather than laziness or lack of expertise, then public policy which increases the demands made on managerial resources at the time of choosing a new site will be likely to encourage firms to settle for a satisfactory rather than a best site. This may then result in an aggregate loss of locational efficiency. Public policy making may not be aware of this imposed cost, especially in the United States where so many different public agencies are involved. Rondinelli's (1975, pp.196–7) outline of the consents and permissions required by a firm seeking to settle in north-eastern Pennsylvania with regional development aid is an apt illustration of the point.

Notes

[1] Chapter 2 of the author's 1971 study, (P.M. Townroe, 1971, pp.10 −27). The model is an adaption of that proposed in J.K. Friend and W. N. Jessop (1969, chapter 2) as a basis for analysing decision making in the context of local government.

[2] A representation of this is offered in D.J. North (1974, p.215).

[3] Remembering Machlup's distinction between: (i) the entire environment, (ii) the relevant aspects of the entire environment, and (iii) the relevant changes in environmental conditions (F. Machlup, 1967, p.25).

[4] Krumme (1969, p.37), in his conceptual framework of location decision making alternatives, distinguishes 'active' or spatially oriented decision making from 'passive' or spatially indifferent decision making.

[5] Very small but rapidly growing companies may also be choosing new locations relatively frequently as they expand out of one set of premises into another.

[6] In the 1969 survey by the present author, a harassed managing director in a new plant, when asked the question: 'If you were to go through the process of establishing a new plant once again, what would you do that was different from last time?' replied: 'Select better management.' (P.M. Townroe, 1971, p.93). As Schmenner suggests (1978, p.4−125), because so many aspects of the location decision are largely non-quantitative in nature it is not altogether surprising that many of the procedures employed in the decision making process are informal, qualitive and judgemental.

[7] See also, for example, P.E. Lloyd and P. Dicken (1972, pp.145 and 147); M.J.M. Cooper (1975, pp.53−60); S. Soderman (1975, p.84).

[8] P.M. Townroe, (1971, p.14); and D.J. North (1974, pp.216−17).

[9] This is discussed at length in P.M. Townroe (1969, pp.15−24, and 1971, pp.17−27).

[10] Slow growing companies may go through the search process fairly quickly if they are subject to leases falling due or to compulsory purchase orders by the public authorities, or if a new management decides upon a change in policy which requires a new location.

[11] These alternatives are discussed at length in P.M. Townroe (1976, pp.22−4). See also W.F. Luttrell (1962, pp.45−7).

[12] In the thirteen branch moves which did consider complete relocation, the cost of disruption involved was the factor deciding against a transfer in ten cases. Loss of an existing work force and speed were other reasons (P.M. Townroe, 1971, p.49).

[13] The availability of government advance factories allowed some companies to drop construction plans, and a fuller realisation of the scale of regional development incentives allowed other firms to revise the planned size of the project upwards.

[14] Although in many cases there is no explicit plan for the search activity, e.g. 'Evidence confirms that search activity is severely limited, casual and unsystematic. This is the overriding impression from the questionnaire responses.' (A.S. Murie et al. 1974, p.76).

[15] See also D. Howard (1972, p.207).

[16] C.P. Rahe's survey (1972, p.6) of 159 firms newly locating in Denver 1965−70 found that industrial development agencies in the metropolitan area initiated very little of the movement, they were not important as sources of information, and had a strong influence on the location of only six firms. This was in spite of further evidence that location decision makers held industrial development agencies in high regard.

[17] Location consultants were used by only 5 per cent of firms in the British government survey (Department of Trade and Industry, 1973, p. 613), by 2 per cent in the Cameron and Clark survey (1966, p.116), and by 4 per cent in the Townroe survey (1971, p.68). In the United States the use of location consultants seems largely restricted to larger firms (C.P. Rahe, 1972, p.5).

[18] Comparative cost analyses are undertaken in 54 per cent of parent companies employing 5,000 or more, in 38 per cent of those employing 500 to 4,999 and only 5 per cent of the smaller firms. Such analyses were much more common for a move involving a division than for a branch production unit or a transfer (G.C. Cameron and B.D. Clark, 1966, pp.120−2).

[19] 'Imitation affords relief from the necessity of really making decision innovations, which, if wrong, become inexcusable.' (A. Alchain, 1950, p.215).

[20] See Also W.F. Luttrell, 1962, p.74, M.J.M. Cooper, 1975, p.88.

[21] See the general discussion in P.E. Lloyd and P. Dicken (1972, pp. 150−60); and the evidence in D.H. Green (1977). And M.L. Greenhut, (1956, pp.175−6 and pp.233−47).

[22] See also A.S. Murie, et al. (1974, p.77) and G.C. Cameron and G.L. Reid (1966, p.15).

[23] See also D.J. North's characterisations of the different search and locational selection processes by different types and distances of move among 100 firms in the UK plastics industry (1974, pp.232−41).

7 The transition into the new plant

As suggested at the beginning of the last chapter, in the literature on industrial movement relatively little attention has been paid to those issues which arise for a company in the course of transition into a new plant at a new location. Yet success in achieving a smooth transition and run up to full production must be a concern both for those interested in industrial efficiency and those interested in the successful operation of public policies to influence industrial mobility. In designated development areas especially, the more painless the transition the more secure will be the jobs created by the new plant and the sooner the company will feel able to increase their original investment.

The process of moving into a new plant, even if it is only a subsidiary production unit, tends to place great stress upon those involved. Here, as in the choice of location, lack of experience and precedent can result in unnecessary mistakes and important ommissions in the planning process, or alternatively it can result in over-planning; thus introducing needless complexity. The strain will be increased if the move is used as an opportunity to change structures and procedures within the organisation of the company; if the move is related to new products and/or new production processes. The survey evidence referred to in this chapter and the next will reveal how some of these stresses may be so severe as to result in the closure of the new plant; although the early closure of a new plant is perhaps more frequently associated with a change in market conditions or parent company policy (M.E.C. Sant, 1975b).

In this chapter, four aspects of the transition into the new plant will be considered: the first managerial appointments, the planning of construction and moving in plant and machinery, the transfer of employees and the recruitment and training of labour.

Managerial appointments

Many initial post-move problems are exacerbated by inadequate management in the new plant (P.M. Townroe, 1971, pp.91–2, and 97–100). The managers in a transfer move may be facing internal problems and an external environment outside their previous experience; and branch plants, particularly production only units, tend to be administered by relatively junior or inexperienced managers. Yet ' . . . many firms consider the quality of the manager to be the key to success in a new venture of this sort' (W.F. Luttrell, 1962, p.149). The personality of the first chief resident manager in the new plant seems to be crucial in drawing the new plant through an initial problem filled period.

In the second Townroe survey of mobile industrial plants in the UK 38 of 202 chief managers were appointed after the choice of location had been made (1974, p.300). For these managers, there is the problem of having to live with someone else's choice of site for the new plant and hence with any inadequate decision making procedure.[1] This occurred in one-quarter of the branch plant moves in the survey. It was also common, as may be expected, in the larger new plants with large parent companies; and in the longer distance moves. As Luttrell also noticed in his survey (1962, p.151), existing senior managers avoid appointments in a new but distant plant. Seven of the Townroe companies made temporary appointments, offering a short term (2–5 years) contract to either a professional manager experienced at running a new plant or to a younger man on a 'prove thyself' basis. In three of the Luttrell firms, a very senior man was sent to overcome initial difficulties before handing over to a more junior man whom he had been training. ' . . . the arrangement worked very satisfactorily' (1962, p.151). In the majority of branch plants in both surveys the manager was appointed from within the firm, although more usually a junior rather than a senior man. Obviously, in the transfer moves, the owner manager was normally the chief executive in the new location.

In the Townroe survey (1974, p.301), the owner managers had more problems recruiting and training labour than other managers. And externally recruited managers in branch plants had relatively fewer problems than managers from within the company. Younger first managers (under the age of forty) were more likely to be in fast growing and larger plants than older managers, in both branch plants and transfer moves. The younger men were more likely to have problems with finance and the development of markets compared with their older counterparts who in turn were more likely to have labour problems in their new plant. Younger men seem to be prepared to move further than older men to run a new plant, reflecting natural ambition.

The problems which face these first managers in newly located plants are clearly too much for some of their number, or for their employers. In 209 firms in the Townroe survey (1974, pp.301–3), 68 first managers had moved on by the time of the interview (up to five years after the move). The reasons given by their successors for their departures were varied. Direct inadequacy was given as the reason on only twelve cases, although organisational changes and takeovers accounted for a further fourteen cases. One man left because of a personal dislike for the location. Some left for further promotion and seven left because they were on temporary contracts anyway. Twenty-five of the 68 stayed with the company in another capacity. Clearly a change of chief executive does not necessarily indicate the existence of a problem, but it is interesting that in this survey a significant relation-ship was found between slow growth rates of both turnover and employment and the rapid replacement of first managers.

Replacement rates were also higher in firms giving labour as the principal cost problem in the first two years of operations. Unfamiliar-ity with a new labour relations environment in a part of the country new to the manager, coupled with inflexibility and a lack of consulta-tion on labour affairs in the locational decision making seem to lead to a cluster of managerial problems in a significant minority of mobile companies.

Turning to managerial staff in general, a very high proportion (84 per cent) of the firms in the British government survey transferred personnel with the company (Department of Trade and Industry, 1973, p.641). This proportion dropped to only 76 per cent in the longest distance moves (250 miles and over) and to only 75 per cent in firms originating overseas. Six per cent of firms did not plan to retain staff permanently and in 5 per cent the firm was unable to retain the staff. But the transferees stayed on in the remaining 89 per cent, a proportion which dropped to only 84 per cent for moves to the assisted areas, countering the belief often expressed that white collar personnel will not transfer to those parts of the United Kingdom distant from London and the South East.[2] Only 3 per cent of the respondents claimed that the operation of the new plant had been seriously handicapped by difficulties in transferring managerial staff; a further 5 per cent replying 'Yes, but not seriously'.

Recruitment of middle and supervisory management in the area of the new plant may be a problem for the mobile company, if the area is relatively thinly populated, or does not have a strong base in manufac-turing industry, or is characterised by those sectors of industry (steel, shipbuilding, coal etc.) in which the proportion of middle management in the labour force is low and in which there has not been a tradition of internal promotion and upward occupational mobility. In the British government survey (Department of Trade and Industry, 1973, pp.644–6) 41 per cent of firms replied that they did not try to recruit manager-ial staff locally (many of these would have been small transfers). But 29 per cent had been able to recruit new management within forty miles of the new plant; a further 17 per cent only with difficulty; and 13 per cent had failed. Local recruiting was especially difficult for those firms locating in the new and expanding towns, presumably due to competit-ion from other fast growing firms. Forty-three per cent tried to recruit from elsewhere in the country, 21 per cent recruiting staff easily, 16 with difficulty and 6 per cent failing to obtain the personnel required. This country wide recruiting proved to be relatively more difficult for branch plant moves, for moves to the assisted areas (especially Scotland), and for moves in labour intensive sectors of industry.

In a large transfer move, senior management has a difficult choice before it in respect of middle managers and supervisors: should the emphasis be on maintaining good general staff relations by encouraging everyone to relocate, or should the opportunity be taken to get rid of the less qualified and the poor performers before the move? Certainly, to transfer personnel only to subsequently dismiss them when problems occur in the new plant causes great personal anguish, and a strong backlash in staff relations in the new plant. After a division of General Foods Limited moved forty miles from Birmingham to Banbury, England in 1965, a dismissal incident in the production planning department contributed to a strong sense of uncertainty, and insecurity in many managers. Mann suggests (1973, pp.191–3), this incident, together with a measure of administrative reorganisation and a worsening of relationships between the workforce and the supervisors (brought on by insecurities in the workforce associated with the move), resulted in a marked increase in membership of white collar trade unions.[3]

Planning construction and moving equipment

There has been little empirical investigation into the problems faced by mobile companies in planning the construction of their new plant and then planning the move-in of all the necessary machinery and equipment. This is true in both the United States and the United Kingdom. Perhaps these tasks have been regarded by those interested in industrial movement as essentially engineering and organisational problems, for which a company will typically seek external advice and employ specialists to find solutions. Or perhaps potential investigators have been deterred by the difficulties in contacting the relevant personnel in companies just on the point of movement. Anyway, it is not clear whether long distance moves face greater problems in these two tasks than short distance moves, whether managerial inexperience in smaller companies leads to additional problems, whether a phased move-in works better than a single point of time start-up, whether it is sensible for the company to employ a single main contractor or to employ the sub-contractors directly itself, how far stocks are built up before a transfer move, and so forth. Because there has been little empirical investigation of these questions and little in the way of discussion, it is therefore unclear whether public policy could or should try to influence the responses made by companies.

One element of British regional development policy which can remove the concerns of the construction of a factory building from the management of a mobile company is the advance factory unit. These units are constructed under the Department of Industry in England and under the Scottish and Welsh Development Agencies.[4] Between 1945 and 1975 over 600 units (ranging from 5,000 to 50,000 square feet in size and on sites allowing for expansion) were authorised, providing an estimated 50,000 jobs.[5] The units are designed to be as flexible as possible and so to be suitable for the widest possible range of manufacturing industry operations. Eighteen per cent of all the firms moving to assisted area locations in the British government survey agreed that a government factory to rent and the immediate availability of a government factory were major factors in their choice of location (Department of Trade and Industry, 1973, p.579).[6] There has been no published study of the net financial or resource costs of this programme.

Also in Great Britain, up to 80 per cent of the cost of moving a factory into an assisted area will be repaid by the government as a grant, on condition that sufficient additional jobs are created. This grant may rise to 100 per cent in Northern Ireland. These grants may encourage firms to use specialist contractors who can offer advice on the basis of experience which the mobile company itself often does not possess.

Transferring employees

The transfer of existing employees to the new location will obviously be an issue of greater concern to the management involved in a transfer move than those opening a new branch, but even in a new branch a number of existing employees of the company may be required to train other workers and/or to generally speed up the build up to full production. The proportion of companies requiring such transferred employees in the UK is shown in Table 7.1

Of the firms transferring workers, 18 per cent were unable to retain them, a proportion which rose to 22 per cent of moves under 20 miles, to 24 per cent of the moves 250 miles and over and to 40 per cent of transfer moves to development areas. Only 6 per cent of all the firms agreed that their operations had been seriously handicapped as a result of the difficulties in getting existing employees to transfer to the new location a further 8 per cent saying 'Yes, but not seriously'. This handicap was greatest among single plant companies and transfers, especially those moving to development areas and to new and expanding towns. Ninety-one per cent of the firms moving workers from the old

180

Table 7.1
The transfer of workers already on the payroll to the new location
(Percentages)

Category of move	A substantial proportion of requirements	A nucleus	None
Transfers	36	52	12
Branches	4	54	42
1 – 19 miles	49	35	16
Over 250 miles	2	48	51
To development areas	6	48	46
To new & expanding towns	42	45	13
To rest of Great Britain	16	57	27
All cases	16	50	34

Source: Department of Trade and Industry, Inquiry into Location Attitudes and Experience, *Memorandum Submitted to the Expenditure Committee (Trade and Industry Subcommittee) on Regional Development Incentives,* 1973, p.636, HC 85-1, HMSO, London.

location offered financial assistance with the cost of moving (Department of Trade and Industry, 1973, pp.636–9).

Existing employees will only rarely actively want to move and so they will require a measure of incentive and certainly full compensation from the company. The cash cost to the company in the UK today would be over £1,500 per employee, by the standards of the 1965 General Foods Ltd. move (M. Mann, 1973, p.239).[7] The full cost to the company, including the management resources involved in planning and overseeing the employment relocation, would be even greater.

In both of the two detailed British case histories of a relocation — that of General Foods Limited, and that of W.H. Smith and Sons Ltd from London to Swindon (B.J. Loasby, 1973) — there are descriptions of how the companies tried to relocate all of their employees while recognising that not all would go. In both companies, policies of equal movement terms to all and of continued employment to all who wished to move reduced trade union disquiet about the move.[8] In both companies, success in encouraging employees to transfer was only achieved by constant publicity and very detailed work in the personnel department.[9] The publicity included visits for employees to the towns; and rental housing was provided for those who required it through the local town councils.[10] As the Finance Director of W.H. Smith said at the time of their move, the relocation plan 'must be sold at all levels' (B.J. Loasby, 1973, p.34). Failure to do so will have the result recorded in an account of the attempt by the British Aluminium Company to transfer workers from Milton in Staffordshire to South Wales on the closure of a plant. The company ' . . . presented its employees with a coolly prepared profit-and-loss account, stepped back and told them to do their own sums' (A. Fox, 1965, p.61). The only positive inducement was compensation for the cost of moving. Only nine workers transferred.

Mann found that the propensity of workers in his study to relocate did not correlate with job satisfaction. 'Movers were not significantly more likely than non-movers to have favourable opinions of the company as a whole, of the work pressure upon them, of supervision, of intrinsic job content, of security or of promotion chances' (1973, p. 133). Mann argues that job satisfaction merely removes an obstacle to employee relocation. The two main positive inducements to relocate for his sample of workers were: housing need, often linked with an increasing dislike of inner urban area life, and ties of job dependence. This job dependence on the company was strong for older salaried and often poorly qualified employees, as may be expected; but it was also strong for those manual workers with company specific skills and who were benefitting from the company policy of internal promotion (1973, pp.162–4).

Studies such as those of Mann and Loasby point to the considerable difficulties involved in transferring existing employees to a new plant location. Is it worth the trouble, especially if a large labour pool exists in the new area? The verdict of General Foods Limited and W.H. Smith was certainly affirmative, a view that was supported by companies transferring so-called key workers in the second Townroe survey. Indirect evidence from that survey suggests that companies transferring key workers had fewer problems with labour supply and labour costs; and, in the Northern region sample, moved more quickly to profitability (P.M. Townroe, 1975, p.337). The transferred workers pass on relevant skills to the new workforce, and also transmit work attitudes and practices to the new plant; even if the key workers are transferred only

182

on a temporary basis, as in 6 per cent of the Department of Trade and Industry survey firms (1973, p.638).

For transfer moves, a corollary to building up the new plant and relocating existing employees is the run down of the old plant and necessary redundancies. In the W.H. Smith move the run down was planned by a joint management-union committee (B.J. Loasby, 1973, chapter 7). One potential problem was a pre-move staff shortage caused by the loss of those unwilling to transfer or to stay on until declared redundant. In fact the terms of redundancy were attractive enough to keep the early loss of workers very low, and eventual redundancies were announced in stages with full union cooperation. In the General Foods move, the run down was not so smooth, partly because the original schedule of opening the new plant could not be kept to but also because of the need to employ temporary workers in Birmingham prior to the move. These temporary workers changed the industrial relations climate within the firm, lowering productivity, challenging the discipline of supervisors, and resulting in a closed shop negotiating agreement with a trade union (M. Mann, 1973, pp.117—28). In both firms a generous redundancy policy seems to have been taken by employees as a sign of faith and goodwill, encouraging those who did relocate that they would be treated fairly by the company.

Advance recruitment and training

In both branch plants and in transfer moves, moving existing employees is unlikely to provide all of the workforce required in the new plant, even if the move is over a relatively short distance. New employees have to be recruited locally in the new community, or recruited elsewhere and moved to the new location. The company will have to decide how early before the opening new employees should be sought and what sort of advance training they should receive. One possibility used by companies is to recruit in the area of origin new employees willing to make the move with the company when the time comes, although they may arouse suspicions among the original employees that they are not really wanted at the new site. Another is to recruit in the destination area prior to the move, bringing the new employees back to the parent plant for training. Either course can be expensive for the company if the timing of the move means that groups of workers have to temporarily commute (by the day or the week) from one site to the other and the expenses involved have to be borne by the company.[11]

The majority of employees for the new plant in all but the short distance transfers, however, will be sought in the destination area. Indeed, as seen in earlier chapters, the search for additional employees

Table 7.2
Ease of recruitment of labour in new location in the UK
(Percentages)

Location	Skilled labour			Semi-skilled & unskilled		
	Yes easily	Yes with difficulty	Not suff-icient	Yes easily	Yes with difficulty	Not suff-icient
Development areas	31	35	34	73	23	4
New & expanding towns	33	33	34	65	26	9
Rest of Great Britain	46	29	25	75	18	7
All cases	35	33	32	72	22	6

Source: Department of Trade and Industry, 1973, pp.618–19, op.cit.
Table 7.1

is one of the prime reasons for undertaking a move in the first place. The ease with which over 500 firms in the British government survey discovered new employees is shown in Table 7.2. Unfortunately, a more detailed breakdown by category of move is not possible; but the table does show, as expected *a priori,* greater difficulties in obtaining skilled workers, especially in the development areas and the new and expanding towns, as well as the effects of strong competition for even semi and unskilled labour in the new towns compared with an easier supply situation in the development areas (which are anyway areas of relatively high unemployment). In reply to a more general question, 52 per cent of the firms said that they found their 'labour situation' 'easier' compared with the previous location, while for 27 per cent it was 'similar' and for 21 per cent 'more difficult'. With the exception of the North West region, the labour situation was easier in the development area regions that elsewhere. It was more difficult for 27 per cent of firms locating in the new and expanding towns, and for 25 per cent of those moving less than twenty miles (Department of Trade and Industry, 1973, p.617).

The 1972 Townroe survey compared labour recruitment in branch plants and transfer moves (1975, p.338), showing no strong differences between the two categories. That survey again demonstrated the difficulties in recruiting skilled employees. It also showed regional differences in firms finding difficulty in recruiting unskilled employees. In London and East Anglia they tended to be small, slow growing concerns, perhaps unable to meet the competition; while in the Northern region the firms with problems were the larger, faster growing concerns, reflecting the different labour supply situation in the development area.

The 1972 Townroe survey also shows the importance of the size of the labour pool within which the new plant is established (1975, p.339). The smaller the town chosen, the more likely the firms were to face recruitment difficulties. Even in two town expansion schemes, Thetford and Haverhill in the East Anglian region of the UK, with planned expansion of the labour pool and high local unemployment levels, only 45 per cent and 30 per cent of firms had been able to recruit all of their requirements locally in 1971. Fifty-nine per cent and 53 per cent of the company managers interviewed by Moseley (1973, p.275) in the two towns favoured continued expansion of the towns because that would enlarge the pool of labour.

Expenses in recruiting new labour in the new location are matched by necessary expenditures by the firm on training. Clearly difficulties in recruiting required skills will encourage a company to undertake its own training, while for many industrial processes on-the-job training, perhaps supplemented by more formal instruction, will be required at all skill levels. In general, the higher the proportion of skilled workers in the total workforce, the greater proportion of the skilled workers it is likely that the company will need to train. This is shown to be so in Table 7.3, again taken from the British government survey. Once the proportion of skilled workers in the total force is over 20 per cent, then more than half of them have to be trained in more than half the cases. More than 80 per cent of the companies replying to this question also had to train more than half of their semi-skilled employees, once the proportion of semi-skilled workers in the labour force was over 20 per cent. In 48 per cent of all firms, over half the skilled workers needed training to that level, although no training for skilled workers was required in 24 per cent of firms. And in 79 per cent of firms, more than half the semi-skilled workers needed training and only in 11 per cent of firms no training was required at this level. Forty per cent of firms did not have an adult training scheme for skilled workers (Department of Trade and Industry, 1973, pp.622–5).

One way of preparing all or part of the new labour force for new work tasks is to undertake a training programme in advance of opening the new plant. This may allow an acceleration of the build-up time once the plant does open. Such training could be undertaken in premises rented temporarily for the purpose (old church halls have been

Table 7.3

Training requirements in mobile plants

Skilled and semi-skilled as a percentage of labour force	Proportion of skilled and semi-skilled labour who needed training to that level									
	Over 50%(1)		11—50%		Under 11%		None		All cases	
	S	M	S	M	S	M	S	M	S	M
0– 19	32	56	10	4	12	3	46	37	100	
20– 39	54	85	18	6	13	5	15	4	100	
40– 59	59	82	17	11	17	5	7	2	100	
60– 79	61	89	16	6	11	3	11	2	100	
80–100	64	95	17	2	13	2	6	1	100	

(1) S = Skilled   M = Semi-skilled

Source: Department of Trade and Industry, 1973a, p.622 and p.624, op.cit. Table 7.1

used), or in a corner of the partially completed factory, or back at the parent plant. In fact, advance training programmes do not seem to be popular with British industrial movers. Among movers to the three areas studied in 1972 Townroe survey, only 5 of the 51 London companies attempted any form of advance training, a proportion which rose to 25 per cent of the East Anglian firms and 28 per cent of the Northern region movers. These programmes were concentrated among the larger new plants or in new plants of larger parent companies. There is no evidence that advance training programmes in general give a new plant a 'head start' in terms of faster than average growth (P.M. Townroe, 1975, p.340).

In the United Kingdom, the training undertaken internally by the mobile company can be supplemented by various programmes of assistance administered by the Manpower Services Commission of the Department of Employment.[12] These include the schemes organised on an industry basis by twenty-three industrial training boards, coordinated by the Training Services Agency of the Commission; the Training Opportunities Schemes, run in fifty-five special government training centres and within companies, and a range of direct services, including the provision of mobile instructors to train people on the premises of the employer, the training of the firm's own instructors, the training of experienced workers on instructional techniques, and the training of supervisors. In addition the Employment Services Agency of the Commission provides financial assistance to companies for key workers moving to the new plant, and also for training recruits from the new area back at the parent factory (under the nucleus labour force scheme). [13]

Public funds for industrial training come from both Federal and state sources in the United States. Prior to 1973 at the Federal level funds for institutional and on-the-job training were available nationwide under the Department of Labor. In redevelopment areas this would be supplemented by programmes under the Area Redevelopment Act of 1961, organised since 1965 by the Economic Development Administration (EDA). This included operating funds for training institutions built with the Agency's public works support; the aim being to upgrade the skills of the unemployed and to retain workers with obsolescent skills. The EDA did not have a separate manpower budget, however, and the lack of investment in human resources, particularly in Appalachia, relative to expenditures on roads was criticised (N.M. Hansen, 1974, pp.291–2). With the passage of the Comprehensive Employment and Training Act (CETA) in 1973, the separate programme for redevelopment areas ended.[14]   CETA was an attempt to decentralise and decategorise manpower programmes by unifying the federally supported programmes, by freeing city, county and state budgets from fund-matching, and by leaving the design of programmes to state and local levels to meet local requirements, the programmes to be funded by federal block grants to some 500 local and state 'prime sponsors'. The local programmes can be closely tied in with efforts to attract mobile industry.[15]

CETA encourages state and local programmes using local funds, to be planned in coordination with activities funded by the federal block grant. Most states have had vocational training programmes for many years, and in many instances these programmes can be closely tailored to the needs of an incoming industrial plant. For example, Hunker (1974, p.124) describes the success of the South Carolina programme which relieves a new company of the cost on in-plant or on-the-job training. Looking to the future, Hunker (1974, p.126) forsees ' . . . further development and improvement of state supported training programs as but another factor in helping to reduce regional variations in labor costs'.

In both countries a lack of knowledge of the training facilities offered by both central government and the local authorities in destination areas of mobile firms well away from a familiar home base may slow up the growth and development of those firms. A report on training for mobile industry in North East England suggested that it took up to 6 or 7 years for the external education and training facilities to be fully appreciated and used by companies new to the area (H.C. Baker, 1969).

Notes

[1] This difficulty was voiced by managers in the earlier Townroe survey (1971, p.91).

[2] The civil service unions have opposed the transfer of civil servants from London for example, in response to the Hardman report on the dispersal of government offices (Hardman, 1973).

[3] The move from a large city to a small country town increased the level of dependence of the employees on the company. Any trouble is therefore magnified (M. Mann, 1973, p.194). Similar issues are discussed in a case history of the move of a General Foods plant within the United States (E.S. Whitman and W.J. Schmidt, 1966).

[4] Central government factory estates up to the end of 1975 were the responsibility of the English, Scottish and Welsh Industrial Estates Corporation, controlled and financed by the Department of Industry.

[5] The programme has recently been accelerated. The total floor-space area accounted for by these public sectors advance units and custom built units, both let and available to let now totals approximately 75 million square feet.

[6] Building grants towards own construction were a major location factor for 49 per cent of the firms and a minor factor for a further 13 per cent.

[7] Assistance for transferred workers for companies moving to the assisted areas in the UK includes settling-in grants, separation and disturbance allowances, and allowances for travel and removal expenses.

[8] Trade union concern about the terms of the move was especially strong in the case of the W.H. Smith move because of an associated restructuring of wage rates (B.J. Loasby, 1973, p.42).

[9] 205 out of 970 employees in the Swindon move; 65 per cent of the male manual staff and 85 per cent of the male salaried staff in the Banbury move.

[10] In her study of the provisions British local government authorities make for new industry, Camina (1974, p.107) found that 60 per cent offer public housing for key workers.

[11] In the General Foods move, because of delays in opening the new plant, the number of employees commuting from Banbury to Birmingham reached 700. This caused considerable dissatisfaction among transferred employees (M.Mann, 1973, pp.117—19).

[12] Established under the 1973 Employment and Training Act.

[13] Further details are given in Central Office of Information (1976,

pp.30—3).

[14] The history of these measures is briefly outlined by S.A. Levitan and J.K. Zickler (1976, pp.76—8) and N.M. Hansen (1976, pp.93—6).

[15] Hansen (1976, chapter 6) describes the general problems of organising a CETA programme in non-metropolitan areas, using a case study of Tennessee, focussing on one development district: Upper Cumberland. He concludes: '. . . although CETA does not represent a panacea for the vast range of manpower problems in non-metropolitan areas, Tennessee experience indicates that with the cooperation of federal and state government, local planning can, given strong leadership and a spirit of cooperation among local elected officials, be effective in formulating and implementing integrated area development and man-power service programmes'. (1975, p.115)

[16] Supplemented in turn by county and city programmes. The efforts of Utica are described as one of the five case studies of the Committee for Economic Development (1966).

8 Experience after the move

A new plant in a new location, just as much as an old plant, will suffer when it is managed badly or when the demand for its product fluctuates wildly or when additional costs and duties are imposed upon it from outside. But a new plant is also vulnerable in a number of ways because it is new. This vulnerability appears to be reflected in the statistics on the closures of plants in new locations. In the United Kingdom, more than 4,000 branch plant and transfer moves took place between sub-regions in the period 1945—65; by the end of 1966, 953 had closed down again. Of 1,600 moves between sub-regions in the period 1966—71, 140 had closed by the end of 1972 (see Figure 4.3).

The true relative vulnerability of new plants compared with long standing establishments cannot be assessed in the absence of reliable statistics of the rates of closure in all plants generally in UK manufacturing industry. But the proportion closing does seem high enough to be a cause for concern by regional policy administrators as well as being some sort of reflection of particular managerial pressures and problems. Sant (1975a, pp.101—9 and 1975b) has calculated the age specific closure rates from the 1945—66 figures, and he finds that closure is relatively uncommon in the earliest years of the life of a new plant. However, the rate rises sharply until in the fifth year after opening something over 2·5 per cent of the plants in the cohort close. This high rate continues in each of the years up to the ninth year, after which the annual rate falls to about 1·5 per cent. Branch plants do not seem to be more prone to closure than transfer moves, and are substantially less prone to closure in the assisted areas in the 1966—71 period (P.M. Townroe, 1975, p.54). Branch plants, contrary to some expectations, were found by Atkins (1973, pp.437—9) to be no more vulnerable in assisted area locations than in non-assisted areas.

The reasons for closures of mobile plants are difficult to determine, given that there is no one left behind to answer survey questions. Clearly the reasons will include higher than planned unit costs or a failure to reduce costs sufficiently as the plant is run-in. Liquidity problems may be particularly important for smaller firms (Z. Malinowski and W. Kinnard, 1963, p.108), particularly for a small transfer move caught in a credit squeeze. O'Farrell's study of the closure experience of plants in the Republic of Ireland[1] related closure to a number of plant variables. He concluded (1976, p.445) that the chance of survival is a linear function of increasing size but he could not find any relationship with the category of industry, the nationality of origin, the organisational type or area of location within Ireland or to the town size of the chosen site.

Keeble's (1968) study of firms moving from North West London between 1940 and 1964 showed that those locating more than 100 miles from London were twice as likely to close as those staying closer to the metropolis: a 20 per cent closure rate compared with 9 per cent. This importance of distance is supported by the Sant (1975b, p.366) analysis of the Department of Trade and Industry statistics for the period up to 1960. But in the 1966—71 group of movers, he shows (1975b, p.367) that the highest relative closure rates are to be found among those firms which move between sub-regions within the same region. These are frequently smaller firms, moving away from the benefits of their previous familiar location, but not moving far enough to obtain the benefit of regional economic policies. Of twenty-one branch plants closing in Luttrell's study (1962, p.337), nine closed because of recession and five in part because of location. Location was a predominant reason for only one closure. These results strengthen the contention that many initial post-move problems are more functions of inadequate managerial skills than anything else (P.M. Townroe, 1971, pp.91—2 and 97—100).

In this chapter we consider four different aspects of the experience of new plants in the first five years or so after the date of establishment: the build-up period to full output and planned levels of efficiency; the changes over time in the access of the new plant to markets, supplies and to services; experience in labour relations and labour turnover; and changes in managerial surveillance and delegation. The chapter concludes with a brief reference to stability and subsequent investment in the new plant, and a comparison of moving and staying plants.

The build-up to viability

There are three elements to the build-up of production in a new plant: (i) the attainment of initial production targets; (ii) the speed with which unit costs can be reduced to an anticipated break-even level; and (iii) how soon the plant can be deemed to be profitable for the company. There has been only one study of the build-up of production of new factories. In thirty-six cases Luttrell (1962, p.299) found that on average 37 per cent of the third year output level was achieved in the first year and 73 per cent in the second. There is some variation as in some firms a carefully staged build-up is planned while in others the management exerts maximum pressure to achieve the planned output levels as quickly as possible. No information is available on these details. More information is available on costs however.

In the 1972 Townroe survey (1976, pp.67–70), of 180 plants answering the question, 62 per cent agreed that their costs had been high by their own standards in the first three months of operations at the new location. High initial costs are, of course, to be expected: '. . . having some establishments working inefficiently because they are at the "running-in" stage is an inevitable cost of growth and economic change, and the extra dislocation caused by combining change of location with growth or change may not be very great' (A.J. Brown, 1972, p.279). Nevertheless, the faster a new plant manages to reduce unit costs, the more secure will be its future and the sooner the management will be able to think about expansion. Among Luttrell's comparisons of thirty-six branch plants and their parent establishments, unit costs in the first year in the branches were twice those in the parent establishments. These fell to 42 per cent higher in the second year and 15 per cent higher in the third year (W.F. Luttrell, 1962, p.298). For 35 per cent of the respondents in the Townroe survey costs began to fall between three and twelve months from the date of opening, although a fall had not occurred by the time of the interview for 46 per cent of those with high initial costs. Twenty per cent of respondents felt that they reached cost stability within the first year of operations, 30 per cent in the second year, and 25 per cent in the third and fourth years, the remainder taking more than four years. This cost stability came somewhat faster to the transfer and shorter distance moves than to the branch plant and larger distance moves. Costs fell for a number of reasons: finding new local suppliers and local services, running in new equipment and the reduction in avoidable overheads.[2] But the prime reason quoted by the majority of respondents was greater experience, both on the part of management and of labour.

The efficient use of labour is clearly the key to unit costs in a new plant. At the beginning, labour turnover is high, leading to high recruitment and training costs, and both the workforce and the supervisors lack experience. Fifteen per cent of the respondents suggested that better experience of the management was the prime reason for a fall in costs. In the Department of Trade and Industry survey (1973, p.633), 36 per cent of all respondents felt that labour costs per unit of output were lower than those experienced at the previous or parent location, and 32 per cent felt that they were higher. Forty-four per cent of moves to development areas had higher labour costs (cf. 31 per cent lower) but only 24 per cent of moves to new and expanding towns had higher labour costs (cf. 32 per cent lower). Both surveys point to lower labour costs in new locations in labour intensive industries, in short distance moves and in single plant companies.

Questions on costs in an interview survey can only yield broadly impressionistic answers. Respondents can be more exact, however, on the time taken from opening to break-even financially. For 168 plants in the 1972 survey, 34 per cent reached a break-even point within three months plus a further 21 per cent within twelve months. The longer the distance of the move, the longer it took to break-even. Transfers attained break-even faster than branch plants, perhaps due to shorter distances moved and to smaller average size, but also resulting from the pressure on liquidity and cash flow when there is no parent company to carry continuing losses. Profitability for those companies, using the standard of profitability normally used by the company involved, took longer to achieve: 38 per cent within a year, 57 per cent within two years. Again branch plants and longer distance moves took longer. Only 26 per cent of branch plants in the survey felt that they were achieving a return on capital better than their company average (P.M. Townroe, 1976, p.69).

A question which has frequently been asked in respect of British mobility of industry policy is whether mobile plants suffer a permanent cost disadvantage as a result of establishing the plant in a new location. This question is extremely difficult to answer with authority. We have seen in earlier chapters that companies will often choose distant locations for cost saving reasons: lower transport costs to serve a market, lower wages for the labour force, elements of subsidy from public authorities. Yet in the British situation there has been concern that those longer distance moves, 'forced' to the assisted areas by the industrial development certificate control or encouraged by the transitory elements of subsidy, will suffer a long term cost penalty.[3] This is a concern which might also arise in the area redevelopment programmes of the economics development administration in the United States. Luttrell's very detailed work on ninety-two branch plants in the immediate post World War II period in the UK suggested that any permanent cost disadvantage tends to be small and no firm evidence has yet emerged to counter this verdict[4] (W.F. Luttrell, 1962, pp.296–321). Long term high unit costs were found most often in those factories in which output levels remained well below the design potential (1962, p.325).

Access to local markets,
supplies and services

In chapter 3, reference was made to six studies (four British, two American)[5] all of which played down the importance of local linkages with suppliers, markets and services for the firms studied in general. For individual companies, of course, these local linkages may be profoundly important, especially as a restraining influence on movement out of an area. For another minority of firms, the possibility of establishing new local linkages will be a significant factor in the choice of location. Only two studies have examined the significance of new local linkages for recently mobile plants.

On the basis of two separate interview surveys, Moseley and Townroe (1973) found relatively small proportions of recently mobile companies taking up local linkages. For example, among two groups of 82 and 67 companies moving in the East Anglia region of the UK, only 32 per cent and 17 per cent were making more purchases in the region than pre-move. Among fifty-four firms in the Northern region (an assisted area) the proportion dropped to 11 per cent.[6] Analysis showed that new plants changing to more local sources of components and raw materials were concentrated in the engineering sector and were plants in which the product line had changed. Supply changes in general, when defined as being to both local and non-local sources, were significantly associated with plants having what was defined as 'non-routine and batch' production processes, with plants moving between twenty-five (the minimum in the survey) and 100 miles, and with 'forced movers' rather than moves which took place because of growth problems.

In the Department of Trade and Industry survey (1973, p.653), only 19 per cent of respondents did not 'largely rely' on the same source of materials and components as at the first location. Those firms more likely to rely on new sources included the longer (250 miles and over) distance movers, firms in the chemicals and mechanical engineering industries, and new plants of overseas origin and ownership. Single plant companies were very (90 per cent) likely to rely on previous sources of supply. Only 24 per cent of respondents obtained more than 50 per cent of materials and components from within forty miles of the new plant, while for 63 per cent of the new plants less than 20 per cent of requirements were obtained locally. Only 14 per cent of the firms could ' . . . at present, if the need arose, obtain at similar prices and qualities a larger part of supplies of materials and components from within forty miles' and only 13 per cent of the respondents thought it likely that the proportion of local purchases would rise in the future. In 20 per cent of the new plants (and in 33 per cent of those that were branch plants) more than 50 per cent of the input came from other plants of the same company. This proportion rose, as may be expected, among plants of larger companies (Department of Trade and Industry, 1973, pp.634–59. See also Rees, 1978a).

Table 3.5 shows that market forces were a major locational influence for only 30 per cent of the new plants in the British government survey. It is therefore not surprising to find that only 16 per cent of the respondents sold more than 50 per cent of their output within forty miles of the new plant, and 70 per cent of the firms sold less than 20 per cent of

their output within forty miles. The tendency to have a higher proportion of local outlets was higher among very short distance moves, as
may be expected. Only 12 per cent of the new plants supplied more
than 50 per cent of their output to other plants within the same
company (this rose to 19 per cent of branch plants). While of those
plants producing for final consumers (79 per cent were producing
intermediate goods for other industrial processes), only 12 per cent
served a regional market at most; the majority of plants were serving
national or international markets. In 23 per cent of the new plants the
new location was felt to have enabled entry into a new geographical
market. These proportions would be likely to be significantly higher
among industrial movers in the United States (Department of Trade and
Industry, 1973, pp.660–4).

The study of Economic Consultants Ltd of firms in South East
England showed (1971, p.6) that sub-contracting was regional rather
than local. Among the mobile companies of the British government
survey, 37 per cent said that they put work out on sub-contract to
other firms within forty miles. This proportion rose among new plants
in the mechanical and electrical engineering sector, among labour
intensive plants, among short moves and among plants originating overseas. Sub-contracting by new plants was less common among capital
intensive, branch plants, and larger distance moves. Only 10 per cent of
the firms not putting out local sub-contract work said that it was
because there were no suitable firms locally (Department of Trade and
Industry, 1973, pp.657–8). In the Townroe 1972 survey, 27 per cent
of 117 firms moving more than twenty-five miles changed to more local
sources of supply of services of all sorts (including legal, financial and
technical services as well as sub-contracting).

In both the US and the UK the fear has been expressed that an undue
concentration of branch plants in a local or regional economy, attracted
there by public incentives, fails to build up allied sectors through the
development of local linkages, as compared with a more balanced build-
up of both branch plants and transfers together with indigenous
industry. In Tennessee, for example:

> A number of officials even fear that encouraging northern owned
> branch plants to enter the state will weaken Tennessee's develop-
> ment. According to this argument, firms owned in New York,
> Chicago, Pittsburgh and other northern metropolitan centers are
> not hiring local engineers and architects, and home grown middle
> management is not being developed. Moreover, marketing and
> advertising services are imported, profits are exported, and local
> resource employment is generally neglected (N.M. Hansen, 1973,
> p.96).

Statistical support for these statements is not available, and British evidence on branch plant linkages would not support these fears. Local 'spin-off' from new branch plants does not seem to be so very different to that from newly transferred plants; ' . . . concern at an over concentration of branch plant establishments with few local linkages would be warranted only if a very strong contrast existed with the transferred plants. This strong contrast does not exist.' (P.M. Townroe, 1975a, p. 59).

Labour relations and labour turnover

A learning process can be expected to take place in a new plant between the new employees and the management. The employees have to decide if they find the work tasks and conditions to be adequately satisfying, while the management has to adapt to what may be new employee attitudes and to perhaps a new technology and new required styles of working. This mutual adaptation on both sides of the labour market may be expected to result in high but declining rates of labour turnover in the early years of life in the new plant. However this supposition is not entirely borne out by the evidence.

The British government survey shows that labour turnover experience in recently established plants is very mixed. For 29 per cent of the responding firms labour turnover was higher than at the previous location, while it was lower for 41 per cent and the same for 30 per cent. These figures conceal considerable variation by region however, and higher turnover seemed to be particularly likely among two groups of firms: the longer distance branch plant moves to the assisted areas, and the short distance (up to fifty miles) transfer moves (Department of Trade and Industry, 1973, p.628). In the 1972 Townroe survey a distinction was made between the first year and then subsequently. In the first year labour turnover was higher for 34 per cent of the branch plants (and 44 per cent of branch plants employing 150 or more) and for 22 per cent of the transfers; but was lower in 45 per cent of branches and 56 per cent of transfer (P.M. Townroe, 1975b, p.341). This conflicts with the trial and error adjustment theory. A move may heighten managerial effort and the expectations of employees: a point that is reinforced by the favourable figures for transfer moves, except the short distance transfers in which the existing pre-move employees may be taken too much for granted in the new location. Worries about high labour turnover did however drop significantly in successive years in the life of the new plants (1975b, p.342).

The same survey also showed that high rates of labour turnover tended to be found in those plants exhibiting indicators of stress. These included closely associated problems such as in the area of labour training and labour costs, but also the more fundamental of a low return on capital. High labour turnover also seemed to be a problem in plants with older first managers rather than younger (perhaps surprisingly); and in plants in which the resident management did not have responsibility for all management functions (i.e. wages, hire and fire, purchasing, marketing, etc.) (P.M. Townroe, 1975b, p.342). This finding lends strength to the argument that area development policies must seek to attract plants with all managerial functions rather than just production plants supervised from elsewhere. Recruiting managerial staff locally in order that the plant may be in touch with the local labour relations environment does not ensure low labour turnover, as might have been expected. But high turnover does associate with organisational change early in the life of the new plant, seeming to suggest a managerial and supervisory problem.

Labour turnover rates are one indicator of the climate of labour relations in a new plant. One might expect labour relations to be worse in the new plant compared with the home base if the move is over a long distance to a local environment very different from that previously experienced, particularly by branch plant moves with weak supervision. This expectation is in part supported by the British government survey evidence (Department of Trade and Industry, 1973, p.635). Labour relations were better in the new location for 26 per cent of those firms, the same for 60 per cent and worse for 14 per cent. But relations were better for only 19 per cent of branch plant moves over 150 miles, and worse for 20 per cent. One interesting contrast in this survey is that moves from origins in the West Midlands experienced a more than average deterioration in labour relations, while those moving from Greater London experienced a better than average improvement.

Some local environments on the other hand do seem to be conducive to an improvement in labour relations. This is often felt to be one argument for a company to establish its new plant in a rural area. For example, Hansen (1973, p.74) refers to a consultants' study in non-metropolitan Minnesota and Wisconsin:

> All company spokesmen felt that both the supply and the productivity of non-metropolitan labor were good. Non-metropolitan workers were said to be more appreciative of jobs and to bring a better work attitude to the plant. Farmers and farm wives especially were praised for good work habits. Most of the companies experienced less turnover and less absenteeism in their non-metropolitan branch plants . . . . Only one company executive ranked metropolitan workers generally higher than non-

metropolitan workers.

This experience is somewhat countered however by the admitted difficulties with productivity in rural Mississippi until the largely black labour force acquired the relevant job skills (N.M. Hansen, 1973, p.107).

Does the presence of strong labour unions in the new local area and/or within the new plants help or hinder good labour relations? The 1972 Townroe survey (1975b, p.343) suggests that the influence is not strong either way, especially in the transfer moves.[7] Also, no strong evidence could be found for a link between union representation in the new plant and the speed of build-up and time taken to break-even and profit. Therefore the findings in Mann's case study (1973, p.193), that the increased social dependence of transferred employees on their employers will result in higher rates of trade union membership, are not to be feared or resisted by the management of the relocated plant.

Managerial surveillance
and delegation

The issue of the control of branch plants and the allocation of responsibilities to branch plant management has already been touched upon. It is one more factor which can influence the success of the build-up period in the new plant. There are essentially three issues here: (i) the degree of delegation of decision making powers, both in routine or operational areas or in strategic or developmental areas; (ii) the control exercised by a parent company or headquarters over the delegated powers; and, (iii) the timing of the transition towards greater delegation as the new plant becomes firmly established. These are all essentially managerial housekeeping questions, but it is sometimes felt that lack of authority within many new branch units in an area will in time reduce that area to the status of a 'branch plant economy', with associated notions of lack of autonomy and susceptibility to swings in the external economic climate.

The 1972 Townroe survey (1975a, pp.49–52) included seventy-five branch plants, established in the 1966–68 period in East Anglia and the Northern region of the United Kingdom, and which had moved at least twenty-five miles. Of the total, twenty-eight at the time of the interview held all the prime operational managerial functions: labour hire and fire, determining wage levels, purchasing and marketing. Two more held everything except purchasing; sixteen more everything except marketing. The range of managerial functions given to the branch did not increase with the size of the plant but did, in general, increase with the distance of the move. The delegation was significantly higher in plants producing goods to customers' orders or in small batches, and in plants with a younger rather than older first manager. The greater the degree of delegation, the faster the plant built up to full production and then subsequent expansion. The survey did not investigate how closely the parent managements supervised these delegated powers, but it did show relatively little movement towards greater delegation (no change in forty-five plants) than that decided at the outset of operations. Luttrell's study (1962, p.155) refers to cases of inadequate control over, and assistance to, branch managers. These seemed to result partly from poor record keeping in the branch plant plus inadequate monitoring, and then from an insufficient response by managers in the parent plant when troubles occurred. Luttrell (1962, pp.156–7) lays great stress on the significance of visits by senior managers to the new plants.

In the area of strategic or long term decision making, reception areas of mobile industry might be concerned that local growth would be lost if local managements are unable to take significant investment decisions. [8] The evidence for this concern is unclear. No evidence was found in the 1972 survey of a link between the degree of delegation of authority to a branch plant manager and to the level of investment undertaken in the new establishment after the initial financial commitment. Of sixty respondents forty-one branch plant managements could not spend more than £1,000 without an examination by the parent plant of the reasons for the expenditure. This might be felt to support local fears of a lack of discretion in the new plant. However, 'It was found that the level of capital expenditure a local manager could allocate without reference to a parent (other than formal notification) was much more closely related to the management structure of the company as a whole, and the type of accounting and financial reporting system used, than to the size of the branch or the parent or to the problems encountered by the branch or to the industrial process characteristics of the plant' (P.M. Townroe, 1975a, p.51). Rees (1978b), in his Dallas-Fort Worth study could find little evidence for the external control argument either. This is an area in which local sensitivities in both the United States and the United Kingdom will encourage further research.

Further investment

Expansion of capacity is a dominant reason for companies undertaking a movement. Therefore a plant that is successfully established in a new location may find fairly quickly that further expansion is desirable. The speed with which this can happen will normally depend upon the time taken for the build-up to full production and to reach financial viability on the original investment. But since mobile plants are

199

concentrated in the growing sectors of manufacturing industry, vigorous post-move growth is to be expected.

The evidence on the speed and scale of post-move investment is limited. Some indication comes from the 1972 survey. Among the twenty-nine plants in that survey moving to the Northern region (P.M. Townroe and R. Morley, 1974, pp.29–30) contacted between four and six years later, only seven employed fewer than the initial planning target and over half the plants, large and small, had already committed as much in subsequent investment as in the initial investment. The total employment in those plants at the time of the interview was 60 per cent up on the total planned initial employment. Among the British government survey firms (opening the new plant between two and five years previously), 26 per cent had extended their production floor space by 50 per cent or more of the originals by the time of the interview; 56 per cent reported no change. Expansion was found particularly among overseas owned plants, while no change was found particularly among short distance transfers (many of which, as we saw earlier would not have moved for growth reasons) (Department of Trade and Industry, 1973, p.649). In some companies, this growth may have been the result of a phased move, an initial branch plant unit perhaps turning into a transfer move as the parent plant is closed down at its original location (D.H.W. Atkins, 1973, p.439).

After the initial building period, a mobile firm or plant may of course no longer be regarded as being in the 'mobile' category but rather as now being in the 'indigenous' sector. It is perhaps rather obvious (sic) to point out that the more successful an area development policy is in attracting new plants to locate within the designated region, then the more important it becomes to have a set of area development policy instruments which focus as much on the encouragement of the growth of indigenous plants as on the attraction of yet more externally based mobile plants.

Further expansion will be hindered by poor locational choice initially and then by poor management of the build-up period as well as by adverse exogenous economic factors. Cooper (1975, p.92), for example, found that 60 per cent of his sample of firms were affected in some degree by expected and unexpected difficulties. These difficulties included: government policy requirements in the assisted areas, inadequate provision of services and buildings, inadequate transport provision, and changes in the character of the labour force. Neither Cooper or any other investigator has managed to show, however, that establishing a plant in a new location will result in one specific problem or set of problems which hinder subsequent growth; nor that more than a minority of mobile plants are seriously affected by such problems. General satisfaction is generally the outcome of a move. Of 631 firms in the British government survey, only 10 per cent replied 'No' when asked: 'On balance are you satisfied with the development you undertook at the new location?' It was too early to say for 11 per cent, but 79 per cent could answer 'Yes' (Department of Trade and Industry, 1973, p.667).

Changes in plant characteristics

If certain conditions within a company act as a 'trigger' for a move, the new plant should be an improvement over the pre-transfer or the parent -of-the-branch establishment. Schmenner's results allow a comparison of 'before and after' profiles of mover plants (1978, p.4–81–4–95).

In both New England and Cincinnati both the plant area and the employment increased for a majority of relocations, although in large plants in New England the average square footage per worker fell. The movers in the survey also tended to show increased complexity: more products, additional corporate functions and greater self-containedness in transfers of plants in multiplant companies. The capital-labour ratio rose, frequently resulting from new production technologies, although 'Only after the need for additional space surfaces does the opportunity the move presents to alter production appear to achieve prominence in corporate thought.' (R.W. Schmenner, 1978, p.4–93). The new plants were much more likely to be single storey units (up from one-third to over three-quarters in New England), not to be built by the company (under one-half) and to be sited in an industrial park or estate (up to one-half of the smaller plants and one-third of the larger plants).

Other results of these comparisons indicate a broadening of markets, while retaining the bulk of both former customers and suppliers; an improvement in transport access; and improved labour availability and skills. Specific site costs, including rents and taxes did not show a significant change. Unionisation remained the same.

In the Cincinnati sample, 26 per cent of these transfer moves involved combining the operations of two or more plants of the company, nearly three times the number of stationary establishments absorbing the operations of other plants. This consolidation role of a large minority of transfer moves seems to be primarily part of an effort by the company involved to retrench. For plants in a similar subgroup in the New England moves compared to other movers, move further, grow less rapidly, have falling profits and move to sites with lower prevailing wage levels and tax rates (R.W. Schmenner, 1978, p.4–91). Schmenner's studies clearly show that the nature of the post-move experience will depend very much upon the corporate strategy being followed when the move was initiated. This relationship was not investigated in the British studies quoted.

Notes

[1]   An analysis of 418 plants established between 1960 and 1973 and in receipt of funds from the Irish Industrial Development Authority. The mean annual closure rate was 2·6 per cent, and maximum rate was 4·6 per cent in 1965. Closure rates were not time dependent, as in the Sant results in Britain (P.N. O'Farrell, 1976, pp.433–48).

[2]   In Luttrell's thirty-six comparisons, overhead costs in the branch plants were nearly three times as high as in the parent company in the first year of life of the branch. This fell to 80 per cent higher in the second year and 30 per cent higher in the third year (W.F. Luttrell, 1962, p.300).

[3]   As argued by a number of large British companies giving evidence to a House of Commons Select Committee (Expenditure Committee, 1973).

[4]   Linked to Luttrell's work detailed cost studies were undertaken on the UK radio and clothing industries. See D.C. Hague and P.K. Newman (1952) and D.C. Hague and J.H. Dunning (1954).

[5]   Department of Trade and Industry, 1973; Economic Consultants Ltd, 1971; W. Lever, 1974; M.J. Moseley and P.M. Townroe, 1973; A. Hamer, 1973; and M. Segal, 1960. J. Rees (1978a) obtained information on backward linkages for 33 acquisitions and 15 new branch plant in Dallas-Fort Worth, finding changes in linkages only in the branch plants and then mainly in intra-company transactions.

[6]   The wording of the question was slightly different in the two surveys, as was the nature of the sampled firms (M.J. Moseley and P.M. Townroe, 1973, p.139).

[7]   The Department of Trade and Industry survey included new plants with overseas ownership among the group tending to worsen labour relations (1973, p.635). Forsyth found that American companies in Scotland experienced more strikes per employee in 1964, 1966 and 1969 than did indigenous firms (1973, p.26), although Gennard and Steur (1971, p.157) showed that foreign owned subsidies in general in the UK had fewer strikes than domestic companies in the years 1963 and 1968.

[8]   J.R. Firn (1975, pp.393–414). Dicken (1976) has clarified the concept of external control, agreeing with Rees (1978b) that the effective impact of external control depends very much on the strategy and organisational structure of each company concerned. He concludes (p. 405) ' . . . there is a real need for much more substantive empirical work to confirm or refute the deduced effects of external control.'

9 Summary and conclusions

This review of the literature on industrial movement in the United States and the United Kingdom has concentrated on major sources only. Potentially significant contributions among theses, consultants reports and internal central, state and local government documents have not been included. Important local studies with more than local relevance may therefore have been missed, especially in the American literature. The review has also been restricted to the British definition of industrial movement i.e. focussing on the opening of new plants, both new branch plants and complete relocations. Only limited use has been made of literature which examines aggregate industrial changes by geographical area. This has cut out many references, especially from the United States. This final chapter briefly summarises some of the principal themes of the earlier chapters before suggesting potentially profitable avenues for further research into industrial movement in both countries.

Industrial movement and urban growth

Certain common trends in the pattern of industrial movement in both countries have emerged over the past thirty years or so. Manufacturing industry, a declining sector in terms of employment in both economies, has been decentralising out of the cities, both leading and following a suburbanisation of population. This process has gone further at lower densities in the United States than in the United Kingdom for reasons of a lower transportation cost to average income ratio in the US and stronger restraints of land use planning policy in the UK. This decentralisation process has been shifting its focus in the 1970s towards the non-metropolitan hinterland areas in the United States, firms now moving further out than the suburbs of metropolitan areas to intermediate sized centres between the major cities. Similar forces seem to be present in the UK, although there is not such a clear cut shift as compared with the 1950s and early 1960s.

Some new towns and many expanding town schemes have been developing in British non-metropolitan areas since the late 1950s. Elements of the assisted area regional development programme have always been focussed on smaller centres (such as some of the government owned factory estates). Also with the relatively stagnant state of the British economy in the early 1970s, there has been a sharp drop in the total volume of industry choosing new locations. Figure 9.1 devised by Keeble (1977, p.308), illustrates the shift in locational preferences of manufacturing industry which will in turn be reflected in the pattern of destinations of mobile industrial plants.

In both countries, although more recently in the UK, concern has been expressed at the decline of the inner metropolitan areas as both sources of manufacturing employment in general and sources of manufacturing industrial moves (branches and transfers) in particular. The inner areas of large cities in both countries no longer seem to be the 'seed beds' they once were, although longitudinal evidence is scarce. Given the rise of service industry employment, it is unclear to what degree this inner area manufacturing decline should be regarded as a social and economic problem in itself, although it clearly links to, and possibly contributes to, other agreed symptoms of urban malaise.

The movement of offices in both countries has been rather different to that of manufacturing plants. As redevelopment has taken place within city centres many office employees have moved very locally from older premises to the new buildings, (and there is very little information on the downtown 'readjustment' process). A certain amount of movement has also taken place of white collar units between American large city centres, primarily of the headquarters of large corporations, but also of new branches of banks, finance houses etc. This movement has been much less common between the largest British cities. In both countries studies of mobile office industry have focussed upon decentralisation, both to suburban complexes and office parks and further out to intermediate sized centres within the metropolitan commuting hinterland. This is a continuing pattern of moves. In the United Kingdom, the central government has been (and will continue to be under present plans) a significant contributor to this decentralisation, and to the less common longer distance office moves, primarily from London to the assisted areas. In the United States it is felt that both federal and state government relocation to, and expansion of, activities in non-Washington and non-metropolitan locations must also have been significant in the past fifteen years or so, but the patterns of this movement have not been defined.

As the discussion of the evidence in chapters 2, 3 and 4 made clear, there can now be considerable agreement as to the principal factors involved in encouraging industrial movement to take place; and some agreement about their general ranking and how this ranking might change for different categories of moves. Certain differences were suggested between the two countries in the push factors. These include the greater significance of public policy measures in the UK (the industrial development certificate system, and possible local land use

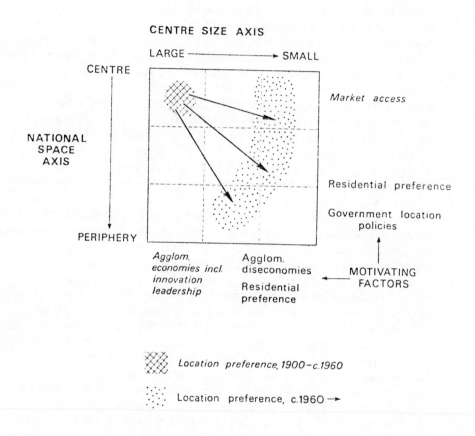

CENTRE SIZE AXIS

LARGE ——————→ SMALL

CENTRE

NATIONAL
SPACE
AXIS

PERIPHERY

Market access

Residential preference

Government location
policies

Agglom.
economies incl.
innovation
leadership

Agglom.
diseconomies

Residential
preference

← MOTIVATING
FACTORS
↑

Location preference, 1900–c.1960

Location preference, c.1960 →

Figure 9.1 Location Preference Matrix

Source: D.E. Keeble, Industrial geography, *Progress in Human Geography*, 1(2), 1977, p.308.

controls); and the possible stronger influences in the United States of urban environmental decay (including crime) and of local industrial taxation differences. But in both countries the central pressure is growth and the need for additional floorspace, associated with a more general re-evaluation of the locational requirements of a company that accompanies planning for growth.

Similar broad agreement can be found in the survey and the regression evidence on the locational attraction factors, again with the rankings changing for different categories of move. Longer distance moves in both countries are more influenced by considerations of new market access and transportation and/or the financial inducement of public policy; shorter distance moves by continuing existing linkages of access to markets, supplies and services and to an existing labour force (or more generally to a known labour environment). In all moves, the factor of labour ranks high, in terms of supply, quality, attitudes and training. The lower the national rates of unemployment, the more significant this factor will be. Differences in wage rates are more important for long distance moves in the US than in the UK, where national wage bargaining in a sector or a company is more common. But geographical differences in unit wage costs, reflecting differences in labour productivity, are important in both countries, although perhaps more as a determinant of the speed and extent of subsequent growth in the new location than for the choice of the location initially.

The nature of the relationship between these patterns and pressures in industrial movement and the resulting patterns of urban growth and change has not been examined in this review, other than in general references. However, it seems safe to suggest that in both countries the patterns of industrial movement, as defined for this survey will not be so important as an influence on urban growth in the near future as they have been in the recent past. In both countries the rate of population increase is slowing; the job search element in household imigration is possibly becoming less important relative to 'quality of life' factors; national imigration trends are being heavily influenced by retirement imigrations, especially in the US; the regional economies are in general (with a few significant exceptions) becoming more balanced in their industrial structures; and both economies seem to be moving towards an era of consistently higher average unemployment rates. These changes in turn have implications for area economic development policies.

Industrial movement and
regional development

In both the United States and the United Kingdom the perception of

206

'regional problems' is rather different in the mid-1970s as compared with the mid-1960s. Although certain regions of each country still have the long term problems associated with high rates of structural unemployment, these problems are becoming increasingly identified with more localised smaller areas, even to the scale of areas within those cities previously regarded as uniformly prosperous when judged on the basis of regional aggregates. In both countries, the problems of relative imbalance in the spatial patterns of social and economic welfare have become more diffuse across the national space economy. Broad brush policies of regional incentives and regional commissions may be less relevant in the future than more selective assistance by central and state governments to designated local sectors of industry and to local public authorities. At this scale national policies to influence the locational choices of manufacturing industry may be less important than hitherto; irrespective of the fact that the pool of mobile manufacturing industry is anyway likely to be smaller than in recent past.

One possible exception to this local focus of area development policies where both central governments may wish to exercise considerable influence over locational choice, may be the inflow of overseas investments in manufacturing. This has been an important contribution to regional development in the UK in the past, particularly in Scotland and Northern Ireland. Such investment has been growing in the United States, as the balance of labour costs has changed, particularly against Japan and Western Germany; and as non-US companies seek the multinational stance of their US owned rivals. Many states (Pennsylvania, Maryland, South Carolina, California, Washington, for example) have actively sought investment from outside the US with some success.

In both countries area economic development initiatives from local government administrations have been increasing. In the UK these efforts have been encouraged by the reorganisation of local government and the devolution of powers and responsibilities, particularly to Scotland and Wales (Northern Ireland has had its own powers to encourage industrial development for many years). In the US the acceptance by local governments of responsibilities and organisation which allows them to receive assistance from the Economic Development Administration and under the Central Employment and Training Act has accompanied local efforts at industrial promotion, often using industrial bonds and offering tax concessions. The local initiatives in both countries involve considerable competition and they potentially waste resources. Not all the officials involved realise the changing national environment within which they are being forced to operate. This is particularly true of the perceptions of the size of the pool of mobile industry.

The literature reviewed in chapters 6, 7 and 8 had two objectives, which sometimes have overlapped. The first was to seek empirically a greater understanding of the ways in which location decisions are taken, and of the early experience of companies in new plants. These studies provide an empirical reaction to many of the assumptions used in deductive theories of location as well as one form of empirical test of the predictions of those theories. They link locational choice to locational growth and decline, and link into a wider perception of the industrial firm as an organisation undergoing internal change while subject to external pressures. These studies have set the choice of a new plant site into its context of a wider investment decision which in turn relates to a longer term corporate strategy. In doing this, these studies have redirected considerable research attention away from locational choice towards a focus upon the spatial interactions of the company (rather than just the plant) and its socio-economic environment.[1] This is a recognition that the space economy of any developed industrial nation is dominated by relatively few large corporate organisations. Changes in plant locations therefore may be seen as an expression of the corporate strategies of these large companies, or as a reaction to the same by smaller competitors.

The second objective of the study of managerial processes and outputs related to industrial movement is more normative than the first. This objective, in turn, has two aspects to it. By the accumulation of a greater knowledge of how locational decisions are made and of how a new plant establishes itself in its new environment, critiques of public policies which seek to influence those decisions and the success of the subsequent growth will be more informed. So revisions made to the existing policy instruments and the specification of new instruments should be able to produce a policy package that is more effective in achieving specified goals and is more efficient in terms of increasing general socio-economic welfare. The resource costs of the policy may be lower, and such costs as are incurred may be more clearly set against the benefits gained.

Public policies which influence the industrial movement process do so by encouraging or forcing changes in managerial behaviour and decisions. Such changes may in part be induced merely by the provision of information to the relevant managers, information which would not otherwise be a part of the decision. The findings of the studies reviewed in chapters 6, 7 and 8 may also have this information serving function, thereby answering a normative objective of improving the efficiency with which a company takes decisions in relation to location and allied matters (efficiency being defined in relation to the company and its profits alone). As was argued in chapter 6, the decision on a site for a new plant is not a common decision in most companies, and is even less common for an individual manager within a company. There tends to be considerable uncertainty as to relevant procedures: there are few precedents to fall back upon. It is unclear as to what information is relevant and how the information sought should be evaluated. The links between the location decisions and related areas of planning and decision making are ill-defined. Information on how other companies have approached the movement process is therefore of considerable value. The total collective experience of a large number of companies provides guidelines for both problem avoidance and improved efficiency. This second use of industrial movement studies, as an input into managerial knowledge and technology, is less common in both the United States and the United Kingdom than the use made of the research for the purposes of formulating public policy.

Future directions for
research activity

At a number of points in the preceeding eight chapters, reference has been made to gaps in the knowledge provided by the existing literature on industrial movement. At one or two points, a specific comment emerged on the need for additional research. This final section will do no more than point to some general directions for useful future research activity in both the United States and the United Kingdom.

As pointed out in the Introduction, the direction of research on industrial movement in both countries has depended crucially on two things. One is the enthusiasm of individuals and large organisations to sponsor and/or undertake sample interview surveys. The second is the availability of sources of relevant secondary data. Undoubtedly British research, both empirical and conceptual, has been given a big boost by the availability since 1968 of figures collected by the government of the full pattern of inter-subregional industrial movement. Likewise, in the United States the recent availability of the even better Dun and Bradstreet establishment information has provided new avenues for research. New sources of data which allow the monitoring of industrial establishment over time[2] will greatly increase the potential range and depth of industrial movement studies.

In both countries, at the metropolitan scale further work is required on the link between local industrial movement and the birth and death of firms continuing studies such as those on Glasgow and Boston referred to in chapter 2. In particular, the role of local agglomeration economies, local labour markets and local land use planning policies is unclear. The importance of labour as a location factor, discovered in existing surveys, also suggests the need for more attention to the relevance of the nature of a local labour market to a mobile firm, as well as the size of that market. In particular, the occupational structure and the local wage structure may be more important in locational choice and certainly in subsequent growth than previously suspected. The relative efficiency of the labour input in different parts of both countries will also be an important determinant of subsequent growth rates.

Also at the metropolitan scale, relatively little is known about the mobility of offices outside of London and New York. Other than in general terms, it is not known what sort of companies or parts of companies are centralising, what prompts moves out beyond the suburbs, whether labour supply is as important a factor elsewhere as Quante suggests it is in New York, and whether public sector organisations respond to the same locational pressures as office-type companies in the private sector. Looking further ahead, improvements in all manner of telecommunications may erode the apparent strength of forces of agglomeration in the office sector for downtown locations. This has obvious implications for land use planning, investment in mass transit etc. It is therefore somewhat surprising that the whole area of communication and information studies, related to locational choice and efficiency in performance, which has been pioneered in Sweden, and to some extent pursued in the United Kingdom, has yet to make any impact on industrial location research in the United States.

The shift in population growth to the non-metropolitan areas of the United States outlined in chapter 3, implies links to the destinations of mobile firms in both the manufacturing and service sector which have yet to be fully investigated. It is not clear why companies are establishing new plants in these locations (although existing studies would probably allow predictions which would be up to 70 per cent accurate). The experience of plants in these locations in terms of growth, efficiency and propensity to close, is unknown; as is the significance of local industrial development promotion and incentives in encouraging the trend. The impacts upon public spending and revenues of an immigrant industrial plant are also unknown. In terms of US policy, it will be important to investigate whether non-metropolitan movement is at the expense of socially deprived metropolitan locations and whether areas previously defined as being depressed are included in the extended decentralisation. Little is known about patterns of long distance industrial movement in the United States also: except by implication through studies of relative rates of growth and decline in different regions, states or countries. Therefore the origin to destination linkages which have been examined and modelled in the UK have not been identified in the US.

Examination of origin to destination linkages is the first step towards investigation of the corporate organisational parameters in industrial movement and locational choice. This is a research area which is starting to develop in both countries, linking movement to growth and decline decisions for individual plants within the management of multiplant firms, seeing the relationship between the geographical space of the company and its organisational space. There are implications here for understanding shifts in the space economy of both countries, and also for the design of instruments to influence locational behaviour as well as for the changes in locational forces which may be induced by significantly higher costs of energy in both countries.

The study of individual industrial moves within their corporate contexts also has two further implications for future research. The first is in the study of location decision making. As chapter 6 made clear, in both countries understanding has moved beyond lists and rankings of locational factors. The complexity and heterogeneity of location decision making has been revealed. Further studies of locational decision making behaviour might allow greater predictive power to emerge from relationships identified between behavioural attributes and outcomes of the decision, and would certainly allow more helpful prescriptions for companies faced with the need to choose a new plant site. Again such studies should assist in improved policy design.

The second implication of the realisation of the importance of the corporate context lies in the post-move experience studies. As implied in chapters 7 and 8, relatively little work has been undertaken on this theme, especially in the United States. Yet the full success of policies designed to influence locational behaviour only comes after a new plant has run up to full design production and efficiency levels. Problems which lengthen the running in period reduce the cost effectiveness of subsidies. The determinants of subsequent investment and expansion in the new plant, both corporate and locational, are known only in general terms. Perhaps understandably, very little is known about the reasons for the closure of the unsuccessful ventures.

In both countries the study of industrial movement is now beginning to be seen within the context of what is sometimes referred to as the 'components of change'. Arrivals and departures of firms to and from an area are only one part of changes in economic activity. Births and deaths, and more especially, expansions and contractions are of greater significance in many areas. However, fundamental changes in the industrial structure of an area, especially over short periods of time, both encouraged or resisted by public policy, are unlikely to take place without considerable industrial movement taking place. The subject of this review will continue to attract and deserve substantial resources for future research activity in both countries.

Notes

[1] A review of writings on industrial geography in 1975 and 1976 charts this trend (D.E. Keeble, 1977).
[2] These sources may include information originally collected for commercial purposes, as well as improved access for research workers to government data, such as the census of production. In both countries undertakings of confidentiality debar the identification of individual establishments or companies from government sources.

Bibliography of literature on industrial movement in the United Kingdom

Archibald, G.C., (1967), 'Regional multiplier effects in the UK', *Oxford Economic Papers*, 19, pp.22—45.

Ashcroft, B. and Taylor, J. (1977), 'The movement of manufacturing industry and the effect of regional policy', *Oxford Economic Papers*, 29 (1), pp.84—99.

Atkins, D.H.W. (1973), 'Employment change in branch and parent manufacturing plants in the UK: 1966—71', *Trade and Industry*, August 1973, pp.437—9.

Aucott, J.V. (1960), 'Dispersal of offices from London', *Town Planning Review*, 31.

Bale, J.R. (1973), 'Industrialists' attitudes towards location on industrial estates', *Tijdschrift voor Economische en Sociale Geografie*, 5, p. 320.

Baker, H.C. et al. (1969), *Location, Education and Training in Mobile Technological Industry: A Survey*, University of Durham Business School for the North East Development Council.

Bateman, M. and Burtenshaw, D. (1971), 'Office staff on the move', *Location of Offices Bureau Research Paper*, no.6.

Barlow Report (1940), *Royal Commission on the Distribution of the Industrial Population: Report*, Cmnd: 6153, HMSO, London.

Beacham, A. and Osborn, W.T. (1970), 'The movement of manufacturing industry', *Regional Studies*, 4 (3) pp.41—7.

Beesley, M. (1955), 'The birth and death of industrial establishments: experience in the West Midlands conurbation', *Journal of Industrial Economics*, 4 (1), pp.45—61.

Brown, A.J. (1969), 'Surveys of applied economics: regional economics, with special reference to the United Kingdom', *Economic Journal*, 79, no.316, pp.759—96.

Brown, A.J. (1972), *The Framework of Regional Economics in the United Kingdom*, Cambridge University Press, London.

Buck, T.W. and Atkins, M.H. (1976), 'Capital subsidies and unemployed labour, a regional production function approach', *Regional Studies*, 10 (2), pp.215—22.

Bull, P.J. (1978), 'The spatial components of intra-urban manufacturing change: suburbanisation in Clydeside, 1958—68', *Transactions of the Institute of British Geographers, New Series,* 3 (1), pp.92—100.

Burrows, E.M. (1973), 'Office employment and the regional problem', *Regional Studies,* 7 (1), pp.17—31.

Buswell, R.J. and Lewis, E.W. (1970), 'The geographical distribution of industrial research activity in the United Kingdom', *Regional Studies,* 4 (3), pp.297—306.

Cameron, G.C. and Reid, G.L. (1966), *Scottish Economic Planning and the Attraction of Industry,* University of Glasgow, Social and Economic Studies, Occasional Paper, no.6, Oliver and Boyd, Edinburgh.

Cameron, G.C. and Clark, B.D. (1966), *Industrial Movement and the Regional Problem,* University of Glasgow, Social and Economic Studies, Occasional Paper, no.5, Oliver and Boyd, Edinburgh.

Cameron, G.C. and Johnson, K.M. (1969), 'Comprehensive urban renewal and industrial relocation — the Glasgow case' in J.B. Cullingworth and S.C. Orr (eds), *Regional and Urban Studies,* Allen and Unwin, London.

Cameron, G.C. (1970), 'Growth areas, growth centres and regional conversion', *Scottish Journal of Political Economy,* 17, (1), pp.19—38.

Cameron, G.C. and Evans, A.W. (1973), 'The British conurbation centres', *Regional Studies,* 7 (1), pp.47—55.

Cameron, G.C. (1973), 'Intra-urban location and the new plant', *Papers and Proceedings, Regional Science Association,* 29, pp.1—16.

Cameron, G.C. (1974), 'Regional economic policy in the United Kingdom', in N.M. Hansen (ed.), *Public Policy and Regional Economic Development: the Experience of Nine Western Countries,* Ballinger, Cambridge, Mass.

Cameron, G.C., Firn, J.R., Latham, M. and MacLennan, D. (1975), 'The determinants of urban manufacturing location — a simple model', in E.L. Cripps (ed.), *Regional Science: New Concepts and Old Problems,* Pion Press, London.

Camina, M.M. (1974), *Local Authorities and the Attraction of Industry,* Pergamon (Progress in Planning Series), Oxford.

Carey, S.J. (1969), 'Relocation of office staff: a study of the reactions of office staff decentralised to Ashford', *Location of Offices Bureau Research Paper,* no.4.

Carey, S.J. (1970), 'Relocation of office staff: a follow-up survey', *Location of Offices Bureay Research Paper,* no.7.

Channon, D.F. (1973), *The Strategy and Structure of British Enterprise,* Macmillan, London.

Child, P. (1971), 'Office Development in Croydon', *Location of Offices Bureau Research Paper,* no.7.

Chisholm, M. (1971), 'Freight transport costs, industrial location and regional development', chapter 8 in *Spatial Policy Problems of the British Economy*, M. Chisholm and G. Manners (eds), Cambridge University Press, Cambridge.

Chisholm, M. (1970), 'On the making of a myth? How capital intensive is industry investing in the development areas?', *Urban Studies*, 7, pp. 289—93.

Chisholm, M. and Oeppen, J. (1973), *The Changing Pattern of Employment: Regional Specialisation and Industrial Location in Britain*, Croom Helm, London.

Chisholm, M. (1976), 'Regional policies in an era of slow population growth and higher unemployment', *Regional Studies*, 10 (2), pp.201—14.

Clark, V.E.G. (1976), 'The cyclical sensitivity of employment in branch and parent plants', *Regional Studies*, 10 (3), pp.293—8.

Committee of inquiry on small firms (1971), *Dynamics of Small Firms*, Research Report 12, HMSO, London.

Cook, W.M. (1967), 'Transport decisions of Black Country firms', *Journal of Transport Economics and Policy*, 1 (3), pp.325—44.

Cooper, M.J.M. (1975), *The Industrial Location Decision Making Process*, Occasional Paper no.34, Centre for Urban and Regional Studies, University of Birmingham.

Cooper, M.J.M. (1976), 'Government influence on industrial location: case studies in the North West and West Midlands of England', *Town Planning Review*, 47, pp.384—97.

Cullingworth, J.B. (1975), *Town and Country Planning in Britain*, Allan and Unwin, London.

Daniels, P.W. (1977), 'Office location in the British conurbations: trends and strategies', *Urban Studies*, 14 (3), pp.261—74.

Department of Trade and Industry (1973), 'Inquiry into location attitudes and experience', *Memorandum submitted to the Expenditure Committee (Trade and Industry Subcommittee) on Regional Development Incentives*, (Session 1973—74, pp.525—668), HC 85-1, HMSO, London.

Dennis, R. (1978), 'The decline of manufacturing employment in Greater London: 1966—74', *Urban Studies*, 15 (1), pp.63—74.

Dicken, P. (1976), 'The multiplant business enterprise and geographical space: some issues in the study of external control and regional development', *Regional Studies*, 10 (4), pp.401—12.

Dicken, P. and Lloyd, P.E. (1976), 'Geographical perspectives on United States investment in the United Kingdom', *Environment and Planning*, A, 7, pp.393—414.

Dicken, P. and Lloyd, P.E. (1978), 'Inner metropolitan industrial change, enterprise structures and policy issues: case studies of Manchester and Merseyside', *Regional Studies*, 12 (2), pp.181—98.

Dixon, R.J. and Thirlwall, A.P. (1975), *Regional Growth and Unemployment in the United Kingdom*, Macmillan, London.

Donnison, D. and Eversley, D. (1973), *London: Urban Patterns, Problems and Policies*, Heinemann, London.

Drewett, R., Goddard, J. and Spence, J. (1976), *British Cities: Urban Population and Employment Trends 1951–71*, Research Report 10, Department of the Environment, London.

Dunning, J.H. and Hague, D.C. (1954), 'Costs in alternative locations: the radio industry', *Review of Economic Studies*, 22, pp.203–13.

Economic Consultants Ltd (1971), *Strategic Plan for the South East: Studies Volume 5*, HMSO, London.

Edwards, S.L. (1970), 'Transport costs in British industry', *Journal of Transport Economics and Policy*, volume 4 (3), pp.265–85.

Eversley, D.E.C. (1965), 'Social and psychological factors in the determination of industrial location', in T. Wilson (ed.), *Papers on Regional Development*, Basil Blackwell, Oxford.

Eversley, D.E.C. (1972), 'Rising costs and static incomes: some economic consequences of regional planning in London', *Urban Studies*, 9 (3), pp.347–68.

Facey, M.V. and Smith, G.B. (1968), 'Offices in a regional centre: a study of office location in Leeds', *Location of Offices Bureau Research Report*, no.2.

Firn, J.R. (1973), *Memorandum to the Sub-Committee on Regional Development Incentives*, Expenditure Committee, Appendix 4, HC 85-1, HMSO, London.

Firn, J.R. (1975), 'External control and regional development: the case of Scotland', *Environment and Planning*, 7 (4), pp.393–414.

Firn, J.R. and Swales, J.K. (1978), 'The formation of new manufacturing establishments in the Central Clydeside and West Midlands conurbations 1963–72: a comparative analysis', *Regional Studies*, 12 (2), pp.199–214.

Forsyth, D.J.C. (1977), *US Investment in Scotland*, Praeger, New York.

Forsyth, D.J.C. (1973), 'Foreign-owned firms and labour relations: a regional perspective', *British Journal of Industrial Relations*, 11 (1), pp.20–8.

Fox, A. (1965), *The Milton Plan*, Institute of Personnel Management, London.

Garbett-Edwards, D.P. (1972), 'The establishment of new industries. with particular reference to recent experience in Mid-Wales', in J. Ashton and W. Long (eds), *The Remoter Rural Areas of Britain*, Oliver and Boyd, Edinburgh.

Gennard, J. and Steuer, M.D. (1971), 'The industrial relations of foreign owned subsidiaries in the United Kingdom', *British Journal of Industrial Relations*, 9 (2), pp.143–59.

216

Goddard, J.B. (1973), *Office Linkages and Location*, Pergamon (Progress in Planning Series), Oxford.

Goddard, J.B. and Morris, D.M. (1976), *The Communications Factor in Office Decentralisation*, Pergamon (Progress in Planning Series), Oxford.

Goddard, J.B. and Pye, R. (1977), 'Telecommunications and office location', *Regional Studies*, 11 (1), pp.19–30.

Goodman, J.F.B. and Samuel, P.J. (1966), 'The motor industry in a development area: a case study of the labour factor', *British Journal of Industrial Relations*, 4, pp.336–65.

Green, D.H. (1977), 'Industrialists information level of regional incentives', *Regional Studies*, 11 (1), pp. 7–18.

Griffith, E.J.L. (1955), 'Moving industry from London', *Town Planning Review*, 26, pp.51–63.

Gripaios, P. (1977a), 'The closure of firms in the inner city: the South East London case 1970–75', *Regional Studies*, 11 (1), pp.1–6.

Gripaios, P. (1977b), 'Industrial decline in London: an examination of its causes', *Urban Studies*, 14 (2), pp.181–90.

Gudgin, G. (1978), *Industrial Location Processes and Regional Development Growth*, Saxon House, Farnborough.

Hague, D.C. and Newman, P.K. (1952), *Costs in Alternative Locations: the Clothing Industry*, NIESR and Cambridge University Press, Cambridge.

Hall, J. (1971), 'Industry grows where the grass is greener', *New Society*, 4 February, pp.187–90.

Hall, P., Gracey, H., Drewett, R. and Thomas, R. (1973), *The Containment of Urban England*, volume 1, Allen and Unwin, London.

Hall, R.K. (1972), 'The movement of offices from Central London', *Regional Studies*, 6 (4), pp.385–92.

Hamilton, F.E.I. (1978), 'Aspects of industrial mobility in the British economy', *Regional Studies*, 12 (2), pp.153–66.

Hammond, E. (1967), 'Dispersal of government offices: a survey', *Urban Studies*, 4 (3), pp.250–75.

Hardman, (1973), *The Dispersal of Government Work from London*, ('The Hardman Report'), Cmnd. 5322, HMSO, London.

Harris, R.J.P. (1974), 'The intra-regional movement of manufacturing industry: a comparative evaluation of findings in the Notts-Derbyshire sub-region', *Town Planning Review*, 45, pp.416–31.

Hart, R.A. (1971), 'The distribution of new industrial building in the 1960s', *Scottish Journal of Political Economy*, 18 (2), pp.181–97.

Hart, R.A. (1972), 'The regional growth in employment in the manufacturing and service sectors, 1960–75: the United Kingdom experience and expectation', *Tijdschrift voor Economische en Sociale Geografie*, 63 (2), pp.88–93.

Henderson, R.A. (1974), 'Industrial overspill from Glasgow: 1958—68', *Urban Studies,* 11 (1), pp.61—79.

Hoare, A.G. (1975), 'Linkage flows, locational evaluation and industrial geography: a case study of Greater London', *Environment and Planning,* 7, pp.41—58.

Holmans, A.E. (1964), 'Industrial Development Certificates and the growth of employment in S.E. England', *Urban Studies,* 1, pp.138—52.

Howard, R.S. (1968), *The Movement of Manufacturing Industry in the United Kingdom, 1945—65,* HMSO for the Board of Trade, London.

Hunt Report (1969), *The Intermediate Areas,* Cmnd. 3998, HMSO, London.

Jones, R.M. (1968), 'The direction of industrial movement and its impact on recepient regions', *Manchester School,* 36, pp.149—72.

Jones, R.M. (1970), 'Local labour markets, the journey to work and government location policy', *Town Planning Review,* 41, pp.168—77.

Kaldor, N. (1970), 'The case for regional policies', *Scottish Journal of Political Economy,* 17, pp.337—48.

Keeble, D.E. (1965), 'Industrial migration from North-West London, 1940—64', *Urban Studies,* 2 (1), pp.15—32.

Keeble, D.E. (1968), 'Industrial decentralisation and the metropolis: the North-West London case', *Transactions of the Institute of British Geographers,* 44, pp.1—54.

Keeble, D.E. (1969), 'Local industrial linkage and manufacturing growth in Outer London', *Town Planning Review,* 40 (2), pp.163—88, Liverpool University Press.

Keeble, D.E. (1971), 'Industrial mobility in Britain', chapter 2 in *Spatial Policy Problems of the British Economy,* M. Chisholm and G. Manners (eds), Cambridge University Press, Cambridge.

Keeble, D.E. and Hauser, D.P. (1971), 'Spatial analysis of manufacturing growth in Outer South East England, 1960—67, I. Hypotheses and variables', *Regional Studies,* 5, pp.229—62.

Keeble, D.E. and Hauser, D.P. (1972), 'Spatial analysis of manufacturing growth in Outer South East England, 1960—67, II. Methods and results', *Regional Studies,* 6, pp.11—36.

Keeble, D.E. (1972), 'Industrial movement and regional development in the United Kingdom', *Town Planning Review,* 43 (1), pp.163—88.

Keeble, D.E. (1974), *The Movement of Firms* (Unit 8 for Course D342, Regional Analysis and Development), The Open University Press, Milton Keynes.

Keeble, D.E. (1976), *Industrial Location and Planning in Britain,* Methuen, London.

Keeble, D.E. (1977), 'Industrial geography', *Progress in Human Geography,* 1 (2), pp.304—12.

Keeble, D.E. (1978), 'Industrial decline in the inner city and conurbation', *Transactions of the Institute of British Geographers*, New Series, 3 (1), pp.102—14.

Law, D. (1964), 'Industrial movement and locational advantage', *Manchester School*, 32, pp.131—54.

Leigh, R. and North, D.J. (1978), 'Regional aspects of acquisition activity in British manufacturing industry', *Regional Studies*, 12 (2), pp.227—46.

Lever, W.F. (1972), 'The intra-urban movement of manufacturing: a Markov approach', *Transactions of the Institute of British Geographers*, 56, pp.21—38.

Lever, W.F. (1972), 'Industrial movement, spatial association and functional linkages', *Regional Studies*, 6 (4), pp.371—84.

Lever, W.F. (1973), 'Cyclical changes in factors affecting industrial location', *Land Economics*, 49, pp.218—21.

Lever, W.F. (1974), 'Manufacturing linkages and the search for suppliers and markets', in F.E.I. Hamilton (ed.), *Spatial Perspectives on Industrial Organisation and Decision Making*, Wiley, London.

Lever, W.F. (1975a), 'Mobile industry and levels of integration in sub-regional economic structures', *Regional Studies*, 9 (3), pp.265—78.

Lever, W.F. (1975b), 'Manufacturing decentralization and shifts in factor costs and external economies', in L. Collins and D.F. Walker (eds), *Locational Dynamics of Manufacturing Activity*, Wiley, London.

Lloyd, P.E. and Mason, C.M. (1978), 'Manufacturing industry in the inner city: a case study of Greater Manchester', *Transactions of the Institute of British Geographers*, New Series, 3 (1), pp.66—89.

Livesey, F. (1970), 'The composition of employment in branch factories', *Oxford Economic Papers*, 22, pp.420—36.

Livesey, F. (1972), 'Industrial complexity and regional economic development', *Town Planning Review*, volume 43 (3), pp.225—42.

Loasby, B.J. (1973), *The Swindon Project*, Pitman, London.

Luttrell, W.F. (1962), *Factory Location and Industrial Movement*, National Institute of Economic and Social Research, London.

Mann, M. (1973), *Workers on the Move: the Sociology of Relocation*, Cambridge University Press, London.

McCallum, J.D. (1973), 'UK regional policy 1964—72', in G.C. Cameron and L. Wingo (eds), *Cities, Regions and Public Policy*, Oliver and Boyd, Edinburgh.

McCrone, G. (1969), *Regional Policy in Britain*, Allen and Unwin, London.

McDermott, P.J. (1976), 'Ownership, organisation and regional dependence in the Scottish electronics industry', *Regional Studies*, 10 (3), pp.319—36.

219

McGovern, P.D. (1965), 'Industrial dispersal', *Planning*, PEP, volume 31, no.485.

Melliss, C.L. and Richardson, P.W. (1976), 'Value of investment incentives for manufacturing industry 1946 to 1974', in A. Whiting (ed.), *The Economics of Industrial Subsidies*, HMSO, London.

Moore, B., Rhodes, J. and Tyler, P. (1977), 'The impact of regional policy in the 1970s', *Centre for Environmental Studies Review*, 1, pp. 67–77.

Morley, R. (1976), 'Unemployment, profits share and regional policy', in A. Whiting (ed.), *The Economics of Industrial Subsidies*, HMSO, London.

Morrison, W.I. (1973), 'The development of an urban interindustry model: 3. Input-output multipliers for Peterborough', *Environment and Planning*, 5, pp.433–60.

Moseley, M.J. and Townroe, P.M. (1973), 'Linkage adjustment following industrial movement', *Tijdschrift voor Economische en Sociale Geografie*, 64 (3), pp.137–44.

Moseley, M.J. (1973), 'Some problems of small expanding towns', *Town Planning Review*, volume 44 (3), pp.263–78.

Moxon, J.W.J. (1972), 'The industrial development certificate system and employment creation', *Urban Studies*, 9, pp.229–33.

Munby, D.L. (1951), 'The cost of industrial dispersal from London, *Planning Outlook*, 2 (3), pp.5–16.

Murie, A.S. et al. (1973), 'A survey of industrial movement in Northern Ireland between 1965 and 1969', *Economic and Social Review*, 4 (2), pp.231–44.

Murie, A.S., Birrell, W.D., Roche, D.J.D. and Hillyard, P.A.R. (1974), *Regional Planning and the Attraction of Manufacturing Industry in Northern Ireland*, CES RP4, Centre for Environmental Studies, London.

Nicholson, R.J. (1956), 'The regional location of industry: an empirical study based on the regional tables of the 1948 Census of Production', *Economic Journal*, 66, pp.467–81.

North, D.J. (1974), 'The process of locational change in different manufacturing organisations', in F.E.I. Hamilton (ed.), *Spatial Perspectives on Industrial Organisation and Decision Making*, John Wiley, London.

Picton, G. (1953), 'Notes on the establishment of branch factories', *Journal of Industrial Economics*, 1, pp.126–31.

Rake, D.J. (1974), 'Spatial changes in industrial activity in the East Midlands since 1945: changes through movement and acquisition', *The East Midland Geographer*, 6, pp.1–16.

Rhodes, J. and Kan, A. (1971), *Office Dispersal and Regional Policy*, Cambridge University Press, Cambridge.

Rhodes, J. and Moore, B. (1973a), 'Evaluating the effects of British regional economic policy', *Economic Journal*, 83, pp.87—110.

Rhodes, J. and Moore, B.C. (1973b), *The Economic and Exchequer Implications of Regional Policy*, Evidence to the House of Commons Expenditure Committee, HC 42, XVI, HMSO, London.

Rhodes, J. and Moore, B.C. (1976a), 'Regional economic policy and the movement of manufacturing firms to development areas', *Economica*, 43, pp.17—31.

Rhodes, J. and Moore, B.C. (1976b), 'A quantitive analysis of the effects of the regional employment premium and other regional policy instruments', in A. Whiting (ed.), *The Economics of Industrial Subsidies*, HMSO, London.

Richardson, H.W. and West, E.G. (1964), 'Must we always take work to the workers?', *Lloyds Bank Review*, no.71, January 1964, pp.35—48.

Rodgers, P.B. and Smith, C.R. (1977), 'The local authority's role in economic development: the Tyne and Wear Act 1976', *Regional Studies*, 11 (3), pp.153—64.

Ruddy, S.A. (1969), *Industrial Selection Schemes*, Centre for Urban and Regional Studies, Occasional Paper no.5, University of Birmingham.

Salt, J. (1965), 'The impact of the Ford and Vauxhall plants on the employment situation of Merseyside', *Tijdschrift voor Economische en Sociale Geografie*, volume 56, pp.145—55.

Sant, M.E.C. (1975a), *Industrial Movement and Regional Development: the British Case*, Pergamon Press, Oxford.

Sant, M.E.C. (1975b), 'Inter-regional industrial movement: the case of the non-survivors', in B.J. Turton and A.D.M. Phillips (eds), *Environment, Man and Economic Change*, Longman, London.

Schofield, J.A. (1976), 'Economic efficiency and regional policy in Britain', *Urban Studies*, 13 (2), pp.181—92.

Seeley, I.H. (1967), 'Planned dispersal by town development schemes', *Chartered Surveyor*, 100, pp.189—91.

Smith, B.M.D. (1970), 'Industrial overspill in theory and practice: the case of the West Midlands', *Urban Studies*, volume 7 (2), pp.189—204.

Smith, B.M.D. (1972), *The Administration of Industrial Overspill*, Centre for Urban and Regional Studies Occasional Paper no.22, University of Birmingham.

Smith, B.M.D. (1975), 'Industrial mobility — in which industries has plant location changed most?', *Regional Studies*, 9 (1), pp.27—38.

Smith, D.M. (1969), 'Industrial location and regional development — some recent trends in North-West England', *Environment and Planning*, 1 (2), pp.173—91.

Spooner, D.J. (1972), 'Industrial movement and the rural periphery: the case of Devon and Cornwall', *Regional Studies*, 6 (2), pp.197—215.

Spooner, D.J. (1974), 'Some qualitative aspects of industrial movement in a problem region in the United Kingdom', *Town Planning Review*, 45 (1), pp.63—83.

Stacey, M. (1960), *Tradition and Change: a Study of Banbury*, Oxford University Press.

Stacey, M., Batstone, E., Bell, C. and Murcott, A. (1975), *Power, Persistence and Change: a Second Study of Banbury*, Routledge and Kegan Paul, London.

Steed, G.P.F. (1971), 'Internal organisation, firm integration and locational change: the Northern Ireland linen complex, 1954—64', *Economic Geography*, volume 47, (3), pp.371—83.

Steed, G.P.F. (1968), 'The changing milieu of a firm: a case study of a shipbuilding concern', *Annals of the Association of American Geographers*, 58 (3), pp.506—25.

Steed, G.P.F. (1970), 'Changing linkages and internal multiplier of an industrial complex', *The Canadian Geographer*, XIV (3), pp.229—42.

Steele, G.R. (1972), 'The migration of industrial firms from Sheffield in the post-war period', *The East Midland Geographer*, December, pp. 283—95.

Steele, D.B. (1969), 'Regional multipliers in Great Britain', *Oxford Economic Papers*, 21, pp.268—92.

Stephen, F.H. (1975), 'The Hardman Report: a critique', *Regional Studies*, 9 (1), pp.111—16.

Taylor, M.J. (1970), 'Location decisions of small firms', *Area*, 2, pp.51—4.

Taylor, M.J. and Wood, P.A. (1973), 'Industrial linkage and local agglomeration in the West Midlands metal industries', *Transactions, Institute of British Geographers*, no.59, pp.129—54.

Taylor, M.J. (1973), 'Local linkage, external economies and the iron foundry industry of the West Midlands and East Lancashire conurbations', *Regional Studies*, 7 (4), pp.387—400.

Taylor, M.J. (1975), 'Organisational growth, spatial interaction and location decision making', *Regional Studies*, 9 (4), pp.313—24.

Tolley, R.S. (1972), 'Telford New Town: conception and reality in West Midlands industrial overspill', *Town Planning Review*, 43 (4), pp.343—60.

Tooze, M.J. (1976), 'Regional elasticities of substitution in the United Kingdom in 1968', *Urban Studies*, 13 (1), pp.35—44.

Townroe, P.M. (1969), 'Locational choice and the individual firm', *Regional Studies*, 3 (1), pp.15—24.

Townroe, P.M. (1970), 'Industrial linkage, agglomeration and external economies', *Journal of the Town Planning Institute*, 56 (1), pp.18—20.

Townroe, P.M. (1971), *Industrial Location Decisions: a Study in Management Behaviour,* Occasional Paper no.15, Centre for Urban and Regional Studies, University of Birmingham.

Townroe, P.M. (1972), 'Some behavioural considerations in the industrial location decision', *Regional Studies,* 6 (3), pp.261—72.

Townroe, P.M. (1973), 'The supply of mobile industry: a cross sectional analysis', *Regional and Urban Economics,* 2 (4), pp.371—86.

Townroe, P.M. (1974), 'Regional policy planning: future research priorities', chapter 13 in M.E.C. Sant (ed.), *Regional Policy and Planning for Europe,* Saxon House, London.

Townroe, P.M. (1974a), 'Industrial location search behaviour and regional development', chapter in J. Rees and P. Newby (eds), *Behavioural Perspectives on Geography,* Monographs in Geography no.1, Middlesex Polytechnic.

Townroe, P.M. (1974b), 'Post-move stability and the location decision', in F.E.I. Hamilton (ed.), *Spatial Perspectives on Industrial Organisation and Decision Making,* Wiley, London.

Townroe, P.M. (1975a), 'Branch plants and regional development', *Town Planning Review,* 46 (1), pp.47—62.

Townroe, P.M. (1975b), 'The labour factor in the post-move experience of mobile companies', *Regional Studies,* 9 (4), pp.335—48.

Townroe, P.M. (1976a), 'Settling-in costs in mobile plants', *Urban Studies,* 13 (1), pp.67—70.

Townroe, P.M. (1976b), *Planning Industrial Location,* Leonard Hill, London.

Townroe, P.M. and Morley, R. (1974), 'The experience of migrant industrial plants in the Northern Region', *Planning Outlook,* 15, pp.18—34.

Townsend, A.R. and Gault, F.D. (1972), 'A national model of factory movement and resulting employment', *Area,* 4 (2), pp.92—8.

Tulpule, A.H. (1969), 'Dispersion of industrial employment in the Greater London area', *Regional Studies,* 3, pp.25—40.

Turner, D.M. (1974), 'Location decisions and Industrial Development Certificate policy in the United Kingdom', in F.E. I. Hamilton (ed.), *Spatial Perspectives on Industrial Organisation and Decision Making,* Wiley, London.

Wabe, J.S. (1966), 'Office decentralisation: an empirical study', *Urban Studies,* 3, pp.35—53.

Wallace, I. (1974), 'The relationship between freight transport organisation and industrial linkage in Britain', *Transactions of the Institute of British Geographers,* 62, pp.25—43.

Welch, R.V. (1970), 'Immigrant manufacturing industry established in Scotland between 1945 and 1968: some structural and locational characteristics', *Scottish Geographical Magazine,* 86, pp.134—48.

West Midland Regional Study (1972), *A Developing Strategy for the West Midlands: Technical Appendix 3: Economic Study 3,* (Industrial Mobility).

Westaway, J. (1974a), 'Contact potential and the occupational structure of the British urban system 1961—66: an empirical study', *Regional Studies,* 8 (1), pp.57—73.

Westaway, J. (1974b), 'The spatial hierarchy of business organisations and its implications for the British urban system', *Regional Studies,* 8 (2), pp.145—55.

Whitelegg, J. (1976), 'Births and deaths of firms in the inner city', *Urban Studies,* 13 (3), pp.333—8.

Wood, P.A. (1969), 'Industrial location and linkage', *Area,* 2, pp.32—9.

Wood, P.A. (1974), 'Urban manufacturing: a view from the fringe', in J.M. Johnson (ed.), *Suburban Growth,* Wiley, London.

Yannopoulos, George N. (1973), 'The local impact of decentralised offices', *Location of Offices Bureau Research Paper,* no.7.

Bibliography of literature on industrial movement in the United States

Albin, P.S. (1971), 'Unbalanced growth and the intensification of the urban crisis', *Urban Studies,* 8, pp.139–46.

Allaman, P.A. and Birch, D.L. (1975), *Components of Employment Change for States by Industry Group, 1970–72,* Harvard University – Massachusetts Institute of Technology Joint Center for Urban Studies, Working Paper no.5, Cambridge, Mass.

Armstrong, R.B. and Pushkarev, B. (1972), *The Office Industry: Patterns of Growth and Location,* The MIT Press, Cambridge, Mass.

Barabba, U.P. (1975), 'The national setting: regional shifts, metropolitan decline, and urban decay', in G. Sternlieb and J.W. Hughes (eds), *Post Industrial America: Metropolitan Decline and Inter-regional Job Shifts,* Rutgers University, New Brunswick, NJ.

Barloon, M.J. (1965), 'The interrelationship of the changing structure of American transportation and changes in industrial location', *Land Economics,* 41, pp.164–79.

Beale, C.L. (1974), 'Rural development, population and settlement prospects', *Journal of Soil and Water Conservation,* 29 (1), pp.23–7.

Beale, C.L. (1976), 'A further look at non-metropolitan population growth since 1970', *American Journal of Agricultural Economics,* 58 (5), pp.953–1,958.

Beckman, N. and Langdon, B. (1972), *National Growth Policy: Legislative Actions,* Urban Land Institute, Washington DC.

Bergsman, J., Greenston, P. and Healy, R. (1975), 'A classification of economic activities based on location patterns', *Journal of Urban Economics,* 2, pp.1–28.

Bergsman, J., Greenston, P. and Healy, R. (1972), 'The agglomeration process in urban growth', *Urban Studies,* 9 (3), pp.263–88.

Berry, B.J.L. (1970), 'The geography of the United States in the Year 2000', *Ekistics,* 29, pp.6–13.

Berry, B.J.L. (ed) (1973), *Growth Centers in the American Urban System,* Ballinger, Cambridge, Mass.

Berry, B.J.L. and Gillard, Q. (1977), *The Changing Shape of Metropolitan America: Commuting Patterns, Urban Fields and Decentralisation Processes 1960–70,* Ballinger, Cambridge, Mass.

Biggs, J.R. (1973), 'Emigration of industry from Ohio', *Bulletin of*

Business Research.

Bryant, C.G. (1971), 'An analysis of municipal financial assistance to industry', *AIDC Journal,* 6 (1), pp.51—69.

Burrows, J.C., Metcalf, C.E. and Kaler, J.B. (1971), *Industrial Location in the United States,* D.C. Heath, Lexington, Mass.

Camberton, C.E. (1976), 'State and local tax exemption programs: comment', *Southern Economic Journal,* 42 (4), pp.736—40.

Cameron, G.C. (1970), *Regional Economic Development: the Federal Role,* Johns Hopkins University Press for RFF, Baltimore.

Cameron, M.A. (1969), 'Property taxation as a location factor', *Bulletin of Business Research,* 44 (4), pp.5—8.

Carroll, J.J. and Sacks, S. (1962), 'The property tax base and the pattern of local government expenditures: the influence of industry', *Pages and Proceedings of the Regional Science Association,* 9, pp.16—20.

Chinitz, B. (1960), 'Contrasts in agglomeration: New York and Pittsburgh', *American Economic Review,* 51, pp.92—106.

Chinitz, B. (ed.) (1977), *The Decline of New York in the 1970s,* Center for Social Analysis, State University of New York, Binghampton.

Chinitz, B. (ed.) (1978), *The Declining North-East: Demographic and Economic Analysis,* Praeger, New York.

Choguill, C.L. (1977), 'Regional planning in the United States and the United Kingdom: a comparative analysis', *Regional Studies,* 11 (3), pp.135—46.

Clawson, M. (1971), *Suburban Land Conversion in the United States,* The Johns Hopkins Press, Baltimore.

Clemente, F. and Sturgis, R.B. (1971), 'Population size and industrial diversification', *Urban Studies,* 8, pp.65—8.

Cohen, B.I. (1971), 'Trends in negro employment within large metropolitan areas', *Public Policy,* 19 (4), pp.614—15.

Committee for Economic Development (1966), *Community Economic Development Efforts: Five Case Studies,* Praeger, New York.

Creamer, D. (1963), 'Changing location of manufacturing employment', *Studies in Business Economics,* no.83, National Industrial Conference Board, New York.

Creamer, D. (1969), *Manufacturing Employment by Type of Location,* National Industrial Conference Board Studies in Economics, no.106, New York.

Cumberland, J.H. and Van Beek, F. (1967), 'Regional economic development objectives and subsidisation of local industry', *Land Economics,* 43, pp.253—64.

Cumberland, J.H. (1971), *Regional Development: Experience and Projects in the United States of America,* Monton and Co., The Hague.

Dean, R.D. (1972), 'Computerized community and site selection programs', *AIDC Journal,* 7 (3), pp.19—25.

Dean, R.D. (1973), *Suburbanisation of Industry in the US,* Oak Ridge National Laboratory, Oak Ridge, Tenn.

De Vyver, F.T. (1951), 'Labor factors in the industrial development of the South', *Southern Economic Journal,* 18, pp.189—205.

Due, J.F. (1961), 'Studies of state-local tax influences on the location of industry', *National Tax Journal,* 14 (2), pp.163—73.

Economic Development Administration (1974), *The EDA Experience in the Evolution of Policy. A Brief History September 1965 — June 1973,* US Department of Commerce, Washington DC.

Edel, M. et al. (1975), 'Urban concentration and deconcentration', in A. H. Hawley and V.P. Rock, *Metropolitan American in Contemporary Perspective,* Sage Publications, New York.

Eichner, A.S. (1970), *State Development Agencies and Employment Expansion,* University of Michigan and Wayne State University Institute of Labor Relations, Ann Arbor, Mich.

Erickson, R.A. (1976), 'The filtering-down process: industrial location in a non-metropolitan area', *Professional Geographer,* 28 (3), pp.254—60.

Estall, R.C. (1966), *New England: a Study in Industrial Adjustment,* Bell, London.

Evans, A.W. (1975), 'A note on the intra-urban location of wholesalers and local market manufacturers', *Land Economics,* 51 (3), pp.268—74.

Fischel, W.A. (1975), 'Fiscal and environmental considerations in the location of firms in suburban communities', in E.S. Mills and W.E. Oates, *Fiscal Zoning and Land Use Controls: the Economic Issues,* Lexington Books, Lexington, Mass.

Floyd, J.S. (1952), *Effects of Taxation on Industrial Location,* University of North Carolina Press, Chapel Hill, NC.

Friedmann, J. and Miller, J. (1965), 'The urban field', *Journal of the American Institute of Planners,* 31 (4), pp.312—18.

Fuchs, V.R. (1962), *Changes in the Location of Manufacturing in the United States Since 1929,* Yale University Press, New Haven, Conn.

Fuchs, V.R. (1967), *Differentials in Hourly Earnings by Region and City Size,* Occasional Paper no.101, National Bureau for Economic Research, Columbia University Press, New York.

Fulton, M. (1971), 'New factors in plant location', *Harvard Business Review,* May—June, pp.4—6.

Ganz, A. and O.'Brien, T. (1973), 'The City: Sandbox Reservation or Dynamo?', *Public Policy,* 21.

Garrison, C.B. (1971), 'New industry in small towns: the impact on local government', *National Tax Journal,* 24 (4), pp.493—500.

Garwood, J.D. (1953), 'An analysis of postwar industrial migration to Utah and Colorado', *Economic Geography,* 29 (1), pp.79—88.

Gillette, A.F. (1976), 'Section 302(a) Economic Development Planning Assistance to States', *Economic Development Administration Research Review,* pp.1—11.

Gilmore, D.R. (1960), *Developing the 'Little' Economies. (A Survey of Area Development Programs in the United States.),* a supplementary paper of the Area Development Committee, Committee for Economic Development, New York.

Gordon, M.S. and McCorry, A.H. (1957), 'Plant relocation and job security in a case study', *Industrial and Labour Relations Review,* 11.

Gray, I. (1969), 'Employment effect of a new industry in a rural area', *Monthly Labor Review,* 92 (b), pp.26—30.

Greenhut, M.L. (1956), *Plant Location in Theory and in Practice,* University of North Carolina Press, Chapel Hill.

Greenhut, M.L. (1959), 'An empirical model and survey; new plant locations in Florida', *Review of Economics and Statistics,* 49, pp.433 —7.

Guest, A.M. (1976a), 'Occupation and the journey to work', *Social Forces,* 55 (1), pp.166—81.

Guest, A.M. (1976b), 'Night-time and day-time populations of large American suburbs', *Urban Affairs Quarterly,* 12 (1), pp.57—81.

Hamer, A. (1973), *Industrial Exodus from the Central City,* Lexington Books, Lexington, Mass.

Hamman, C.L. (1966), *Industrial Location as a Factor in Regional Economic Development,* Management and Economic Research, Inc., Pao Alto.

Hamrick, J.G. (1973), *Industrial Location Determinants, 1971—75,* US Department of Commerce, Washington DC.

Hansen, R. and Munsinger, G.M. (1972), 'A prescriptive model for industrial development', *Land Economics,* 48, pp.76—81.

Hansen, N.M. (1972), *Intermediate Size Cities as Growth Centers,* Praeger, New York.

Hansen, N.M. (1973a), *Location Preferences, Migration and Regional Growth,* Praeger, New York.

Hansen, N.M. (1973b), *The Future of Non-metropolitan America,* Lexington Books, Lexington, Mass.

Hansen, N.M. (1974), 'Regional policy in the United States', in N.M. Hansen (ed.), *Public Policy and Regional Economic Development: the Experience of Nine Western Countries,* Ballinger, Cambridge, Mass.

Hansen, N.M. (1975), *The Challenge of Urban Growth,* Lexington Books, Lexington, Mass.

Hansen, N.M. (1976), *Improving Access to Economic Opportunity: Non-metropolitan Labour Markets in an Urban Society*, Ballinger, Cambridge, Mass.

Haren, C.A. (1970), 'Rural industrial growth in the 1960s', *American Journal of Agricultural Economics*, 52 (3), pp.431—7.

Harris, C.C. and Hopkins, F.E. (1972), *Locational Analysis: an Inter-regional Econometric Model of Agriculture, Mining, Manufacturing, and Services*, Lexington Books, Lexington, Mass.

Harrison, B. (1974), *Urban Economic Development: Suburbanisation, Minority Opportunity and the Condition of the Central City*, The Urban Institute, Washington DC.

Hellman, D.A., Wassall, G.H. and Falk, L.H. (1976), *State Financial Incentives to Industry*, Lexington Books, Lexington, Mass.

Hovey, H.A. (1977), *State Urban Development Strategies*, State Planning Series 5, Council of State Planning Agencies, Washington DC.

Howard, D. (ed.) (1972), *Guide to Industrial Development*, Prentice Hall, Englewood Cliffs, New Jersey.

Huff, D.L. (1973), 'The delineation of a national system of planning regions on the basis of urban spheres of influence', *Regional Studies*, 7, pp.323—9.

Hughes, J.W. (1974), *Suburbanisation Dynamics and the Future of the City*, Center for Urban Policy Research, Rutgers University, New Brunswick, New Jersey.

Hunker, H.L. (1974), *Industrial Development: Concepts and Principles*, Lexington Books, Lexington, Mass.

James, F.J. and Hughes, J.W. (1973), 'The process of employment location change: an empirical analysis', *Land Economics*, 69 (4), pp. 404—13.

Joun, Y.P. and Beaton, C.R. (1969), 'The effect of property taxation on industrial location', *The Annals of Regional Science*, pp.67—75.

Jusenius, C.L. and Ledebur, L.C. (1976), *A Myth in the Making: the Southern Economic Challenge and Northern Economic Decline*, Economic Development Research Report, US Department of Commerce.

Jusenius, C.L. and Ledebur, L.C. (1977a), *The Migration of Firms and Workers in Ohio, 1970—75*, Academy for Contemporary Problems, Washington DC.

Jusenius, C.L. and Ledebur, L.C. (1977b), *Federal and Regional Responses to the Economic Decline of the Northern Industrial Tier*, Economic Development Research Report, US Department of Commerce.

Kain, J.F. (1975), 'The distribution and movement of jobs and industry', in *Essays in Urban Spatial Structure*, Ballinger, Cambridge, Mass.

Kain, J.F. (1975), 'Housing market discrimination and negro employment', in *Essays on Urban Spatial Structure*, Ballinger, Cambridge, Mass.

Karaska, G.J. (1969), 'Manufacturing linkages in the Philadelphia economy: some evidence of external agglomeration forces', *Geographical Analysis*, 1 (4), pp.354–69.

Katona, G. and Morgan, J.N. (1952), 'The quantitative study of factors determining business decisions', *Quarterly Journal of Economics*, 66 (1), pp.67–90.

Kemper, P. and Schmenner, R. (1974), 'The density gradient for manufacturing industry', *Journal of Urban Economics*, 1 (2), pp.16–32.

King, P.E. (1975), 'Mobility of manufacturing and the inter-state redistribution of employment', *Professional Geographer*, 27, pp.441–8.

Kinnard, W.N. and Messner, S.D. (1970), *Effective Business Relocation: a Guide to Workable Approaches for Relocating Business Displaced by Urban Renewal*, Center for Real Estate and Urban Economic Studies, University of Connecticut.

Kennard, W.N. and Messner, S.D. (1971), *Industrial Real Estate*, Society of Industrial Realtors, Washington DC.

Kitagawa, E.M. and Bogue, D.J. (1955), *Suburbanisation of Manufacturing Activity within Standard Metropolitan Areas*, University of Chicago Population and Training Centre, Chicago.

Klemme, R.T. (1959), 'Regional analysis as a business tool', *Proceeding of the Regional Science Association*, 5, pp.71–7.

Knight, R.V. (1973), *Employment Expansion and Metropolitan Trade*, Praeger Publishers, New York.

Kraft, G. et al. (1971), *The Role of Transportation in Regional Economic Development*, Lexington Books, Lexington, Mass.

Krumme, G. and Hayter, R. (1975), 'Implications of corporate strategies and product cycle adjustments for regional employment changes', chapter 13 in L. Collins and D.F. Walker (eds), *Locational Dynamics of Manufacturing Activity*, Wiley, London.

Lampard, E.E. (1968), 'The evolving system of cities in the United States', in H.S. Perloff and L. Wingo (eds), *Issues in Urban Economics*, The Johns Hopkins University Press, Baltimore, Md.

Le Heron, R.B. (1973), 'Best-practice technology, technical leadership and regional economic development', *Environment and Planning*, 5, pp.735–49.

Ledebur, L.C. (1976), 'The dynamics of change: the urban-rural distribution of work and residence in the United States', *Economic Development Administration Research Review*, pp.12–24.

Ledebur, L.C. (1977a), *Issues in the Economic Development of*

Non-metropolitan United States, Economic Development Research
Report, US Department of Commerce.

Ledebur, L.C. (1977b), *The Economic Development Context of
Population Distribution Issues,* Economic Development Research
Report, US Department of Commerce.

Leone, R.A. (1972), 'The role of data availability in metropolitan
workplace location studies', *Annals of Economic and Social
Measurement,* pp.171–82.

Leone, R. (1976), *Location of Manufacturing Activity in the New York
Metropolitan Area.*

Leone, R.A. and Struyk, R. (1976), 'The incubator hypothesis:
evidence from five SMSAs', *Urban Studies,* 13 (3), pp.325–32.

Levitan, S.A. (1964), *Federal Aid to Depressed Areas: an Evaluation of
the Area Redevelopment Administration,* Johns Hopkins Press,
Baltimore.

Levitan, S.A. and Zicker, J.K. (1976), *Too Little But Not Too Late:
Federal Aid to Lagging Areas,* Lexington Books, Lexington, Mass.

Logan, M. (1966), 'Locational behaviour of manufacturing firms in
urban areas', *Annals of the Association of American Geographers,* 56
(3), pp.451–66.

Logan, M.I. (1970), 'Location decisions in industrial plants in Wisconsin',
Land Economics, 46, pp.325–28.

Mandell, L. (1975), *Industrial Location Decisions: Detroit Compared
with Atlanta and Chicago,* Praeger, New York.

Manners, G. (1974), 'The office in the metropolis: an opportunity for
shaping metropolitan America', *Economic Geography,* 50, pp.93–
110.

Martin, C.H. and Leone, R.A. (1977), *Local Economic Development.
The Federal Connection,* Lexington Books, Lexington, Mass.

McCarthy, K.F. and Morrison, P.A. (1978), 'The changing demographic
and economic structure of non-metropolitan areas in the 1970s',
Rand Paper, P-6062.

McLaughlin, G.E. and Robock, S. (1949), *Why Industry Moves South,*
National Planning Association, Washington DC.

McMilan, T.E. (1965), 'Why manufacturers choose plant locations vs.
determinants of plant location', *Land Economics,* 41, pp.239–46.

Miernyk, W.H. (1971), 'Local labor market effects of new plant locations', in J.F. Kain and J.R. Meyer (eds), *Essays in Regional
Economics,* Harvard University Press, Cambridge, Mass.

Miernyk, W.H. (1977), 'Rising energy prices and regional economic
development', *Growth and Change.*

Millman, R.H. et al. (1972), *Alleviating Economic Distress: Evaluating
a Federal Effort,* DC Heath, Lexington, Mass.

Mills, E. (1972), *Studies in the Structure of the Urban Economy,* Johns

Moes, J.E. (1962), *Local Subsidies for Industry,* University of North Carolina Press, Chapel Hill, NC.

Montello, P.A. (1972), 'The importance of education factors in industrial and business site selections', chapter 18 in D. Howard (ed.), *Guide to Industrial Development,* Prentice Hall, Englewood Cliffs, NJ.

Moonaw, R. (1971), 'Regional development programs: a critical view', *The Review of Regional Studies,* 1 (2), p.99.

Mooney, J.D. (1969), 'Housing segregation, negro employment and metropolitan decentralisation: an alternative perspective', *Quarterly Journal of Economics,* pp.299—311.

Moore, C.W. (1973), 'Industrial linkage development paths: a case study of two industrial complexes in the Puget Sound Region', *Tijdschrift voor Economische en Sociale Geografie,* G4 (2), pp.93—107.

Morgan, W.E. and Hackbart, M.M. (1974), 'An analysis of state and local industrial tax exemption programs', *Southern Economic Journal,* 41 (2), pp.200—5.

Moses, L. and Williamson, H.F. (1967), 'The location of economic activity in cities', *American Economic Review Papers and Proceedings,* 57 (2), pp.211—22.

Mueller, E. and Morgan, J.N. (1962), 'Location decisions of manufacturers', *American Economic Review,* 52 (2), pp.204—17.

Mueller, E. et al. (1961), *Location Decisions and Industrial Mobility in Michigan 1961,* Institute of Social Research, University of Michigan, Ann Arbor.

Neuhoff, M.C. (1955), *Trends in Industrial Location,* Tax Institute, Princeton.

Newman, D.K. (1967), 'The decentralization of jobs', *Monthly Labor Review,* May, pp.7—13.

Newman, M. (1972), *The Political Economy of Appalachia: a Case Study in Regional Integration,* DC Heath, Lexington, Mass.

Niebank, P.L. (1968), *Relocation in Urban Planning: From Obstacle to Opportunity,* University of Philadelphia Press, Philadelphia.

Parsons, S. (1966), *Displacement Effects of Urban Renewal upon Small Business: a Survey of the Literature,* Center for Urban Studies, University of Chicago, Chicago.

Patrich, C.M. (1973), *Decentralization of Manufacturing Employment,* Oak Ridge National Laboratory, Oak Ridge, Tenn.

Perloff, H.S. et al. (1960), *Regions, Resources and Economic Growth,* The Johns Hopkins Press, Baltimore.

Pred, A.R. (1975), 'On the spatial structure of organizations and the complexity of metropolitan interdependence', *Papers of the Regional Science Association,* 33, pp.115—42.

Pred, A.R. (1976), 'The inter-urban transmission of growth in advanced economics: empirical findings versus regional planning assumptions', *Regional Studies,* 10 (2), pp.151–72.

Quante, W. (1976), *The Exodus of Corporate Headquarters from New York City,* Praeger, New York.

Rahe, C.P. (1972), 'Industrial development agencies and the location of new plants', *Growth and Change,* 3 (4), pp.3–8.

Ray, C.P. (1971), 'The location of United States manufacturing subsidiaries in Canada', *Economic Geography,* 87, pp.389–400.

Rees, J. (1978a), 'Industrial location decisions, post decision effects and firm growth: a study of Dallas-Fort-Worth', in F.E.I. Hamilton (ed.), *Geography and the Industrial Environment,* Wiley, London.

Rees, J. (1978b), 'Manufacturing change, internal control and government spending in a growth region of the United States', in F.E.I. Hamilton (ed.), *Industrial Change: Challenge to Public Policy,* Longman, London.

Rinehart, J.R. (1963), 'Rates of return on municipal subsidies to industry', *Southern Economic Journal,* 24 (4), pp.297–306.

Rinehart, J.R. and Laird, W.E. (1972), 'Community inducements to industry and the zero sum game', *Scottish Journal of Political Economy,* 19, pp.73–90.

Rondinelli, D.A. (1975), *Urban and Regional Development Planning: Policy and Administration,* Cornell UP, Ithaca.

Rothblatt, D.N. (1971), *Regional Planning: the Appalachian Experience,* DC Heath, Lexington, Mass.

Rust, E. (1975), *No Growth: Impacts on Metropolitan Areas,* Lexington Books, Lexington, Mass.

Sazama, G.W. (1970a),'A benefit-cost analysis of a regional development incentive: state loans', *Journal of Regional Sciences,* 10 (3), pp.385–96.

Sazama, G.W. (1970b), 'State industrial development loans', *Land Economics,* 46, pp.171–80.

Schmenner, R.W. (1978), *The Manufacturing Location Decision: Evidence from Cincinnati and New England,* Economic Development Research Report, US Department of Commerce, Washington DC.

Schriver, W.R. (1971), 'The industrialization of the South-east since 1950: some causes of manufacturing relocation with speculation about its effects', *American Journal of Economics and Sociology,* 30, pp.47–69.

Segal, M. (1960), *Wages in the Metropolis: Their Influences on the Locatson of Industries in the New York Region,* Harvard University Press, Cambridge.

Semple, R. (1973), 'Recent trends in the spatial concentration of corporate headquarters', *Economic Geography,* 49, pp.309—18.

Shimshoni, D. (1971), 'Regional development and science-based industry', in J.F. Kain and J.R. Meyer (eds), *Essays in Regional Economics,* Harvard University Press, Cambridge.

Shively, R.W. (1974), 'Decision making for locating industry', in L.R. Whiting (ed.), *Rural Industrialization: Problems and Potentials,* Iowa State University Press, Ames, Iowa.

Smith, T.R. (1954), 'Locational analysis of new manufacturing plants in the United States', *Tijdschrift voor Economische en Sociale Geografie,* 45 (2), pp.46—50.

Stanbach, T.M. and Knight, R.V. (1970), *The Metropolitan Economy: the Process of Employment Expansion,* Columbia University Press, New York.

Steinnes, D.N. (1977), 'Causality and intra-urban location', *Journal of Urban Economics,* 4 (1), pp.64—79.

Sternlieb, G. and Hughes, J.W. (eds), (1975), *Post Industrial America: Metropolitan Decline and Inter-regional Job Shifts,* Center for Urban Policy Research, Rutgers, The State University of New Jersey, New Brunswick, NJ.

Stober, W.J. and Falk, L.H. (1969), 'The effect of financial inducements on the location of firms', *Southern Economic Journal,* 36, pp.25—35.

Stone, D.N. (1974), *Industrial Location in Metropolitan Areas: a General Model Tested for Boston,* Praeger Publishers, New York.

Struyk, R.J. (1972), 'Spatial concentration of manufacturing employment in metropolitan areas: some empirical evidence', *Economic Geography,* 48, pp.189—92.

Struyk, R.J. and James, F.R. (1975), *Intra Metropolitan Location,* Lexington Books, Lexington, Mass.

Sulvetta, A.J., Thompson, N.L. and Tobin, W.J. (1976), *Alleviating Unemployment Through Accelerated Public Works in the United States: an Historical Perspective,* Economic Development Administration, US Department of Commerce.

Summers, G.F. et al. (1976), *Industrial Invasion of Non-metropolitan America: a Quarter Century of Experience,* Praeger Publishers, New York.

Sundquist, J.L. (1975), *Dispersing Population: What America can Learn from Europe,* The Brookings Institution, Washington DC.

Sweet, D.C. (1970), 'An industrial development screening matrix', *The Professional Geographer,* 22 (3), pp.124—7.

Tabb, W.K. (1969), 'Government incentives to private industry to locate in urban poverty areas', *Land Economics.*

Tax Institute of America (1972), *Business Taxes in State and Local Governments,* Lexington Books, Lexington, Mass.

Thompson, J.M. (1961), *Methods of Plant Selection Available to Small*

Manufacturing Firms, West Virginia University.

Thompson, W.R. (1975), 'Economic processes and employment problems in declining metropolitan areas', in G. Sternlieb and J.W. Hughes (eds), pp.187—96.

Till, T.E. (1973), 'The extent of industrialization in Southern labor markets in the 1960s', *Journal of Regional Science,* 13, pp.453—61.

Tucker, J.C. (1976), 'Changing patterns of migration between metropolitan areas in the United States: recent evidence', *Demography,* 13 (4), pp.435—43.

Tybout, R.A. and Mattila, J.M. (1977), 'Agglomeration of manufacturing in Detroit', *Journal of Regional Science,* 17 (1), pp.1—16.

Vaughan, R.J. (1977), *The Urban Impacts of Federal Policies: vol.2, Economic Development,* Rand, Sant Monica.

Vining, D.R. and Strauss, A. (1977), 'A demonstration that the current deconcentration of population in the United States is a clean break with the past', *Environment and Planning A,* 9, pp.751—8.

Waxmonsky, R. (1967), 'Considerations in the location and primary policies of Branch Plants', *AIDC Journal,* 2 (2), pp.29—51.

Weinstein, B.L. (1977), 'Tax incentives for growth', *Society,* 14 (3), pp. 73—5.

Weinstein, R.L. and Firestine, R.E. (1978), *Regional Growth and Decline in the United States. The Rise of the Sunbelt and the Decline of the Northeast,* Praeger Publishers, New York.

Wheat, L.F. (1973), *Regional Economic Growth and Industrial Location,* DC Heath, Lexington, Mass.

White, M.J. (1975), 'Firm location in a zoned metropolitan area', in E. S. Mills and W.E. Oates, *Fiscal Zoning and Land Use Controls: the Economic Issues,* Lexington Books, Lexington, Mass.

Whitman, E.S. and Schmidt, W.J. (1966), *Plant Relocation: a Case History,* American Management Association, New York.

Widner, R.R. (1977a), *Revitalizing the North Eastern Economy. A Survey for Action,* Academy for Contemporary Problems, Washington DC.

Widner, R.R. (1977b), *Stimulating the Economy of the Great Lakes States. A Survey for the Committee for Great Lakes Economic Action,* Academy for Contemporary Problems, Washington DC.

Williams, W.V. (1967), 'A measure of the impact of state and local taxes on industry location', *Journal of Regional Science,* 7 (1), pp. 49—59.

Yaseen, L.C. (1960), *Plant Location,* American Research Council, New York.

Zimmer, B.G. (1964), *Rebuilding Cities: the Effects of Displacement and Relocation on Small Business,* Quadrangle Books, Chicago.

Zimmer, B.G. (1975), 'The urban centrifugal drift', in A.H. Hawley and V.P. Rock, *Metropolitan American in Contemporary Perspective,* Sage Publications, New York.

Supplementary general bibliography on industrial movement

Bos, H.C. (1965), *Spatial Dispersion of Economic Activity*, Rotterdam University Press.

Chisholm, M. (1971), 'In search of a basis for location theory: micro-economics or welfare economics?', in C. Board, R. Chorley, P. Haggett, D. Stoddart (eds), *Progress in Geography. International Reviews of Current Research*, vol.3, Edward Arnold, London.

Cooper, L. (1967), 'Solutions of generalized locational equilibrium models', *Journal of Regional Science*, 7, pp.1–8.

Cyert, R.M. and March, J.G. (1963), *A Behavioural Theory of the Firm*, Prentice Hall, Englewood Cliffs.

Daniels, P.W. (1975), *Office Location: an Urban and Regional Study*, Bell, London.

Danielsson, A. (1966), 'The location decision from the point of view of the individual company', *Economisk Tidskrift*, 66, pp.47–87.

Dicken, P. (1971), 'Some aspects of the decision making behaviour of business organisations', *Economic Geography*, 47, pp.426–37.

EFTA (1971), *Industrial Mobility: Report of a Working Party*, European Free Trade Association, Geneva.

Eliot Hurst, M. (1972), *A Geography of Economic Behaviour*, Duxbury Press.

Erickson, R.A. (1972), 'The "lead firm" concept. An analysis of theoretical elements', *Tijdschrift voor Economische en Sociale Geografie*, 63 (6), pp.426–37.

Friend, J.K. and Jessop, W.N. (1969), *Local Government and Strategic Choice*, Tavistock Publications, London.

Golledge, R.G. and Brown, L.A. (1967), 'Search, learning and the market decision process', *Geografiska Annaler*, 49B, pp.116–24.

Greenhut, M.L. (1963), *Micro-economics and the Space Economy*, Scott Foresman, Chicago.

Haines, V.G. (1970), *Business Relocation: a Guide to Moving a Business*, Business Books, London.

Hamilton, F.E.I. (1967), 'Model of industrial location', in R.J. Chorley and P. Haggett (eds), *Socio-economic Models in Geography*, Methuen, London.

Holland, S. (1976), *Capital Versus the Regions*, Macmillan, London.

Isard, W. (1956), *Location and Space Economy*, MIT Press, Cambridge, Mass.

Isard, W. and Smith, T.E. (1967), 'Location games: with applications to classic location problems', *Papers of the Regional Science Association*, 19, pp.45–80.

Isard, W. et al. (1969), *General Theory: Social Political Economic and Regional*, MIT Press, Cambridge, Mass.

Karaska, G.J. and Bramhall, D.F. (eds), (1969), *Locational Analysis for Manufacturing*, MIT Press, Cambridge, Mass.

Koopmans, T.C. and Beckmann, M. (1957), 'Assignment problems and the location of economic activity', *Econometrica*, 25, pp.53–76.

Krumme, G. (1969), 'Toward a geography of enterprise', *Economic Geography*, 45 (1), pp.30–9.

Kuenne, R.E. (1968), 'Approximate solution to a dynamic combinational problem of space', *Journal of Regional Science*, 8, pp.165–80.

Kuhn, H.W. and Kuenne, R.E. (1962), 'An efficient algorithm for the numerical solution of the generalized Weber problem in space economics', *Journal of Regional Science*, 4, pp.21–33.

Lefeber, L. (1958), *Allocation in Space*, North-Holland, Amsterdam.

Lloyd, P.E. and Dicken, P. (1972), *Location in Space: a Theoretical Approach to Economic Geography*, Harper and Row.

Losch, A. (1954), *The Economics of Location*, Yale University Press, New Haven, Conn.

Machlup, F. (1967), 'Theories of the firm: marginalist, behavioural, managerial', *American Economic Review*, 57 (1), pp.1–33.

McLure, C.E. (1970), 'Taxation, substitution and industrial location', *Journal of Political Economy*, 78 (1), pp.112–32.

Molle, W.T.M. (1977), 'Industrial mobility – a review of empirical studies and an analysis of the migration of industry from the city of Amsterdam', *Regional Studies*, 11 (5), pp.323–36.

Nicholson, T.A.J. (1971), *Optimization in Industry*, volume II, Longman, London.

Nishioka, H. (1974), 'Location decision making by firms in Japan', in F.E.I. Hamilton (ed.), *Spatial Perspectives on Industrial Organisation and Decision Making*, Wiley.

Onyemelukwe, J.O.C. (1974), 'Industrial location in Nigeria', in F.E.I. Hamilton (ed.), *Spatial Perspectives on Industrial Organisation and Decision Making*, Wiley, London.

O'Farrell, P.N. (1976), 'An analysis of industrial closures: Irish experience 1960–73', *Regional Studies*, 10 (4), pp.433–48.

Ohuiginn, P. (1972), *Regional Development and Industrial Location in Ireland*, Gill and Macmillan, Dublin.

Pred, A.R. (1967), *Behaviour and Location: Foundations for a Geographic and Dynamic Location Theory, Part 1*, Lund Studies in

Geography, Series B, 27.

Pred, A.R. (1973), 'The growth and development of systems of cities in advanced economies', in A.R. Pred and G.E. Tornqvist, *Systems of Cities and Information Flows*, Lund Studies in Geography, Series B, N.38.

Richardson, H.W. (1978), *Urban and Regional Economics*, Penguin, London.

Richter, C.E. (1969), 'The impact of industrial linkages on geographic association', *Journal of Regional Science*, 9 (1), pp.19—28.

Serck-Hanssen, J. (1970), *Optimal Patterns of Location*, North-Holland, Amsterdam.

Shimshoni, D. (1971), 'Regional development and science-based industry', in J.F. Kain and J.R. Meyer (eds), *Essays in Regional Economics*, Harvard University Press, Cambridge, Mass.

Smith, D.M. (1966), 'A theoretical framework for geographical studies of industrial location', *Economic Geography*, 42 (2) pp.16—32.

Smith, D.M. (1971), *Industrial Location: an Economic Geographical Analysis*, Wiley, New York.

Soderman, S. (1975), *Industrial Location Planning*, Halsted Press, New York.

Spanger, U. and Truener, P. (1975), 'Statistical analysis of location determinants', *Papers and Proceedings of the Regional Science Association*, 35, pp.143—56.

Stafford, H.A. (1969), 'An industrial location decision model', *Proceedings of the Association of American Geographers*, 1, pp.141—4.

Stafford, H.A. (1972), 'The geography of manufacturers', *Progress in Geography*, 4.

Stafford, H.A. (1974), 'The anatomy of the location decision: content analysis of case studies', in F.E. I. Hamilton (ed.), *Spatial Perspectives on Industrial Organisation and Decision Making*, John Wiley, London.

Steed, G.D.F. (1971), 'Plant adaptation, firm environments and location analysis', *The Professional Geographer*, 23 (4), pp.63—72.

Steed, G.D.F. (1971), 'Forms of corporate environmental adaptations', *Tijdschrift voor Economische en Sociale Geografie*, 62, pp.90—4.

Stevens, B.H. and Brackett, C.A. (1967), *Industrial Location: a Review and Annotated Bibliography of Theoretical, Empirical and Case Studies*, Bibliography Series 3, Regional Science Research Institute, Philadelphia.

Streit, M.E. (1969), 'Spatial associations and economic linkages between industries', *Journal of Regional Science*, 9 (2), pp.177—89.

Thoman, R., Conkling, E.C. and Yeates, M.H. (1968), *The Geography of Economic Activity*, McGraw-Hill, New York.

Thompson, W.R. (1965), *A Preface to Urban Economics*, Johns Hopkins

Press, Baltimore.

Thompson, W.R. (1968), 'Internal and external factors in the development of urban economies', in H.S. Perloff and L. Wingo (eds), *Issues in Urban Economics,* Johns Hopkins Press, Baltimore.

Thompson, W.R. (1969), 'The economic base of urban problems', in N.W. Chamberlain (ed.), *Contemporary Economic Issues,* R.D. Irwin, Homewood, Illinois.

Thorngren, B. (1970), 'How do contact systems affect regional development?', *Environment and Planning,* 2, pp.409—27.

Tiebout, C.M. (1957), 'Location theory, empirical evidence and economic evolution', *Papers and Proceedings of the Regional Science Association,* vol.III, pp.74—86.

Tornqvist, G.E. (1970), *Contact Systems and Regional Development,* Lund Studies in Geography, Series B, No.35.

Tornqvist, G.E. (1973), 'Contact requirements and travel facilities — contact models of Sweden and regional development alternatives in the future', in A.R. Pred and G.E. Tornqvist, *Systems of Cities and Information Flows,* Lund Studies in Geography, Series B, No.38.

Townroe, P.M. (1978), *Employment Decentralization: Policy Instruments for Large Cities in LDCs,* Progress in Planning Series, Pergamon, Oxford.

Vergin, R.C. and Rodgers, J.D. (1967), 'An algorithm and computational procedure for locating economic facilities', *Management Science,* 13, pp.240—54.

Walker, D.F. (1975), 'Governmental influence on manufacturing location: Canadian experience with special reference to the Atlantic provinces', *Regional Studies,* 9, pp.203—17.

Webber, M.J. (1972), *The Impact of Uncertainty on Location,* MIT Press, Cambridge, Mass.

Weber, A. (1929), *Alfred Weber's Theory of the Location of Industries,* translated by C.I. Friedrich, University of Chicago Press, Chicago.

Wheeler, J.O. (1973), 'Industrial location: a bibliography, 1966—72', *Council of Planning Librarians, Exchange Bibliography 436,* Illinois.

Subject index

Author index